THE SPIRITUAL PROPERTIES

OF HERBS

By GURUDAS

CASSANDRA PRESS

SAN RAFAEL, CA. 94915

CASSANDRA PRESS
P.O. BOX 868
SAN RAFAEL, CA. 94915

Printed in the United States of America.

First printing 1988

ISBN 0-961587-57-1

Library of Congress Catalogue Card Number 88-71401

The use of the material described in this text is not meant to replace the services of a physician who should always be consulted for any condition requiring his or her aid.

"That which is looked upon by one generation as the apex of human knowledge is often considered an absurdity by the next, and that which is regarded as a superstition in one century, may form the basis of science for the following one."

Paracelsus

Other books by Gurudas

Flower Essences and Vibrational Healing

Gem Elixirs and Vibrational Healing, Vol. I and II

Front cover art by Susan St. Thomas. Copyright © 1988 Cassandra Press.

TABLE OF CONTENTS

FOREWORD

When Gurudas asked me if he could do some flower essences from the herbs in my back yard garden, I was honored. I had never seen anyone do flower essences before, so I was interested to see how he did it. I knew about the Bach Flower Essence tradition and understood it in association with homeopathy, and I was happy someone could come and demonstrate the procedures. I had planted a large herb garden in my backyard after beginning the Student Garden Project at the University of California, Santa Cruz, with Alan Chadwick, in 1967.

Alan practiced the Biodynamic approach to gardening, which was developed by Rudolf Steiner under the influence of Goethe, who, as well as being the foremost literary figure of Germany, was also an accomplished botanist.

It is clear from the writings of Gurudas on herbs and gem stones that he is part of this tradition, one that you could call a tradition of esoteric vitalism.

I like the references to Lemuria and Atlantis, which are important archaic sources for this tradition, because they tell us of a time when human consciousness was in complete rapport with the plant world—a symbiotic relationship that we have for the most part lost, but one that can, in part, be restored. I have thought about this tradition of human/plant harmony in reference to the re-establishment of the medicinal herbal tradition in this generation. In order to guide my studies, I have formulated a hypothesis that there is an herb code in the immune memory of the DNA. This means we are genetically programmed in our immune memories for herbs that prevent and cure illness. This memory is a deep one and the symbolic meaning of Lemuria and Atlan is is one way of thinking about the roots of this memory.

Another figure who lives in my memory, and with whom Gurudas has great affinity, is St. Hildegard of Bingen, a great mystic and adept who lived in the twelfth century. She worked with gem stones and medicinal herbs and gained all of her knowledge from direct experience and intuition—"Everything I ever wrote came wholly from the source of my heavenly vision," she says. Although she has been unknown in this country until recently, her work is now available in an English translation: *Hildegard of Bingen's Medicine* by Strehlow and Hertzka.

For those readers who want to know more about the background of this work, I would urge them to consult Gurudas' *Flower Essences and Vibrational Healing,* especially the bibliography. I was delighted to see the list of books under "Lemuria and Atlantis" which introduced me to those themes and the available literature.

What Gurudas has done for us in this volume is to increase, the morphic resonance between the plant world and ourselves, and or those of us who see healing as an integral part of salvation (salvation is an act of cosmic healing) this is an act of cosmic healing, this is all to the good.

Paul Lee Ph.D.
The Platonic Academy
September 1988

PREFACE

Most of this text were provided by the master Hilarion through Jon C. Fox, a channel in California. Fox has become increasingly respected for his ability to accurately research a wide variety of technical subjects. He began his channeling career seven years ago as a conscious channel. In recent years, he has expanded his gift to include trance channeling, because that often makes it easier to present technical information. Fox's main interest is to do research channelings that will present new scientific technologies and concepts. Fox now conducts group readings with numerous people in California.

Hilarion focalizes the fifth ray, which consists of technical and scientific information. Some may be aware that Hilarion has recently been the source of an entire series of channeled books from the Marcus press in Toronto. Hilarion has provided inspirational guidance and technical advice to many people for thousands of years.

While almost finishing a master's degree in political science and being in law school for a year, I have also for some years been involved in various spiritual practices. This interest stimulated three trips to India in the early 1970s. Since 1976 I have worked with gem elixirs, homeopathic remedies, and flower essences, first as a student and then from 1978 until 1982, in my own private practice. This work also included giving advice relating to herbs, nutrition, and bath therapies. Since 1978 I for several years taught classes on different natural healing topics.

In early 1983 I founded and ran Pegasus Products until I sold it in the fall of 1987. The company produces about 700 different flower essences, gem elixirs, and homeopathic remedies, including all the remedies described in my books.

In the summer of 1979, I learned of a psychic surgeon from the Philippines, and with my keen interest in this form of healing, I visited him. In the middle of the session, several of my guides appeared, and they stated that my healing research would improve if I worked with a good trance channel. A few days later, a friend returned from San Diego describing Kevin Ryerson's work, and I was interested. I borrowed several tapes of Ryerson's public talks in trance and after listening to John's voice, one of Ryerson's guides, and hearing the information that was being discussed, I felt there might be a deep connection here. After a period of meditation, I called Ryerson and in October 1979 he visited San Francisco. From that period, we did numerous research readings for four years.

The nature of channeled teaching is such that to produce much information many questions must be asked. If one were to just sit back and listen, a fair amount of information would be presented, but it usually would not match what can be given if the inquirer comes prepared with many questions and a good background and training in the field of inquiry.

Fortunately, I have an inquiring mind, an academic background that demands objective information, a natural gift for asking questions to beget specific information, and a fair degree of training in several holistic health modalities. Channeled teaching is a slow time consuming process in which a certain amount of information is discussed, which I gradually assimilate. Then I return to discuss new information and to sometimes ask additional questions to expand on previously discussed material.

In several of my previous books I provided information on the nature of channeling. Since then the subject has become much more popular and respected in the New Age movement, and there are now several good books on the subject. More important is the fact that increasing numbers of people are becoming channels so they do not have to just learn about this fascinating subject from others. Their own guides can provide the teachings!

One reason why Hilarion is allowed to provide much technical information in such detail is because many people are now ready and willing to receive this new material. As a society, we have reached a state of conscious and technological development so that, while some of the information these masters share may seem radical at times, many people now have the capacity to assimilate and apply it. Partly because of these facts, it is now time for channeled data to manifest from the fifth ray, which carries detailed and technically specific information. In the past, most channeled material came from the second ray, which is more a frequency of love and spirituality.[1] (The seven rays are seven primary energies that influence everyone.)

The research presented in this book was obtained in my private readings with Fox from 1986 until the spring of 1988. In my readings with Fox, Hilarion answered all of the questions. Assisting Hilarion in this work are a number of other guides, many of them historically respected spiritual and healing masters. While some of these individuals are also my personal guides, many of them contributed to this work because of their background and expertise in the use of herbs for healing and spiritual growth.

1 Hilarion, *Symbols* (Toronto:Marcus Books,1979), p.25-26.

INTRODUCTION

This book is the first available text that provides a detailed account of how herbs affect us spiritually. This is the first of a series of books which will present approximately 400 herbs. Each book will contain charts, as in the back of this book, to apply this data.

People are always affected by the spiritual properties stored in herbs, even though they may not be aware of these characteristics. It is wise to learn about these qualities in order to better activate an herb's spiritual properties. The spiritual transformation now taking place in our society is unfolding partly because so many people take herbs.

Initially, we will discuss the general principles involved in activating an herb's spiritual qualities. Each herb works with the various laws of God. Then follows a detailed presentation of how herbs were used in Atlantis and Lemuria. The Lemurians and Atlanteans had a deep understanding of the spiritual attributes of herbs. The Lemurians used rituals and a close attunement with the nature spirits to activate the spiritual properties in herbs, while the Atlanteans used quartz crystals and telepathy.

Also included is new information on how herbs were used in ancient China and Egypt. Chinese herbs generally have more spiritual qualities, because for thousands of years they have been surrounded by positive thought forms, and by a race of people who understood the higher qualities stored in herbs.

One of the most important topics discussed in this book is the problem of negative thought form pollution and etheric density. Our negative thoughts play a key role in causing ill health in mind, body, and spirit. Unfortunately, most of us today do not have etheric sight, so we cannot see how we harm ourselves in this area. It is now understood how emotions play a key role in the cause and cure of diseases. This is an important reason why visualization exercises are used to alleviate a wide variety of diseases. Understanding how negative thought forms cause disease is an extension of acknowledging the role the emotions play in health and disease.

While certain herbs are presented that weaken the AIDS virus, I included the chapter on AIDS because I wanted the opportunity to present further information on the cause and cure of AIDS. The Rife ray and related technology will quite possibly have a profound impact on our lives in the coming years. It was used for some years to successfully treat cancer and a host of other serious diseases, and it is already being used to treat AIDS. AIDS is an extension of the cancer virus so there is an intimate relationship between these two diseases.

There is also a chapter on the preparation and taking of herbs, including various ways to prepare and take herbs to activate their spiritual properties. Water is an especially valuable vehicle here. For instance, taking a bath with herbs, flower essences, and gem elixirs can be of great value. There are many ways herbs can be combined with flower essences and gem elixirs. Some material is provided on using herbs with homeopathy. More information will be provided in a future volume.

Through companion planting and crop rotation the spiritual properties of herbs can be activated. Here it is important to work with the nature spirits. Herbs learn from us just as we learn from herbs. The massive use of chemicals in agriculture is also worsening the petrochemical miasm. This is intimately connected to negative thought form pollution and insects.

Animals also greatly benefit from the spiritual properties stored in herbs. Animals attune on a soul level to specific herbs because of their spiritual properties, which helps explain why certain plants and animals have long been interrelated. The relationship between catnip and cats exemplifies this pattern.

A total of 108 individual herbs are discussed in this book, with 15 different points related to each herb. A broad range of herbs has been presented, including rare and common western and Chinese herbs, tropical plants, and trees. Most of these herbs are readily available in stores.

In recent years, many people have come to appreciate and respect channeled teachings as a valuable research vehicle. I believe this trend will continue. This book is presented in a very organized manner based on trance channeled material along with my own insights.

CHAPTER I

GENERAL PRINCIPLES

Herbs have been utilized for centuries, for many different purposes. These purposes have ranged from healing and ritual and the simple beauty of the herb to their utilization for higher spiritual properties. This book will bring some of this information out, both historical and that which is relevant for today. Individuals who understand herbs, who are attracted to them, who feel a love for herbs have this in their makeup for important reasons. This may relate to past lives, but it may also relate to the spiritual properties that act as keys to the barriers and difficulties that individuals may currently experience. It is as if they have laid the pathway or groundwork for their ability to accept the spiritual properties of these herbs for themselves even before coming into this life. It is time for most individuals to begin experimenting with herbs for their spiritual properties, to understand their own subtler vibrations because herbs bring this into greater clarity.

Taking herbs as medicine always produces some physical effect that also relates to some level of spirit or an attitude that keeps you from a fuller understanding, such as some attribute of your own life you have not been willing to look at. Each herb works with various laws of God, usually with certain tendencies towards one or more of these laws.[1] As an individual moves out of harmony with these laws, herbs which are in intrinsic harmony with certain of these laws bring some of this energy as a pattern or morphogenetic field into the individual's personality, into their physical body, into the way they view things, and into the way they think. What occurs as a result of this is spiritual understanding and insight. But this vibration is not usually rooted or grounded unless there is some clear attribute of natural substance within the body.

When an herb, or any substance, is taken into the physical body, there is a corresponding spiritual effect. This is because the vibration of what you take affects your own vibration. The degree to which you are willing to acknowledge and work with this spiritual energy determines how much this vibration becomes more clear. When an individual is clearly out of harmony and experiences disease or difficulty in the physical body, a thought form is usually involved that has two sides. One side is a negative thought form, the question or attribute that shows where a part of you is out of harmony. The question is always asked, "Out of harmony with what?" and this is the other side. Why was this negative thought form brought into a person's existence. An herb as a natural substance provides healing, but it also provides a spiritual message.

This is why you may see deeper spiritual effects in a person who experiences physical illness and takes an herb or herbal formula that has a direct and beneficial effect. It lasts with the person not because the physical effect was so deep or strong, but because on a spiritual level they open to the deeper lesson involved.

It is important to recognize the vibrational shift that is now occurring. This may happen at subtler levels than most people are consciously aware of. Tune into this shift to understand, recognize, and more importantly, welcome it. This is an important part of allowing the spiritual vibration of an herb to come into a person. It is important to see that these vibrational shifts will affect an individual according to their own principals of existence, that is, what is true and important in their life, what is unique about them, the way they approach life, relationships, and all the important day-to-day things. These things will affect the way this vibrational shift is perceived; thus, patience is often needed to understand this energy shift.

A life stream, in the broadest and more general sense, is a morphogenetic field or soul group that is incorporated with the creation of a particular life form on planet Earth. A life stream can extend throughout time, across various incarnations of a being or a species. It does not have to be on planet Earth, of course, but we will confine ourselves to this planet. Therefore, from one lifetime to the next these patterns, or morphogenetic fields, remain with various individuals that make up a particular species. This applies to plants, animals, and humans. Individual tasks such as lessons, difficulties to overcome, cycles, and the attributes of God's laws as they uniquely affect each life form remain associated with a particular life form in lifetime after lifetime. This is what is brought into action. Because it is continued from one lifetime to the next, a life stream usually moves through several cycles.

Life forms and life streams interact. The term life form generally relates to a particular embodiment in a particular species and in a particular body. A life stream is the overall pattern and picture, the flow of this energy from its source, its inception point in first coming into this type of life form and its ultimate goal, realized through the life form because then the life stream can go on and choose another life form.

These cycles embody themselves in several different forms of animate or even inanimate matter. Thus, in the human life stream, being created in the Earth as a mountain region, a dinosaur, or a human being are all the same life stream separated by eons of time. Dinosaurs and humans are part of the same life stream. In each case the lessons were similar, moving towards a common path. Mankind has had many different life forms and one of the most important ones on planet Earth was that of embodiment in mountains—the Himalayan Mountain range was chosen for its strength and majesty and for its wide variations in climate. Then humans, after a period of separation from the Earth and a discussion amongst themselves, incarnated as dinosaurs. Here separateness, the basics of existence, power, and the Earth herself came to be understood better. This life stream has different life forms and each has a different purpose in existence. The beginning of this is not clear; indeed the necessity to recognize it as circular is an important attribute in the unconscious of most people. When you say 'life stream' it implies circularity, the movement of water. But then what? It goes back to its source and again moves.[2]

The soul is divided into finer and finer parts in the continuous life stream of one individual, from one lifetime to the next. Mankind as a whole has a common destiny. This destiny revolves specifically around understanding love. In many of its forms, love, as understood on the scientific level, works with and is intrinsically related to the ever fine substance of the ethers. Love, in its essence, is more than a vibration. Scientifically, one might separate the ethers from vibrations that affect the ethers. And one might assume that love is merely a vibration that affects the ether, but in fact, love is more than this. Love creates etheric substance, binds it together as well as creates vibrations upon it. Therefore, it is not an easy matter to separate, particularly in humanity's existence and understanding, the difference between the ethers and love.

The ethers are seven or more dimensional states that vibrate faster than the speed of light. They exist all about life on Earth. Love is not only a manipulation of this substance, but indeed, is a way to actually create it. However, this is seen as the future rather than the present, because mankind currently merely manipulates and works with the ethers that connect all beings to each other.

However, as the varieties of love understood by the specialization of mankind develop more deeply within individuals, from one lifetime to the next, and as these areas of understanding love become finer and finer, so will the ability to create the ethers. The ability will develop for people to connect more powerfully to change the ethers so that they are more supportive of love vibrations to ultimately join mankind together based upon this fine substance. This will be one of the first stages. Later the ethers may be sufficiently changed so that they will no longer support negative vibrations. This is a unique characteristic that is very difficult to reproduce anywhere else in the galaxy, but it has already been seen around spiritual masters on planet Earth. This is why it seems possible for mankind to be able to do this in the future.

The finer and finer substances of the ethers relate to the finer and finer vibrations of mankind as it grows and works with love. Gradually, however, all of this has a similar point in which oneness is taken. This would seem to be paradox, in that the finer and finer divisions, specialization, and understanding of love become only side benefits and the primary focus after a time becomes oneness itself. This is in perfect harmony and alignment with God's purpose in understanding love through the creation of mankind. Therefore, the full division of mankind into more areas of specialization conveys greater knowledge, which when shared by mankind as a whole becomes the oneness of love itself. In this way, God knows that the deepest way of understanding has been completed. Then the reabsorption, recompletion, and reunification of mankind takes place from the finest substance level upward and complete. That is how we visualize and recognize this onward-moving path.

What occurs with genetic specialization on the physical level is that each plant develops certain unique characteristics and properties. These properties extend to other levels of existence. The plant as a life stream has been on the Earth for a long time and will tend to continue for a long time. This sets up a pattern, which may be called an m-field, or morphogenetic field. This pattern of energy, which is described in Sheldrake's *A New Science of Life*, creates specific vibrations that are in harmony or resonance with it and others that are not.[3] This begins to delineate and define an aspect of being in a plant. This aspect is that which other individuals, in coming to see how the plant operates, see how it affects the physical body and what happens to them when they merge with it. This helps make each plant unique as they view and work with it. This uniqueness is what we refer to as the herbal personality because it is different from one plant to the next. On certain levels, the herbal personality will vibrate or be in harmony and resonance with personalities of devic spirits and of physically incarnated people. You notice this, of course, with individuals who feel drawn to certain herbs, not necessarily because of the healing effects. What occurs is that this herbal personality becomes that which a human can simply know, like they know the personality of another person. (I have long found this to be true with morning glory. I have often chosen to live where they were growing.)

When a plant has completed its life purpose the way it assists humanity, the vibration associated with it has learned the primary lessons that it needs to understand. These could have to do with the particular properties by which it shares its attributes and gifts with humanity, but it may also be that it receives the energy of love and receptivity of what it has to give with mankind. In most cases, in the way this giving and receiving has taken place, the plant will then be able to grow in a new way. Its sentience increases beyond the level of just being a plant. In such cases, the life stream will have a degree of intelligence, love, and strength added to it. Something unique is added that it has learned from this experience.

In working with mankind, there will usually be a deeper sense of love. Then it will pick a new direction. Sometimes this will be influenced by mankind or by the devas associated with that plant. Other subtle beings may be drawn in to create some of these energies. This refers to extraterrestrials, beings from within the Earth, certain angelic forces, and even a manifestation of God and the Christ energy as associated with humanity. However, in most cases, the plant will make many of the decisions itself.

But this is not a decision in the conscious way that you conceive of it. A plant does not think like a human. It is a decision, nevertheless. Sometimes there will be a moving to an entirely different planet or planetary system. Perhaps it will seek to explore the mineral or animal kingdoms, or become an entirely new form of plant. Sometimes it will combine with other plants to create an entirely new species. This is rare, but does take place occasionally.

For instance, in some ways nectarine may be seen as quite separate and different from its antecedents. It was also formed from at least one plant that had already finished its purpose on the physical plane. It is possible for many characteristics associated with a plant to be different from those that contributed to the plant's formation. Elecampane has largely achieved its life cycle purpose, and it may decide to disappear from the planet in a few thousand years. This plant may combine with a number of other forces, including certain gem stones and energies associated with beings from other planets. It may also combine with the energies of amaranthus, a plant that may pass from usefulness in about 50 years. Then these plants may combine to form an entirely new species. This species would likely yield interesting flowering capacities and have the ability to transfer energy into people's hands as they held this plant.

In some cases, a plant has attempted for a long time to assist mankind and this is not being allowed because of the way the energy is received or understood. Sometimes this is seen with rarer plants in which there is the combination of this effect and the plant being an endangered species. Because of environmental conditions and the rarity of the plant, it dies out. However, in many cases seeds of the plant are still available. They have been preserved in locations throughout the world, sometimes by botanists and biologists. This has often been done in secret or is well known to others, but the purpose is to regenerate the plant when the time is appropriate. On the etheric level the vibration will often remain when a plant becomes extinct. In such cases, it is possible, by several technological means not currently available on the planet, to resurrect the species. This involves a technology that will be more understood in 80 or 100 years. If a plant has completed its cycle and has become extinct, it will no longer be available on the etheric plane. But some species that have become endangered and died out are not doing this simply because they have fulfilled their karmic purpose. Sometimes this develops from environmental conditions. When this happens, the seeds will remain in an etheric form for at least 100 years.

It is possible now to present techniques to restore these seeds to the physical plane, but again, most individuals would not understand these methods sufficiently to work with them. And some of the environmental pollutants will still be present, so the plants would have difficulty maintaining their growth patterns even if they were brought back.

What this relates to in terms of the life stream is that, as the plant kingdom continues to divide and learn, as it changes or metamorphoses into another life stream, the inner message that has been learned, the way it has evolved, is shared with the entire plant kingdom. In this way the life stream contributes back into the entire plant life stream.

1 Hilarion, *Vision* (Toronto: Marcus Books, 1983).
2 _____, *Seasons of the Spirit* (Toronto: Marcus Books, 1983).
3 Rupert Sheldrake, *A New Science of Life* (LA: J.B. Tarcher, 1983).
_____, *The Presence of the Past* (NY: Times Books, 1987).

CHAPTER II

HISTORICAL USE OF HERBS
IN ATLANTIS AND LEMURIA

In Lemurian times, the properties of plants were closely associated with the devic orders. The herbs had very specific properties for healing the human body and were more used as sacraments by the devic spirits. They were used as a part of ritual. The specific vibrations associated with each herb on the planet were known as personalities, as you might imagine them. This eventually led to the impression of such personalities deeper within the physical makeup of the plant. In Lemurian times, the understanding of the subtle bodies existed far deeper than you can imagine it now. The subtle bodies of herbs and of the plant kingdom were a part of this. This meant that the personality, friendship, and awareness of all aspects of these plants were known. They were respected as individuals, as a specific life stream. You will notice this in the speech of some of the great herbalists today. They refer to these plants as if they were alive, as if they were beings with personalities.

As a result of this, some of these properties were more defined, refined, and impressed deeply as the plants were nurtured by the Lemurians and devic orders. This allowed some of the plant's vibrational properties to be utilized when needed. The vibrational effects of flowers and flower essences were perceived and known deeply by the Lemurians. But this was not always fully known or used throughout the Lemurian times because these vibrational properties were not always needed. People also worked with plants for joy, knowledge, and sharing.

Herbs were used as food in Lemuria, and the plants were gathered wild with great reverence for their abilities to nourish. It was seen that in taking an herb or plant into the physical body, one was nourishing the physical vehicle and the etheric, mental, and astral bodies. The emotional body was of great importance, but not a direct tie here with plants because this was a mutable thing. The emotional body joined in the joy and love with a plant before it was consumed.

It would be hard for most people to understand this because generally they would see that their emotional bodies react. People do not recognize their control over the emotional body in the sense that their lovingness alone is able to direct it where it is needed. Instead, they react to their environment, to what other people say, how they look, and how they feel before the energy of their heart or even of the will would affect the emotional body. The Lemurians had no such way of working. The emotional body was one by which expression, love, deeper understanding of the Earth, and a direct connection to the will was felt and known. Therefore, it was a simple technique to allow all of the emotions to have a purpose of holding a plant in a position of reverence and love. Nothing interfered with this, and therefore, a great deal of energy was made available. This energy was not just love, it was a channel from the Earth through the person to the plant that was accomplished by the emotional body.

Herbs were often used in Lemurian rituals. The way an herb could be used for purification was the way the herb was involved with the Earth directly. Most rituals were ways of working with Earth energy because the Earth was revered as a living and important being. For instance, one might use the herb sage, as is still done in some areas of the world now, for purification. However, sage was not only burned, it was brought into separation.

During the ritual, the subtle bodies of plants and people were able to merge. When you cast forth to the north, you would be imagining, as the arms would fly forward holding the herb within them, that your etheric body would also move to the north. And the etheric body of the herb sage would also move northward. Then, in facing the east, you would repeat this movement but imagine the astral body moving out of the physical body, joining the herb and standing there. A similar technique applied to the south with the mental body and to the west with the physical body. In imagining this, a ritual was created in all directions while you sat or stood in the middle.

This was a general technique and is still brought into action today by burning an herb in certain North American Indian rituals. This includes burning the herb and casting it into each of the four directions, or moving the smoke. The idea here is to stimulate the sense of smell.

Another aspect of rituals very important in Lemuria was the stimulation of all the senses. Thus, it would be wise in working with an herb to know it. This was naturally done because it was seen as a personality or friend, and in knowing your friend you would come to know it on levels beyond just the verbal. You came to know it by all facets of the senses. Thus, the rituals involved all the senses: the full being was part of the ritual. You would not only know its smell and taste and the oils within it and what they felt like upon the skin, but you would imagine yourself being within the plant and allowing the Earth energy itself, as modified by the personality of the plant, to flow deeply into you. This led to many meditative type activities.

When one merged with the herb in this manner, one could understand more of the herb's point of view of the Earth, its own personality, and its particular refinement. This was a very important ritual. This is currently done sometimes with animals; people merge with an animal during meditation. This was also done with plants in Lemuria. This was done not so much for purification; it was simply a way of knowing the Earth's energies that formed into herbs and other levels.

These different rituals in Lemuria activated the spiritual properties in people. What happened naturally was that, if a particular aspect of your being was in harmony with some of the higher aspects of these plants, this was brought into clarity. You were, of course, given a choice. Free will was just as important then as it is now, but the choice was that, if this was a part of your being you wished to know more deeply, the plant assisted you in this vibrationally.

For instance, in the purification ritual, as you cast the etheric body to the north, you might also be aware that there was some resistance in letting go within you, to seeing yourself in the four directions. Then the individual would ask for assistance. You would not be praying to the plant, but would ask the devas associated with the plant for assistance. The devic spirits associated with the plant were a large part of this ritual. You would be opening to their help in changing your vibration along certain avenues revealed by the ritual. An invocation was often done to bring energy into form.

Secondly, because it was a vibration, there would not necessarily have to be thinking or deciding about it. The vibration itself would lead an individual into other thought and emotional patterns to view themselves differently. Thus, this awakening took place in merging with the herb, to show the individual other possibilities and to simply have this on an experiential level. Each plant focused and concentrated energy in a certain direction, such as for purification or healing of the physical body. In these rituals you had your focus brought into a similar avenue. It was for the experience of it as much as for a direct change.

The natural result of this was that vibrationally an aspect of one's being was further clarified. If the person chose to allow that more firmly in their life, it would be as if the personality of that herb might be with them for quite some time, perhaps for years. And as a result of this, they moved further to a place of awakening, awareness, and enlightenment in a particular direction. It was then that the ritual allowed the individual free choice about that. And that is what is still left today and is the purpose of ritual: to bring us into consciousness as experience so the individual may choose it.

The Lemurians often used crystals during rituals. Crystals in Lemuria were not very refined. Nothing was changed or destroyed; it was unnecessary. Instead, the various locations in the Earth where crystal deposits existed could be felt by many individuals. People wishing to meditate or work with a particular herb sometimes visited these places for a while. Then they become partly affected by the energy of the Earth, as the crystalline deposits modulate such energy.

Crystals found in these regions were employed in rituals. They might be brought into a circle. Sacred sites often had gemstones placed about them. For instance, four or five small amethysts were placed in a circle around a plant. Individuals then sat within the circle and, knowing the Earth vibration was with them, welcomed the Earth's energy deep within their being as well as that of the crystals and the plant. All tended to merge together. Generally, a particular meditation was chosen. It would often be like a fountain of light, pouring up from the Earth, through the person, flowing out from their upper chakras into the circle of stones and then the herb, back down into the Earth all the way to its center, and then again through the individual.

Such a movement of energy by sound was usually then brought into the person's awareness. They found a certain level of vibration by which, in the way they viewed these things etherically, the plant began to glow. There was a certain energy resonance deep within it. Then some joyous attribute of the plant, a spiritual aspect the person was learning, was amplified by the crystals. This was usually established through a meditation of a fountain moving from within the Earth, out through the person and then down through the crystals. There was often a circular motion from one crystal to the next which moved faster and faster. This was viewed by the Lemurians as a crystalline dance.

What occurred as a result of this was an intensification of the energy and joyousness often reached an ecstatic state. This was sometimes used in various rites to celebrate movement through the seasons, the change of various attributes in society such as the celebration of a child's coming of age, the passing of a loved one, or a marriage. Individuals could even do this together in a group. Often this was done by four or five people in separate locations over a few acres of land, creating their own circles of meditation. They were joined by the crystalline deposits deep in the Earth. After this energy had become stronger, they would then seek to join it in the crystalline deposit underneath the Earth and allow that to spring back into their minds. What often occurred was a joining of hearts more than a merging of minds. But it was not like telepathy. The Lemurians were able to be in contact in ways that you would call telepathic, but they also sought a deeper merging at times. It is difficult to explain the purpose of this merging, but it related to levels of the joyousness of Earth herself that are beyond joy as you come to understand and imagine it now.

The release of an herb's spiritual properties in Lemuria enabled various life streams to mingle more directly with people. The natural kingdoms, the beings associated not just with plants, but with the waters of the Earth, with the sky, with the energies of a mountain or a beautiful formation, indeed the energies associated with all natural phenomena, were often more incorporated in a person's life. One would as much enjoy going out to visit a tree spirit or a being associated with a waterfall, or a beautiful energy vortex, the same way you now visit a friend around the corner. As a part of daily life, working with these energies and beautiful spirits was a part of normal existence.

It was understood that you had a friend or guide, and this related to the devic spirit, but also to some attribute of the plant. This is a very different way of seeing and working with these things. It is not so much that one attempted to come into resonance with a plant. Rather in seeing the herb and knowing its joyousness because of its form and beauty, you danced with it. This is a hard analogy to make, but indeed in the Lemurian way, there was this merging and oneness. This is hard to express in words because thought, as you understand it, was not employed in Lemuria. Then the specialization of a plant, its own particular way, was enjoyed. This great joy that was felt opened an individual to many aspects of beingness. It opened them to the joy by which they had come into this incarnation, the joy they wish to share with others, and the joy they wish to bring more clearly into form for other people and other civilizations later to come.

Many individuals now on the Earth are again coming to know this joy in working with plants, especially through working with herbs. It is not only for the scientific purposes that there is benefit in exploring this, but rather simply for reawakening that joy. As the spiritual properties of an herb are better known by an individual, that person may decide there is something particularly entrancing and joyous about those properties, about what they are learning from the plant. That is because there is a part of them, usually unacknowledged, that is joyous about existence on the Earth. Ultimately, this joyousness is resolved by how the Earth is known more fully. There is always some component of the spiritual side of each herb relating to joyousness of the Earth and acknowledgment of the Earth being.

In Lemuria, the individual applied some of this without full conscious understanding. Thus, joyousness was felt deeply and in the acknowledgment of the particular attribute of the plant unique to its own being; the person felt it within them and shared this with others. The way this was shared and loved with others made the dance of life easier and better. Because of this, there was a great deal of sharing and enjoyment of life. The full spiritual understanding of what this meant in terms of God, nature, or mental thought forms or exercises was unnecessary in Lemuria. In fact, mental understanding was unnecessary in Lemuria. The willingness to receive the basic energies of the plant through the action of will was quite sufficient. Mental capacities were more powerfully developed later in Atlantis. In Atlantis, there was the ability to understand logic and higher spiritual wisdom from the conscious mind rather than a simple pure understanding of the plant and love itself as was done in Lemuria.

In Atlantis, the spiritual attribute of each herb was known, and as it was taken for a physical difficulty, the individual was telepathically shown possibilities by images, pictures, and various meditations of ways they had fallen out of harmony with God's laws. To be brought into greater harmony with God's laws results not simply from taking nutrients into the physical body, but also from a spiritual understanding that goes deep within the individual.

For instance, someone struggling with throat or lung problems, would take some herbs that assisted with this, bringing greater energy into the throat perhaps easing immune system dysfunction as well. At the same time, the practitioner providing the herb, made suggestions and might meditate with that being. He projected images of soothing words and thought forms using the voice appropriately, and telepathically posed the subtle question: Are you in harmony with this? In general, there would be a clear no in response. The practitioner then allowed this to move into the patient's body providing images and pictures.

Two pictures would be provided. First, there was the image of how the individual was out of harmony, how indeed the voice was used inappropriately. This related, of course, to the law of speech. It showed the way things were said that harmed someone, causing difficulty. But it was always shown as if at a movie, as if separate from the individual. Then the entire movie was replayed in the mind of the person doing this healing work. They then projected these images with speech correctly and in harmony with God's laws. It was done in such a way that the individual could understand that, as they said something, it then came into existence. Thus, the existence created was loving and helpful. Then the individual was given choices. They were shown different paths and asked how they wished to work with this in the future. Then they found a way to create these pictures themselves and these were transmitted to the practitioner. All this was done under the influence of one or more herbs so that they could work closely together. Sometimes a particular gem stone that was associated with this difficulty would also be used. If an individual had difficulty assimilating the telepathic messages, they might touch the gem stone, and the person doing the healing work would also touch it. The images would be transmitted to the patient through the aid of the crystalline structure within that gem stone.

The root cause of a nutritional deficiency was often perceived, so there was a focus on vibrational remedies to correct this. There was a complete system of therapy. If someone was deficient in specific nutrients, the person might be given those nutrients in tablet form, but they would also usually also be given certain vibrational remedies to get at the root cause of the problem.

For about 2,800 years in Atlantis there was a focus on bringing the nutritional properties of certain plants and herbs more clearly into the physical being. This resulted in a number of plants and herbs currently on the Earth that have extra amounts of various minerals, proteins, and nutrients. These were used as food.

An excellent example of this is amaranthus. It has many spiritual properties, but it was also focused upon to develop its protein content. These techniques involved agricultural manipulation, just as is done today to pick the best strains. But in Atlantis the devic order aided this process, so these nature spirits were made more welcome with certain strains. When a particularly strong plant was identified, instead of simply watching for its seeds and crossing them with others, Atlanteans did a great deal of meditation, concentration of energy and purpose upon that plant. This allowed it to grow deeper roots to even more strengthen its particularly properties. This took some time, as you can imagine. But you can also see that the farmers were not only involved in cultivation but also in meditation with these plants. This allowed a deeper connection with the Earth, and indeed, many of those who understood this were able to be successful at it. On a ritualistic level, inspiration from Lemurian times helped these activities.

In later lifetimes, certain individuals used their knowledge and understanding to create specific formulations for supplementing the physical body. During this period, rosehip was identified as a vitamin C source. Later vitamin C was isolated and used when the Atlanteans had some need for it. Similarly, with all the different nutrients there was a long process by which first the nutrient was understood vibrationally, as if the attribute of robustness or health-giving properties of the plant was acknowledged. Then it was focused on by meditation, cross-breeding, and the creation of thought forms to honor the plant and to manifest greater spirituality and love in it. In later lifetimes, individuals completed this process by concentrating through chemical and vibrational means the various individual nutrients that they had worked with previously in Atlantis. This allowed them to understand these things on a purely physical level, to see them in a holistic way, and to go into past lives as well as their current lifetime. People today who find themselves particularly drawn to certain nutritional substances that are grown in the Earth would be wise to look into the herbs in which these things are found plentifully. It would be wise to understand them on a deeper level as they relate to the Earth herself. This would resolve certain levels of this karma in themselves.

Many other techniques were used in Atlantis in which herbs were a part of daily life. They were used around a person's house for decorative purposes, as well as for their effects from growing near an individual. This was a very respected and common practice. Sometimes, after an individual had been associated with a certain plant for most of their life, they felt a particular kinship with it. In certain activities done in old age, when an individual was getting ready to leave the physical body, these herbs were brought more into prominence. These activities included a remembrance of past lives and a dotting on certain past activities. Then, the use of the herb's various attributes such as in aromatherapy, their exact color when ground up, or the herb's feel were brought more clearly into form around the person by painting the herb or by producing a little mat or rug that might have the same energy pattern.

The unconscious bond with the herb was respected, and an individual felt more in tune with the physical Earth as they reached their later years. This is important, because when individuals reach an advanced age, they often have difficulty fully understanding what the purpose of life is and what is happening on the Earth. Today, individuals who have had a particular affinity with specific herbs throughout their life, often forget or overlook this affinity as they reach advanced age. Their friends and people who care for them, may have noted such an affinity, and that is when their action is important. This is partly a ritual, but it is also a physical level pattern, because the vibration of the plant is so close to the vibration of the person. It can have a deep effect in reacquainting an old person with the Earth body.

For around the first ten or twenty years of life, for most of the Atlantean period, parents and those who watched over children would notice a certain affinity with specific herbs. This could have a wide variety of effects, and the ability to observe this was very important with those who watched over the children. They might be drawn to a particular smell brought out by a tea. Or they might be drawn to its shape or form or just like to be near a particular flower or herb for no apparent reason. They were encouraged to explore this more deeply. One reason for this was that deep in the unconscious of many in Atlantis were the ways of Lemuria and the older paths. There was a rekindling in the child of this ritual development and assimilation of the herbal personality. This was very respected with many children.

Herbs were also used extensively for healing the physical body. When a pattern was set up with the child, when a particular herb was seen to be a constitutional remedy—something that would usually help the individual over and over—it was noted that the child had an attunement with the personality of that particular plant. For instance, a child particularly drawn to rosehip tea might be seen to have spiritual gifts, certain attributes of development along the line of the rose itself. That child might aspire to become a priest or to understand the deeper meaning of God's nature as it is permitted mankind to know. These type of attributes were looked for the way parents today notice certain tendencies in a child and then say, "Well, that one will grow up to be a ballerina because she likes to dance." Sometimes these things actually do take place.

Deep within much of this work with children were the devic orders associated with various herbs. This was the attribute that was also a part of this work; the devic orders were allowed to be with the child. This was encouraged by the herb being near the child as they slept and by drinking a tea. However, contact with the devic orders was lost more easily as the individual grew older, as if those were childlike things, no longer necessary.

In Atlantis, it was seen that some connection with the Earth was important and useful, but this was not really part of Atlantean society. There was very little in that society to bolster or support such a connection. Individuals involved with ritual, with the deeper understanding of the Earth may have been paid as geologists or archeologists, but that was about all. They recognized this lack of attunement with nature as a gap in the Atlantean knowledge and learning structures. One reason for this understanding was that some of these beings had strong Lemurian ties from past lives that they were not fully aware of. They voiced their opinions but were ignored. Sometimes these individuals were even ostracized.

Gradually a resistant or negative thought form was formed that created for the Atlanteans an extra barrier to a full understanding of the process of pure will. Because of this, some will was denied to the Atlanteans. The emphasis here was on the pathway of learning through spirit. This was sometimes unrelated to the physical body, to the Earth, or to will. In this emphasis on more purely spiritual concepts and understandings some aspects of love were omitted. What they learned was certainly accurate and useful, but it was missing the part that related more directly to the Earth, to practical levels, and especially to the willingness to bring love into all natural processes. In this way the Atlanteans eventually got themselves into trouble. Overemphasis upon any one characteristic over others is generally to be avoided.

Thus, at a certain point it became very easy for the Atlanteans to go wrong. They found greater attraction to areas of conflict and difficulty as a result of genetic manipulation into areas in which natural processes were no longer an intrinsic part of their own hearts' development. From that point forward, many different things gradually went wrong, including the creation of separate structures for priests and scientists, various mistakes with genetic encoding, and difficulties that led to energy dependence. Ultimately, that dependence released an energy so destructive that Atlantis itself was destroyed. The very seeds of that destruction were inherent in the misuse or ignoring of the deeper energies of the will.

Will relates very much to the Earth and nature. The way physical processes, understood by the individual, allow their own creative force to mingle with nature in a loving harmonious dance unites and strengthens these energies. As the Atlanteans fell out of step with this, it became very difficult for them to fully understand the great gifts that nature gave to humanity. Without this relevant love, they were unable to understand the Earth in a direct fashion through the will center within the body and their own higher self. There was no spiritual understanding of the Earth or of nature. They were unable to use and experience the ways of nature appropriately. Only from such a place could genetic mutations and things commonly reported and known about Atlantis have ever taken place. Thus, genetic manipulation and the combining of completely different species were allowed. The seeds for the destruction of Atlantis were within that culture long before individuals got involved with energy and genetic manipulation difficulties or work with the land. It had to do with an understanding of the will function within people. Now, humanity is to some extent following these steps again. When mankind is out of harmony with nature, nature will make itself known. It is by the will, by the action of knowledge with the physical body, with a sense of empowerment and love of nature that answers are found. Solutions are not just found through the mind or through rational, logical, or scientific understanding.

The properties of distillation, chemical refinement, and extraction became quite well known and much better developed than in current times. Herbal properties were condensed and concentrated to degrees that you do not yet understand today. This involved several treatments using various frequencies of sound, radio waves, thought forms, and vibrations impressed upon the plants for an even purer form of distillation of the essential ingredients. This was not seen from the chemical point of view, but was a way of bringing out the foundation principle—that strongest or more important part within a given herb.

These chemicals, towards the end of Atlantis, made up a large variety of healing substances that could be applied directly to the physical body. However, these substances were also used in genetic manipulation experiments that involved changing the physical body, and they were applied in many other areas of science and technology. You can see this running parallel to what is happening now in the United States, worldwide, and in the petrochemical industry with the broad use of synthetics. Many involved in this industry today know of herbal properties but are applying similar things to synthetic chemicals that are now being derived. These are less likely to cause great genetic change as occurred in Atlantis, although they are clearly causing great difficulty to the environment, just as eventually happened in Atlantis with the misuse of herbs. This is because refinement, beyond a certain degree destroys the life force, and what is left is only a pure substance that does not have with it the life stream intelligence, that very beginning point that we mentioned in the Lemurian times.

In Atlantis, herbs were used for what you would term 'chemical purification.' Primarily physical means were applied. This meant that, for instance, a group of people, particularly interested in refining a particular property of an herb, focused energy, sound, and the vibration of healing in their bodies, perhaps through amplification with a number of crystals, to a little bowl filled with a distilled tar, resin, or component of an herb. This vibration caused a separation or even a filtration of certain parts of the vat or bowl of the herb. On the surface, a liquid might be found as a result of the vibration. This had within it some of the most powerful properties of the purest level of the substance because it was set into vibration with itself. It was set into a place by which its energies related much more than just to the physical. This was done as an experiment at various times in Atlantis with no great harm or difficulty until the later Atlantean phase. Then genetic experiments were carried out so that human components were merged with animal life streams. Various aspects of an animal's body were merged with a humans. Exactly how this was accomplished has not been very detailed in the available literature, for good reason.[1]

The herbs used had to be extremely purified. We are speaking on many levels of such purification—not just that of the physical, but distilled etherically as well. This allowed genetic manipulation and mutations to take place. This is not a level of purity that is very easily achieved, and today it is much more difficult to achieve than in Atlantis because the subtle levels are more dense today.

Certain herbs were changed by the concentrated focusing of various vibrational techniques. However, many times these changes would not take hold. It was very difficult to manipulate from such a level and yet maintain the life force within the plant as the devic spirit brought it in. This was easily done in Lemuria, because the Lemurians were in harmony with the life force. With certain plants genetic changes took place, and you see this today in plants that clearly have influences of a rather unusual nature associated with them.

Corn is an example of this. This substance has been genetically changed through several different stages on the planet. It is relatively easy to manipulate genetically. But if experiments were done today with this substance with any degree of ill will or intent beyond that of seeking truly to help, even though genetic changes might develop, they would not last for more than a few generations. This would happen with substances that had a great focus and energy upon them—those commonly used as food and medicine. But this, of course, excludes the vast majority of plants and herbs. There have been attempts to manipulate these substances, but very few plants still have any of these effects with them today.

Today, there are benefits to genetically manipulating certain herbs, but by and large it seems unnecessary, because the wide variety of herbs seems to cover most of mankind's difficulties. The primary benefit to genetic manipulation would be to understand the devic orders. Any such genetic manipulation should be done in cooperation with the devic orders. You see this in the lives of people like Luther Burbank and others who truly understood the way plants operate. They spoke with them and knew the plant personalities, but even deeper, they were in harmony with the devic orders.

Certain vibrational techniques were used to genetically manipulate plants. Ultrasound of particular frequency patterns may be derived that will affect the DNA chain in the reproductive organs of plants. The flowers and seeds should be focused upon. These various patterns tend to move the genetic chain. It will not disrupt a particular site upon the chain, but rather shift and move some of it. This will, after a few generations of working with the plant, in 99 percent of the cases, develop a sterile plant that will not replicate. In perhaps one percent of these cases, a gene will develop that can change the property of the plant.

The specific frequencies used related to certain wave shapes with high harmonic content, particularly at the second and fourth harmonics, as in things like a triangle or sawtooth wave forms. These are periodic wave forms. The key was that bursts of other wave forms were superimpressed upon these. The particular frequencies involved correspond to a range of ultrasonic frequencies. These disrupt cell membranes of all types. Therefore, when the tuning of the ultrasonic equipment is precise enough and it is singular in frequency, which today is quite easy to do, this resonance that disrupts cell membranes can be avoided. A specific frequency instead will disrupt or change a DNA structure. On the level of hit and miss, certain frequencies would disrupt the molecular arrangement and shift some of the bonding that takes place in the process of cell replication. When this takes place, the new cells have different DNA structures. It can be random. As these plants were worked with, the correct mutations were selected by the usual techniques of cross-breeding.

There is a direct correlation between the exact frequencies and types of ultrasound used and the desired result. Because this might be abused by mankind, it is not something that we will give specific details upon at this time. Also, certain of these techniques may involve a little more energy than was used in Atlantis. It is wise, when exploring these things, even with the highest good in mind, that one do this work far away from any concentrations of negative thought forms. In some of these ultrasound techniques, there is a blank slate type of effect that takes place. In the genetic movement of various DNA chains there is a possibility of outside influence to reposition a particular gene or chain of DNA in a given direction.

You might say, "But if I don't know what the gene's pattern looks like, how can I change it with my thoughts?" That is where the devic order comes into play, because it is able to use the energies of the ultrasound on the physical level and the thought forms of the human to adjust the various attributes genetically in a way that makes a difference in the reproductive attribute of the plant, the actual DNA change. This does not mean that only coordination with the devic spirits is necessary. In addition, the thought forms of the individual must be quite pure for this to take place.

Obviously, there are many other techniques that are currently used to genetically manipulate plants. These techniques involve chemicals, a concentrated focus of energy, and radiation. Generally, these practices lessen the devic spirits' connection with plants. This is how hybrids are often derived. As various plants are manipulated by these techniques and many seeds are grown, a small percentage of them will have some of the attributes an individual is looking for. What is lost is the connection with the life force, and that is why these experiments are usually not good to do.

These changes were dangerous, and several different varieties were created that were ultimately destroyed. It is not wise for some of these techniques to be used blindly at this time. The problem with this is that there are many things that will be affected deeply, more deeply than the usual ways of altering DNA structures through current chemical techniques. There can be several problems with this process. Often the plants created developed without the full understanding of the person involved in the process, and the devic order was not sufficiently involved. The specific frequencies necessary will not be given because of potential misuse. However, a range of frequencies could be given for those who wish to explore this, so that some of the intermediate science could be developed in about ten years, when there might be more of the appropriate consciousness used to present less harm to the environment.

Imagine a simple plant structure that replicates easily, such as a weed. If this was altered genetically so that the weed could rapidly take over large areas, it could be used as a destructive weapon. Alterations in the normal cycles of nature could disrupt crop growth and cause famine. Thus, you see why caution is needed. The particular frequency range will be in the areas of about 26 kilohertz upward. The upper limit of this may be higher than most people who investigate ultrasound have looked at. That is all we are permitted to say at this time.

The Atlanteans also used herbs and crystals together. A particular herb that might affect the physical body in a specific manner was sometimes given a vibrational treatment before being ingested. This was done in many different ways. One way involved the use of crystals. A set of crystals was energized by people who wished to heal an individual. Then the crystals were placed around the herbal formulation, herbal distillation, or even just around the plant. Then the vibration was shifted in this substance by the crystals. This sometimes took a few weeks, so such preparations were made well in advance. When the herb was ingested, it had a greater vibrational match to the individual. It was as if the crystal acted as a transformer.

It generally takes a few hundred years to fully program a crystal, so that it will work for a number of people, at least 12 and, in many cases, 144 to 1098. Such individuals may indeed work with this crystal over and over, bringing energy of transformative vibration-raising ability into it. The crystal will generally change slightly. Cracks and fissures may appear, and it may change its outward appearance.

Some crystals have the ability to allow a rapid transfer of vibrations when placed near other substances. This transfer of energy must be directed by those who understand and can work easily with crystals. Beyond this, they are fairly self-governing, in that the energies are generally harmonious and impossible to harm a person or plant. When it is placed near a plant, this vibrational shifting stirs within the plant the highest spiritual capacities so that some energy may be released into the ethers. This energy will generally swirl into the crystal, if the crystal is a double terminated quartz or any other double terminated type of crystal formation. These energies move into one end of the quartz and out the other forming a circulation. As this resonance and circling take place, the energies shifting through the plant move faster and faster and begin to be perceived by those around it as a glow. Then one would step into the field, moving closer to the crystal and plant to become a part of this circle.

Another common technique involved crystals and devices that activated telepathy. They were set in attunement with a given herb. Here a live plant was always used. It was set up as if a resonance was taking place, and as an individual slept, certain properties of the herb were brought into the physical body. This was done at times for physical healing, but was more applicable to activating the herb's spiritual properties. Some plants were very affected by these experiments. This included some of today's more prominent, useful, and well-understood herbs such as comfrey, peppermint, tansy, and even substances now used in homeopathy such as belladonna and aconite. The thought form was brought as clearly as possible into consciousness while holding the crystal to allow that energy to be amplified, strengthened, and purified by the crystal as it entered the plant. Then the plant was dried and the herbal concoction, tea, or tincture might be burned or in some cases taken internally. In many cases it was not necessary to harm the plant. In fact, the plant was often allowed to live near the person. This is the best way to do this. Keep the living herb near the person with crystals around it. At least once a day, the person should take those crystals around the plant and hold, touch, or squeeze them while focusing and concentrating on the healing thought forms and higher energy that they wish to receive. However, if this is a plant that can be easily dried and taken, nowadays, for most people, the spiritual properties would be better transferred into the plant and into the person if the plant is dried and eaten or taken as tea. This better assists the individual because then some physical component is also present.

Usually a large group worked with these crystals to bring energy into such plants. The thought forms from these treatments were impressed upon the life stream of the herb worldwide. There was no physical change associated with this. What was asked was that the devic kingdom associated with the herb would also take on some of these additional attributes to help transfer spiritual properties into the plant.

Crystals were used to activate an herb's spiritual properties in Atlantis. The crystal was seen as an intervening medium. It therefore was not simply an amplifier, but something which allowed resonance. If an individual was seeking greater spiritual understanding or the understanding of a particular attribute, various plants were employed with crystals to aid that growth experience.

A crystal was held by an individual for three nights. Each time they slept, or each time during meditation, they held the crystal and imparted into it their energies. The individual then focused a pure mental image of the particular herb that they wished to find greater resonance with. This would be like bringing a picture into the crystal. After three days of this, the crystal would be more firmly imbued with the vibration of the pure picture of this plant. This was not just an image like you see on television, but it involved the taste, smell, and feel of the plant as well as all the attributes that a person might know of it. This created a resonance between the crystal and the plant. Then one invoked the devic spirit associated with the plant to create a firmer resonance with the crystal. That same crystal was then placed in close physical proximity to such a plant for three days. After that, the preparation and programming of the crystal was complete.

This can be done now by stimulating the crystal physically or electrically so that the piezoelectric effect is more firmly stimulated and the molecular resonance of the crystal is set into various modes of vibration. Then it more easily absorbs your own thought forms.

If the individual at any time in their life sought healing from this plant, the crystal could be employed. It could be placed upon a particular chakra on the physical body corresponding to where the healing was needed, or it could be placed next to the individual as they slept. It could also be placed behind the plant with a visualization of rays of light pouring from the crystal moving through the plant to the individual.

Because the crystal resonated with the plant, if at any time an individual felt out of harmony with some attribute of life related to that particular plant, they could employ the crystal to reacquaint them with this. They could also place the crystal to their left and the plant to their right. This could even involve other attributes of the plant that were desired. For instance, if the sense of smell for spiritual development was being focused on, then just the aroma from the plant's oil would be sufficient. The crystal placed there would form a circuit, like a circular motion when viewed from above in a clockwise direction, as if the energies of each were pouring into the other. After perhaps a half hour meditation on this, the circle would be reversed and seen counterclockwise.

On a less evolved level, the crystal might be placed next to the herb alone and the devic order invoked to assist. This was usually done with the living plant or the living herb, not with its extract or a dead plant. This was important because the life force associated with the plant is much stronger when the plant is living. Individuals today can experiment with such techniques. Programming a crystal is a little more difficult today, but those who have some affinity with a particular herb or plant may have some success with this.

Other techniques used with crystals involved telepathic communication with the devic orders. Particular messages or information from those orders were made more clearly available to the Atlanteans. They would sometimes be in communion with the nature spirits of such plants worldwide to gather information about the planet—about weather conditions, climatic change, earthquakes, and tidal waves.

This communication often took place with plants that were found in many places about the Earth, such as the various grasses. A dual tetrahedral crystal was usually employed for telepathy in Atlantis. To see this shape, imagine a tetrahedron with its point facing upwards, and another one with its point facing downwards, joined at their bases. Often the triangular prism shape that is created by such a crystal is extended so that between these two tetrahedral crystals is a solid crystal mass. Today, individuals can create such crystals out of quartz. They can also be grown out of silicon if one wishes to explore this. These crystals were then used to resonate and create a telepathic link. This link was best done by individuals involved in agriculture who knew these plants in a more intimate way. But sometimes they employed other means to share this with other individuals.

Children were also involved in this process, because many of them knew the devic orders quite intimately. They played with the devic spirits, and at a later time, perhaps at nine, ten or eleven years of age, they were introduced to these telepathic or dual tetrahedral crystals. Then they were asked to communicate a given thought, not so much just the joyousness of knowing the devic spirit, but a particular attribute. This was not formed as a question quite yet, but rather the individual was given the assignment of, for instance, knowing what the sun is like for the devic order. The link through the crystal became more intense.

Often a field of plants, or a little planter box with some of plants and crystals in it, was placed about four or five feet away from the child. The crystal was hung from the middle of the space at an equal distance between the plant and the child. In focusing their eyes upon the crystal, they imagined romping in a field with the herb, or communicating with the devic spirit, or the enjoyment that they felt in such playfulness. Then the question was interposed about, for instance, focusing on sunrise. At a later time, a more specific question was asked, for instance, about what was happening worldwide, about some particular message the devic order had, or some attribute that the child was working on spiritually. This resonance and communication with the devic orders was encouraged.

Later the magnetic attributes relating to crystals were necessary for this telepathic link because some of these capabilities of communicating with the devic order were lost. More technologically oriented apparatus in Atlantis became necessary. Towards the end of the Atlantean phase, even these were not sufficient to make contact with the devic orders in the most advanced of children.

Crystals have a lattice pattern that can be stimulated by certain techniques to bring the action of magnetic fields into a state of amplification. In these techniques, energy of a highly concentrated magnetic force is impressed across the crystal in certain lattice directions. The key here is the way the magnetic force is concentrated, so that the lines of force, as they move, are in a strongly unidirectional matrix. Most magnetic fields currently created tend to have lines that move in curves. There are many ways to compensate for this, to force the lines into stronger straight lines over small spaces. These are currently being explored by many scientists. This is useful for crystals, because then this energy, as it is applied to quartz, may have a direct stimulating effect—if the magnetic field is varied in its direction at various frequencies that correspond to certain natural resonance structures within the crystal lattice. These may be at frequencies above 64,000 cycles per second and below 200,000 cycles per second. These energies set into resonance certain of the magnetic properties of the crystal.

This energy may be utilized by a human because it is similar to some of the gentler magnetic fields that are created in the brain when these telepathic communication techniques with the devic orders are used. Sometimes etheric sight may be gained by this. As these techniques are explored, one might wish to place a crystal stimulated in such a fashion at the third eye center and notice what effect it has. Devices were constructed in Atlantis that involved placing crystals around the head so that some of these deeper states of communication could be achieved.

The work with crystals and the vibrational resonance of various herbs and plants to the individual was taken simply for their spiritual properties. This meant that an individual in resonating with a particular herb was not doing it for healing or for seeing how they would be more in harmony with God's laws. They wished to explore a part of their being, a certain aspect of their spirit. This resonance was of great benefit for the individual, not so much on the physical level but simply for greater awareness in their lives, their relationships, and all things that a person could put into action in the world. Ultimately, spirituality not brought into action is a burden. This is why in Atlantis these practices were largely discontinued by the end of the Atlantean phase, because the burden of spirituality as a deeper understanding was not brought into physical action. Individuals were not able to fully share emotionally, or in ways of deep relationship or intimacy on a physical level, those lessons and understandings of God that they received.

1 Edgar Cayce, *The Egyptian Heritage* (Virginia Beach, VA: A.R.E. Press, 1972), p. 11-12, 22-23, 37, 60-61, 63, 75, 76, 120.

ELECAMPANE

CHAPTER III

USE OF HERBS IN
ANCIENT EGYPT AND CHINA

The spiritual properties of herbs were activated by the energies of ritual in Egypt in the ways soul energy was focused on by the people. This is where most of the translations and understandings of the hieroglyphics are somewhat in error because it was soul energy, not the energy of death or of movement that was focused on.

In the Egyptian religious rites, it is assumed that death was the doorway to another land, to a place that was in some ways similar to the concepts, particularly important in this century around heaven. It is as if the religious rites of the Egyptians are being interpreted through the filters of Protestant, Catholic, and other Christian based religions. This is not true at all. In fact, the Egyptian rites were to understand, not an afterlife, not a place very different from Earth, but rather a place by which the greater capacities of the soul intermingled and mixed with the individual's consciousness as they understood the world, what their lives were about, and their relationships.

The way this understanding developed amongst the Egyptians was the goal to be taken into the afterlife, as we might call it. The training, rituals, and ability to move into a trancelike state and the ability to shift vibrations to work with what you would call magic assisted the soul to completely understand how to merge with the higher forces. The subtler energies, normally associated with the points known after death, were merged with those drawn from physical life. This is not easy to understand if you look at it from the point of view of the worship of a death state, or some reversal of what is heaven and what is Earth, as is sometimes seen by those interpreting Egyptian hieroglyphics.

This energy was seen as symbolized in many of the plants. The entire Egyptian civilization was based upon the fertility of land near the Nile, and the people were well aware of this because of the desert region all around them. Thus, they focalized the energy of plants as they related to the soul. This meant that an individual, in seeking greater peace, deeper states of meditation, and deeper communion with the Gods, might employ herbs. This was done by eating them, preparing them in teas, and using herbs on the physical body. The herbs were often crushed and the oils applied.

As a part of this, a ritual often took place by which the individual was given greater awareness of the soul. It was seen that with a particular plant the individual's vibration changed. This was not a conscious process.

In Atlantis, a similar process was done in a conscious manner. It was a common practice in much of the Atlantean culture to understand how thought forms were created, how they work with individuals, and what they were made of. This was an entire sequence of studies similar to present day studies of psychology. Specific vibrational states were often initialized by herbs, and these then influenced the construction of thought forms. The spiritual property of the herb was often taken inside an individual as they constructed the thought forms.

In Egypt, various artifacts such as the ankh were dipped into an herb mixture. They were often able to vibrate to the higher vibration of the herb as a result. These objects captured and worked with these thought forms. Another example of this might be a piece of crystal specifically carved and set into vibration by certain energies associated with inert gases, under electrical and magnetic stimulation. As it was set into vibration, the pattern was changed by giving it an herb bath. The herbal vibration gradually penetrated and changed the energy of the structure. The thought form caused the vibrational shift, influencing what was eventually learned from working with an herb and an object. This shift was not just a combination of these two separate vibrations, but a way in which they yielded a third vibration. That vibration was not directly associated with either the physical substance or the herb itself, but was under the control and guidance of the person doing the experiment and working with these thought forms. Thus, it took on the highest characteristics of all the different beings and forces involved including the herb, the devic order associated with it, the physical substance, and the person working with it.

This had very little to do with the herb's actual spiritual property. For instance, in working with certain herbs, one might feel attuned to a particular aspect of life. One might feel greater calmness when in actuality, the herb's higher spiritual property would be in attunement to the soul's calmness, which often meant for the individual an entirely different pattern such as the relaxation of the physical body as it is a symbol. So the person might feel more relaxed in their feet, and decide this herb helped them feel more calm when in actuality the soul's pattern was one of easing life's important duties, and of finding a way to nurture and relax on the soul level. This meant that on the physical or even ritual levels, the full properties of the herbs were not understood, and this was not necessary. Individuals were able to resolve and understand issues with the assistance of the vibration of these herbs. In fact, almost all herbs of a beneficial or health-giving effect had a similar positive property. This is still found today. Individuals who take an herb are affected on levels beyond the physical.

Herbs were an important part of various rituals that were done regarding embalming, scented baths, and dance techniques. Many of these rituals did not directly involve spiritual properties; however, the beginnings of such rituals were inspired by a quest for spiritual understanding. This was how much information about the specific herbal spiritual properties known and used by the techniques of resonance in Atlantis were transferred to Egypt. The rituals created such a resonance. Sometimes herbs were an important part of the ritual, and sometimes they were merely symbolic. Individual often received the message of various rituals, and thus were able to again tune into or create a greater resonance with some of the spiritual techniques that the rituals naturally brought out.

There were sharp class divisions, which created certain difficulties in ancient Egypt. What is not well known about ancient Egypt is that using herbs transcended most classes because they were common and easy to find. Herbs could be found up and down the Nile, and people used plants in many different ways regardless of their station in life. This sometimes provided an overriding spiritual equality amongst the individuals in that society.

Egyptian rituals often invoked knowledge from past lives and the energies they had already dealt with. These things came to them gradually after a ritual. This was an open door to higher consciousness and to other dimensions.

Before the start of an Egyptian ritual, some aromatic herbs, particularly frankincense and myrrh were burned in a room for three days. This prepared the room, and then the incense was removed so that just the soft vibration of these herbs penetrated and remained within the room. This was timed so that rituals usually began at the new or full Moon. Water was placed throughout the room in small bowls around the periphery of the room, and into each of these an herb was added. The herb might be in a tincture or tea, but was often just a little sprig of a plant. These herbs were selected to activate greater memory, understanding, and inner awakening. It was up to each of the individuals working in the group to choose the herb for themselves that they wished to place there. In the center of the room was usually placed one particular plant. Often, it was a live plant in a small pot or a plant that the individuals felt deeply in tune with at that time. In many cases, these plants had beautiful flowers, and the effect was also of simply observing and knowing the beauty of the plant. These included, of course, many different plants such as wild roses or plants taken from foreign lands. The object was that the herb would create a slight shift in vibration; individuals would understand and feel it on levels that responded to the heart, that related to beauty. Thus, an understanding of the plant's spiritual properties developed.

Before individuals came into this room they had already anointed themselves with various aromatic oils. They would generally not be clothed when the ritual began. They sat quietly together for a period of two hours or so. You might call this meditation, but in fact they had been meditating before this, and they came into this room with empty, open minds not focused or concentrated in any particular area. After two hours or so, the priest or priestess entered the room. Often this was a woman who brought a powerful sense of love but also a tie to a particular man in the group. He acted as her partner in grounding some of the energies that were then shared.

The priest or priestess created a vortex. This was generally created by a dance. These people might be sitting in a circle, and she would walk around the circle. Usually this was done in some specific pattern such as 144 times in one direction and 144 in the other direction. As she did this, attempts was made by these individuals to go deeper into a state of opening to her vibrations, to where she was moving. After a while, she would usually sit. When she did this, it was a signal and certain sounds were then made. These sounds matched the frequencies that corresponded to the room, in what was termed a resonator configuration, so that the room began to vibrate. As she added her own energy to this, the other individuals joined in.

Then she asked them to journey to another place, another time, and another way of seeing. From this, individuals would have particular experiences, and they would share what they saw and remembered. This included how the others in the group looked, how they worked, what they wore, and what they shared together. The journey was usually a group interaction. Most important in this process was a discussion of what they had learned. It was the ultimate role of the priestess, to bring out from each of these individuals what they learned from their past experiences, from their understanding between lives, and from their understanding of higher consciousness. After this had taken place, she usually did a dance, and asked, that each of the others join her one-by-one. In this dance, again, a ritual rotary motion might be taken, walking around the room in a circle, moving in various ways. Then each chose one of the bowls of water that had the herbs in it, and they usually drank the water or ate the herbs. The purpose was to cleanse and allow the vibrations of the herb to heal some psychic difficulties that may have arisen during this work. At various times throughout the ritual, there was chanting and working with the vibrations of the voice. This was often under the guidance of the priestess or priest.

After the ritual was done, it was usually suggested that the people involved should fast, to remember, and to meet again just to discuss what had happened. Generally, it was also required that they each make a gift. This was sometimes pure money, something of an economic nature, or simply a gift to the priestess to show that they indeed honored her as a representation of God in that ritual. Many times it was asked that they bring something creative and share this with the priestess and with each other. Then, she usually destroyed the gift. Sometimes the gift was so precious and special that she had it placed in a special chamber to be placed around her at her eventual death. This was a great honor.

As in Lemuria, the Egyptians implanted thoughts into certain plants knowing they would reach and help us today. The plants involved worked on a more subtle level. The Egyptians worked from a place of ritual. There was less consciousness involved, than in Lemuria. This meant that many of the herbs and plants from that time have been imbued with thought forms in a gentler way. It was perceived that at some point in the future mankind would lose the ability to truly understand the value of ritual. Then these gentler thought forms, from this Egyptian period, might again be evoked within humankind. That was the general purpose. It was not done as consciously and with as much focused intent as in Lemuria.

They implanted in papyrus a generalized appreciation of the idea of communication enhanced by ritual. This was done partly to influence people today. Again, we look at generalities here simply because these are more on the level of thought forms and impressions than of specific attributes. Other plants imbued with positive thought forms by the Egyptians include the olive, maný grains, particularly those grown in Egypt, various plants and herbs local to that region, including Christ thorn, and some plants that were used primarily as flower essences such as bamboo, lotus, and papyrus. The list also extends to all the herbs used for essential oils including frankincense and myrrh, as well as many fragrances that were utilized for different rituals.

These thought forms were of a ritualistic nature. They were not always consciously fed into these plants. Part of the idea here was to incorporate them as if to allow a connection to the Earth through these plants. Another reason was simply to receive benefits from the plants. Papyrus, for instance, became scrolls to write on, and various fragrances had utility in ritual because the nose and sinuses were stimulated.

Many of the seeds for these Egyptian rituals were derived from Atlantis in which a clear understanding of how thought forms related in harmony to Earth existence was left to them by the Lemurians. Thus, there was a three-stage development by which the spiritualization and thought form energies from Atlantis derived from the Lemurians was taken into a place of ritual. The Egyptians utilized many of these ideas without knowledge or full understanding. During certain periods, various herbalists and people who understood the plant kingdom in Egypt questioned this and began to understand some parts of this heritage. But their knowledge was not broadly transferred to the Egyptian culture. Various herbs and oils continued to be used in rituals but never with a deep understanding.

In ancient China, plants were experienced more with the Lemurian attitudes. The intrinsic nature, personality, comraderie, and joyousness of plants were known. To experience this attitude while working with plants, understanding that mankind has a united soul, is of great benefit. Each will have their own path, but some will know this through sound. Visualize people throughout the world chanting Om, creating a sound together, and then join in this process. This is discussed and commonly shared through the teachings of Yogananda in what is called the Om technique. It is wise to see that it is expansion to the group that is required to achieve this greater soul unity.

Others will activate the visual sense. Imagine yourself part of a very large circle, connected to these individuals, and that an energy from your heart flows to their hearts. Imagine this circle encompassing the planet. It is a way of imagining an embrace. The one person you embrace becomes ten, and then becomes a hundred and on and on. They are embracing you, and in this way, a feeling develops within you of a close connection to many.

There were many times when life was very difficult in China, especially in growing food for large populations. Individuals found that companion planting and ways of working with herbs combined with food was beneficial. Because of the nature of the language and the way the Chinese culture grew, many questions were asked about this: What is the importance spiritually of such companion planting? What is the message? How can individuals know this? This is an example of one way the Chinese culture learned from herbs to see how they were used, how they grew, and the ways they worked.

Ginseng was honored in such a culture because of its similarity to the human form. In fact, the similarity and relationship of many different herbs to the human form was gradually understood in China. Gradually, what developed as a result of this were many questions regarding the energies provided by using these herbs. This allowed change in a physical body that was not seen to be the result of a drug or direct physical manipulation as might be seen in current times. Instead, it was believed that the Gods, or the energies of nature itself acted through these herbs to affect a person. Questions were then asked about the nature of this energy.

This was one of the important attributes understood in using herbs with acupuncture. Those who worked as herbologists combined this well with acupuncture because the nature of the effect upon the physical body was known as having as its beginning a spiritual direction. Therefore, the herb's point in being was eventually understood by those who studied this technique in ancient China. Its origin and point of being was that of spiritual oneness with the universe, or Earth energy loving mankind. This was to a certain degree in agreement with the Lemurian way of working with nature.

Naturally, this led to individuals experimenting and using herbs in many different ways. Herbs gradually became an intimate part of the culture. That was when it became a bit more ritualized—the various tea ceremonies and the ways herbs were a part of building a house and having a garden with companion planting. This was not because they understood the principles, but simply because that is the way it was always done.

This ritualization however never blinded the eyes of herbologists, herbal healers, or acupuncturists. They understood the properties of herbs on a purer level. They understood the deeper meaning of the five elements, the five directions, the energies of the movement in the physical Earth, and the changes that happened in the body. Heat and cold were often applied here, and the yin-yang principle right from the beginning was very important. All these things affected society, so what was created was a spiritual awakening of society because of the incorporation of herbs. These individuals were able to realize a greater spiritual development as a society than as individuals because of this attention and continual work with herbs.

The continuous use of herbs in China affected the herbs as they now affect mankind. This is partly because the herb gatherers also treated and worked with them. There is an internal spiritual reverence that is created for the beautiful energies of these various herbs. Secondly, the signature in the Chinese system was always of great importance. Those who worked with herbs recognized the signature and honored it deeply. The thought forms of herbalists and those who understood and worked with the signature solidified and strengthened the very factor by which the signature brought some of the higher spiritual properties into Chinese herbs. Therefore, co-working with these herbs, which has gone on for a long period of time, has gradually allowed the permeation of positive, helpful, and uplifting spiritual thought forms of various herbalists and wildcrafters to be more closely associated with the plants. This also gradually affected the devic orders associated with the plants, strengthening the thought forms and therefore the signatures of the plants. This ultimately strengthened the signature and spiritual properties of Chinese herbs. It is a positive cycle that is of great benefit to the plants and people who utilize Chinese herbs. These patterns continue today.

In the most spiritual sense, Chinese herbs as a group are more influenced by interaction with mankind than is true with other herbs. Chinese herbs have developed greater sensitivity and strength. Because of this Chinese herbs will not be as weakened by environmental pollutants, fertilizers, and poor growing methods. This goes across all cultural boundaries. For so many centuries, and in a deep way almost akin to a religion, the Chinese and other Oriental groups have recognized the signature, the energy of healing, and the way these plants work. This has run very deep through the culture. Moreover, this reverential attitude has been cultivated by the nature of the Chinese language and by the way the people understood and worked with herbs whether they were herbalists or not. You see this attitude particularly when looking at panax ginseng. There is a great deal of reverence, almost religious lore, with regards to this plant. This attitude is similar, although extended more in time, to the way the Lemurians worked with the devic orders of these plants and with their karmic purpose. The Chinese, in working with them for thousands of years, often for four or five or six thousand years, have developed this coordinated energy. This attitude is not so developed in Western culture.

HAWTHORNE

CHAPTER IV

THOUGHT FORMS AND ETHERIC DENSITY

Some of the material in this chapter is deliberately presented in a vague style. This is because some of this information could be misused to create weapons. Because of a similar understanding Steiner, especially regarding homeopathy and agriculture, did not reveal certain facts because of the imminent Nazi threat.

The ethers are the ever fine interconnecting substance that connects all beings on all levels in all ways in the universe. It is not a substance that exists in three dimensions the way people normally perceive the three dimensions. This interconnectedness on many levels allows the transfer of vibrations. But it does not allow this transfer in the usual sense of either energy or matter as you perceive it, but it is a way in which waves are set up in this medium.

The movement of the ethers takes place from many sources including physical motion, magnetism, electricity, and thought. It acts as the conducting substance by which telepathy takes place. People's thoughts influence the ethers. Thus, if thoughts are of a positive nature, vibrations in the ethers will normally be uplifting and helpful. If your thoughts relate to power over others, willingness to cause harm, various negative states, or even just adherence to ignorance, such vibrations also set up wave patterns in the ethers. These create densified patches in the ethers in localities where these negative thought forms readily occur. In places where there have been wars or great difficulty, some of these etheric vibrations still remain. It is because of this that historians sometimes experience these things and have difficulty being in such places. Some people get physically ill when visiting a concentration camp partly because of this problem. The etheric density over the entire planet has reached such a state that mankind now has a continuing difficulty with negative thought forms. This influences most people today.

Etheric density developed because of negative thought form pollution. Unfortunately, much of this thought pollution is largely unconscious so people are not aware of it. If mankind still had etheric sight, etheric density and negative thought forms would be far less of a problem. Individuals are usually not aware that the thoughts they create such as their anguishes and worries, the energy associated with these negative vibrational states has no place to go. It simply surrounds them, and gradually the constant expression of such energies co-creates a foundation vibration. This interlinking vibration between many beings all over the planet full of worry, fear, guilt, and other negative states is a receptor mechanism by which energies of a more powerful nature can remain rooted.

In recent years it has become increasingly understood that the emotions play a key role in causing and even curing diseases. Visualization exercises are now used with cancer as part of the treatment. Understanding the deep role that negative thought forms play in our lives is an extension of appreciating the role that the emotions play in health and disease.

On the planet in the past there have, of course, been beings who have been greedy, full of hatred, and misguided in various ways. But the loving response of the general population to these individuals did not allow difficult negative thought forms to prosper. Thus, the ethers remained thin and clear. Individuals filled with hatred, greed, and difficulty simply remained with their own negative thought forms, which did not go much beyond them. In the current day, however, negative thought forms of a more powerful and energetic nature, like those of hatred and greed, are often carried into the general population. You see this with the great fears and the way people approach disease, earthquake, and various environmental difficulties. People often do not just respond with deeper understanding, they experience fear. Negative thought forms get transferred worldwide. As this energy goes around and around the planet, it creates a denser and denser state.

Obviously, it is mankind's attention to these negative and difficult states such as greed, power, and hatred that makes the big difference. However, it is not for you to blame others. It is their hatred, their struggle with power, or their willingness to hurt others. It is not them doing it to us. The way individuals learn to receive this energy often allows it to continue. If individuals, for instance, recognize that a murder described on the front page of a newspaper is not what they are most interested in and stop buying the newspaper, many of these things will change. And so individuals, though they may be filled with love and assistance, tie in to these overall negative thought forms. Gradually, this is what has made the difference and allowed this difficulty to take root. Etheric density is a result of mankind's thoughts, which increase etheric density throughout much of the planet.

At various periods in mankind's history, etheric density has temporarily reached a state of difficulty. This took place a couple of times in Lemuria for short periods when there was general anxiety and fear regarding the coming Atlantean civilization. It was as if a darkness descended on the planet because etheric sight was reduced in all people. They naturally put focus, energy, and attention on this, finding ways, for instance, to provide positive and uplifting plant species and various flower essences to the Atlanteans. The typical example here is the orange. You see in that color and in the fruit itself an uplifting feeling, as if there is a smile on your face, or a happiness vibration associated with the orange itself—not just the orange flower or orange flower essence.

This problem also developed several times in Atlantis. During the mid-Atlantean epic there were difficulties regarding nuclear weapons. Then powerful negative thought forms descended upon the planet, but again they were released. Individuals gathered, using crystals, meditation, group chanting, channeling, and energy from the Earth. Help also came from beings beyond the Earth. Consciousness was raised so that the etheric density was released. Indeed, experiments done then with inert gases to reduce the etheric density yielded information that is applicable to the techniques in which inert gas devices can be used today. Much of that research is applicable now because the vibration today is similar.

The time period between Atlantis and Greece was a relatively awakened period in which etheric density difficulties were often prevented from coming to the Earth by outside influences. In Grecian times, mankind lost the ability to have this etheric sight and so could not discern the darkness that gradually came again upon the Earth.

In the Egyptian civilization, the use of darker energies were seen to cause difficulty. Therefore, much ritual and activities were done, especially in the early Egyptian phase, to raise the vibration of the planet worldwide so that the etheric mists were dispelled before they ever became dark and difficult. They often used frank, myrrh, sage, and sandalwood incense to ease etheric density. One of the characteristics of the beings who became leaders of Egypt was that they had the ability to recognize this density of the ethers more clearly, firmly, and powerfully than most of their brothers. This ability was particularly strong with the Pharoah Aknaton. These kings often planned their reign and what would be done in their time, based on their ability to understand this darkness and how thinning the ethers would be more important at certain times.

Of course, there are astrological influences here. Certain planetary alignments affect overall negatively on the Earth so that etheric density is slightly stronger. This includes all alignments with Saturn and the Sun in opposition or conjunction, the way Pluto is stationary as viewed from the Earth or in the time between retrograde and forward motion, and the way the Earth's density is affected in a positive way as it moves from one galactic transformation point to another as during the harmonic convergence. Galactic movement is also a part of this. These patterns affect the etheric density on the Earth. In many cases it will move backwards before it moves forwards. Sometimes these instances can last for as long as one month on the Earth, particularly the Saturnian influences.

The times when the ethers are the thinnest, when energy can be transmitted from the Earth and moved in many different ways, occurs during the solstice and equinox points. That is usually around the twenty-first or twenty-second of every third month. Seasonal change is a deep part of the unconscious of beings, and so at such times rituals done to dispel the ethers became a part of folklore and myth. This was a deliberate design. The hope was that even though mankind lost the ability to know this etheric darkness, they would still have some capacity to dispel it by these rituals. This is one reason for the current attraction of some to pagan rituals that relate to seasonal activities, particularly during the solstice and equinox.

Today, there are many ways to weaken etheric density. Crystals can be arranged in gridlike patterns with repeated stimulation, and objects that have been imbued with life force by their use in ritual can be placed in a house. Or burn sage in the four directions. (A few months ago, before and after I moved into a house, I burned sage in the four corners of the house for several days as a cleansing.) Because etheric density on the Earth is so strong, it is probable that various rituals will need to be done to overcome some of these energies. Where etheric thinning is required over long periods of time, it is best that the devices or techniques utilized not be those that draw energy out of people.

A series of inert gas devices can also be used. Many of these relate to fields that are omnidirectional in content rather than unidirectional, and imply the use of moving water or highly charged electric fields of high voltage through the inert gases. The particular gases involved are krypton and argon, especially argon. These devices may be constructed more often in the future.

Using water here is quite safe, and it is possible that high voltage electricity can be applied with little ill effects to most inert gases. There are certain limitations on this regarding various pressures and achievable voltage levels, but for the most part there is little difficulty if the frequencies applied to the inert gases are kept sufficiently low. As a medium measure, the frequencies primarily below 20 cycles per second (20 hertz) in high voltage arrangements will be of benefit. There are certain exceptions here, of course, but 7.83 hertz as a vibration, no matter how much voltage is used, is not going to be harmful through any inert gas at any particular pressure. DC high voltage fields will not create much difficulty. Moving water in most of its forms will work well with most inert gases, and indeed this is already being done by certain individuals.

A crystal that has been sufficiently cleared and imbued with pure sunlight energy can be moved through a room in a rapid fashion. It is not usually enough for a person just to do this by holding it. Instead, it is something that may need to take place for a while. There are ceiling fans that people have in some of their homes. Take a crystal that has been purified—exposure to sunlight energy for a whole day—and securely attach it to the blade of the fan. This may cleanse the etheric density and extend downward into the room for perhaps as much as six or even eight feet. These techniques may need to be experimented with to fully perfect them. Further experimentation is necessary partly because conditions are different now than when these patterns with crystals were used in Atlantis. And individuals who have a greater tie to Lemuria than to Atlantis will not respond in the same way. Many will indeed not gain the same results. They will be more sensitive to living things than to gems.

Other techniques involve movement in which dispersion of energy on the etheric level takes place because of the movement of etheric objects. Energy associated with the etheric body moves. This takes place if one has sufficient conscious dreaming ability to manipulate ritual objects in their etheric form in the astral state. It can also take place when individuals dance or move around a room.

There are many others techniques that increase the light vibration in a room such as repeated affirmations or repeated group meditation. These things gradually shift the ethers. However, if the techniques or practices are discontinued, the vibration of the place will gradually slip back, by entropy, to that which matches the vibrational rate of the environment.

During the harmonic convergence, the released energy created an etheric thinning on the highest mental planes. This energy will permeate into those with the ability to receive it over the next two-year period. As these energies of essentially intensified potential come through more powerfully for people, they will be able to manifest this localized etheric effect. In two years there will be a significant clearing for some, particularly when individuals gather in groups.

Many herbs, flowers essences, gem elixirs, and homeopathic remedies ease etheric density. There are two levels of this. There are those that act directly on the ethers themselves. This is not a very common property, because the ability to do this must usually be amplified by humans. However, because of the potent ability of the genuine vibrational state clear quartz, black quartz, white diamond gem elixirs and pennyroyal and lotus flower essences directly clear the ethers. They can be added to the water used around plants or people, or be misted in the air. This effect will generally be temporary because the vibrational nature of mankind's negative thought forms is so powerful that it will gradually counteract this. Therefore, the effects of vibrational remedies will vary depending on the location. In an inner city, the effect of relieving etheric density may pass in only 15 minutes. In a place far into nature and away from urban environments, the effects might be noted for as long as two days.

The other side of this is raising consciousness, particularly of groups. There are many flower essences and gem elixirs that have a powerful cleansing ability. Acting through the person, the negative thought forms are eased. This includes pennyroyal and carob and those flower essences relating to group activity and group meditation. Indeed, many flower essences that work on individuals to raise their consciousness also have the powerful effect of relieving the etheric density around the person.

Many herbs, of course, raise someone's consciousness, which directly eases etheric density. One can also examine the way herbs grow. Those that grow under widely varying conditions and that are not easily changed by various forms of cross-breeding often have the ability to powerfully change and raise the vibration of a person and an area. The ability to assist a person to change their vibration is stronger with such herbs.

Herbs also act directly on the ethers. They primarily have their effects when utilized in ritual or aromatherapy, or when subtle vibrations are transmitted. But, the most powerful way they directly affect the ethers is through the actual presence of growing plants. An herb garden has a very beautiful and important etheric vibration around it. Most herb gardens are excellent places to meditate, study, and activate the higher spiritual bodies.

Sage, orange, lobelia, and Pao d' Oro are very helpful herbs to ease negative thought forms and disease. Most fruits are also beneficial. Certain exceptions to this include fruits that have been exceptionally hybridized and changed, or that have been overtreated with chemicals such as banana. But many of the various fruits have spiritual and uplifting characteristics that tend to intermingle on a spiritual level across humanity. This accelerates and assists the entire process of easing negative thought forms.

Sage, orange, lobelia, and most fruit flower essences also ease negative thought forms. This is also true with lotus and cotton flower essences. Cotton flower essence increases the spiritual properties of one's entire life in many directions at once. There is a likelihood that individuals will gain a greater perspective necessary to deal with negative thought forms. Yarrow is also quite effective in easing negative thought forms, particularly when a person is attuned to that plant, especially the shape of the flower. However, with flower essences you will also see properties relating more directly to the individual, such as pennyroyal essence, in expelling negative thought forms. A greater sense of purpose and deeper understanding may emerge. Individuals may be able to deal with their own thought forms to understand any disease process.

Etheric density also affects the Earth. This is beyond the understanding of most individuals. The Earth is able to inhale and exhale, moving energy through its own being, to work with all energies on its surface, including love and understanding as well as hatred and power. All these things affect it. The way it releases energy that is essentially toxic to its being often occurs on the etheric levels. The blockage created by environmental pollution and mankind's negative thought forms throughout the Earth is similar to how a person who puts a coating of heavy oil upon the skin over the entire body might feel. This is obviously not good for the body for a very long period of time. Some of it will naturally be absorbed and some of it will be released, but the processes of energy inhalation and exhalation of the Earth is reduced because of the densified ethers.[1]

The Earth must do something about this, and will gradually make a change, perhaps by catastrophic Earth changes. But we do not wish to be making predictions here. It is a matter of time. These Earth processes can exist for long periods of time, for hundreds or even thousands of years, before there must be a catastrophic change. An example of one such change was the volcanic eruption of Mt. Saint Helen's. It involved not only the release of physical material, but a powerful etheric wave poured into the stratosphere very high into the atmosphere. Through it, a certain magnetic disturbance was also released. It could be compared to a sneeze. This energy was released into the Van Allen radiation belt then transmitted across the planet and ultimately to the Sun.

This process released negativity from the Earth and caused increased radiation. It also allowed the Earth a greater connection to the Sun. It is very important in the Earth's development that it receive and work with loving, caring energies from the Sun. These energies that are shared back and forth vitalize and nourish the Earth, so it is not only a matter of release. A current exists in the opposite direction, from the Sun to the Earth, through this same pathway that is nourishing to the Earth.

The thoughts of plants, animals, and devas resonate in attunement with mankind. These orders are here to learn and coexist with mankind. If mankind says now is the time for hatred, fear, guilt, and difficulty, some of this will be amplified and created in a state of resonance by certain plants and animals. Many times they simply do not know better because they do not have the experience. They are here to learn of these things. This is especially true with the animal kingdom. They are here to learn of love. They are not simply nourished by it, they are actually here to learn this from mankind.

The devic orders are also nourished by love. They come to learn something from it, but their principle purpose in assisting mankind may be accomplished even if they do not receive this love. Plants receive energy from the devic orders and from mankind. They combine these energies, to make sense genetically and express ways they learn. The trouble is essentially with the animal kingdom, because the creatures that experience fear from mankind and then share it amongst themselves will significantly multiply this on the Earth. This has already had what one might call a boomerang effect, in which the fear thought form relating to animals has closed the minds of many to the difficulty that animals experience when they are slaughtered. Closing one's heart to this destruction allows it to go on even more. Thus, you see the way this downward spiral has been created.

Thought forms on this planet are diverse. They move into many parts of the astral level and some of the mental plane. The powerful etheric levels are filled with thought forms of human beings, plants, animals, devic spirits and many other levels of vibration. Plants vibrate with these thought forms. This often takes many generations. By moving in harmony and synchronization with thought forms, plants become more powerful, prosperous, beautiful, and reproduce more easily. If they develop out of harmony with thought forms, they become debilitated and prone to disease. This is an obvious example of the way thought forms have powerful effects.

However, when a morphogenetic field, which is the superset of all thought forms, is in resonance and works more closely with a specific plant species, it will gradually be imbued with a powerful resistance to outside negative thought forms. A morphogenetic field can be a pattern created by repeated thoughts. It is a repeated process of a particular frequency of energy. That frequency as thought exists on the mental plane. A thought, repeated over and over, begins to form a pattern. Patterns have a characteristic of taking onto themselves, at least on the mental plane level, their own innate intelligence. It is almost as if they become a being. The sentience of the being may vary, but as the pattern is impressed over and over, as more energy is brought into it, this sentience may increase. In such a way the pattern begins to have far-reaching implications.

Positive thought forms protect a plant against negative thought forms that are outside its general sphere of origin. This is what has taken place with herbs that are considered weeds. These plants grow easily and are difficult even to beat back. They often have powerful, long lasting spiritual effects that run deep in an individual because they are resistant to the ebb and flow of many different more transient thought forms. This means that individuals struggling with certain negative thought forms they wish to change, will particularly benefit from the spiritual properties provided by herbs that are considered weeds.

To a degree plants create thought forms for themselves. This is shown in the doctrine of signature. For example, those plants that have voracious growing conditions in certain times of the year such as ivy propagate rapidly with enough moisture. The vibration of this expansion will be transferred into someone who eats ivy. Its signature gets directly transferred to the person. A persistent thought form is felt deep within an individual. This goes beyond the plant's persistence and tenacity; it shows that the plant can transfer the thought form that it is seeking to learn. All plant forms are working with the next level up from beingness, and that is the way they are accepted, used, and seem to become part of Earth society, of something greater than just themselves. This is a good step towards intelligence, but rarely in any systems in current use in the universe has this been allowed to lead to what humankind would consider intelligence.

Plants, in learning of individual characteristics associated with the life stream of all plants, are learning about certain aspects just of being on the Earth, of coordinating with humans. If a plant is killed and taken into the human body, to some extent the vibration of the entire life stream associated with that plant remains around the plant, around the person taking it, and around the excess substance that is inevitably excreted from the physical body. The vibrational level will gradually become more and more dilute, but the lessons learned by the plant as it passes through the physical body of the human contributes to the thought form of the plant. This is an important thing to realize. It is one reason why plants, as food substance for mankind, are in harmony and coordination with people.

You may wonder about death in plants as a thought form. There is some difficulty on this level. But it is quite minor when compared to the karmic lessons for mankind regarding the eating of animal flesh. Ultimately, it is seen that, beyond the current stage of evolution, mankind will eat food that can be consumed without harm to plants. This obviously refers to fruits, flowers, nuts, seeds, and leaves.

The thought forms of mankind and plants are intimately interwoven. Because this takes place primarily on spiritual levels, as you focus attention upon these levels by attuning to the spiritual attributes of herbs, the morphogenetic fields of those who read this book and work with this energy will coordinate and speed up the process of understanding these energies and of eating plant foods that will not harm plants. The overall thought form will be of some benefit to the plant life stream and morphogenetic field associated with it. This is a two-way process. Life force energies associated with the overshadowing morphogenetic field need to move through the person's body appropriately, and then be returned easily to the plant.

The natural kingdom is associated with the devic orders, and this is true throughout nature. As people work with naturally occurring substances, herbs in particular carry many of these properties into a person, and they become allied with nature spirits. Then negative energies of low intelligence and darker vibration have a great deal of difficulty coexisting with these beings. It is as if you raise your vibration somewhat to the level of the nature spirit. But there is a qualification here. It is a shift on one characteristic level, usually the etheric, by which this vibration changes in you. People think they have a single vibration, but the vibration of each subtle body is different. This is partly what makes them separate. As the etheric vibration is in harmony with a resonance, confluence, or vibrational state that is of a higher level than you usually are, the negative energies that might be with you leave. They are dispelled or simply find it uncomfortable to be there. This is a general tendency that is significantly enhanced as your vibration is shifted by the energies of the natural kingdom.

Many entities coexist with man at the current time. These entities may have sentience and be able to exist independently, but the thought forms that are usually most difficult for individuals are those that they have generated. Thought forms are associated with attitudes, behavior patterns, lessons learned or not learned in life, and ways people are unwilling to see themselves as lovable or helpful to others. The accumulation of these energies create a breeding ground for negative thought forms of all kinds. It is like when you are with somebody who is imbued with a powerful negative self image, even though you may seek to struggle against it, you may take on such an image after a time. This is not only due to attempting to sympathize or empathize with the person, it is due energetically to the way negative thought forms work together.

For most individuals, it is enough to deal with negative thought forms they create. They will find the higher vibration that they have in themselves, as they release negative thoughts, to be profound and useful. It is not necessary to clear the ethers or do everything else. When large numbers of people worldwide accomplish this cleansing, there will be a tendency to uplift the vibration of all. The breeding ground for negative thought forms will disappear.

The most difficult negative thought forms that are nonself-generated, that are independent of people, are those of individuals who have left the physical body, and yet have important and powerful emotions driving them. These individuals may easily fall into patterns of hate, negativity, and energy in which they do not know exactly what they are doing. This can go on for many, many years. These entities, as negative thought forms, may need the energy of other people just to survive. And so they may at times be around you. There may be situations where they are harmful, but compared to the amount of life force within a living incarnate being, they cannot be of any harm to you. They can be dissipated relatively easily through various techniques such as invocation, inert gases, surrounding yourself with light, or by thinning the ethers.

However, when not conscious of negative thought processes, these beings have the ability to merge with them from time to time and extract energy from them. You might say a negative thought form is draining you, when you have a negative energy pattern of your own creation and the energy reserves within you are lowered. When your fear or negative thought forms allow you to resonate with such difficulties, then these things can multiply and indeed harm a person. It is as if you only harm yourself. Where does the energy go? It is absorbed by some of these other entities. A mere knowledge or consciousness of this process may be enough to dispel them. It is not so much the focus on beings external to oneself, but rather the negative thought forms that one generates. This is because the life force within an incarnate being is so strong.

Positive thought forms have the ability to manifest an ongoing love and sensitivity. Under such an influence, those entities of a positive nature that coexist with and aid mankind will flourish. This includes the nature kingdom, the angelic realms, and the intermediate realms filled with beings such as elves and nature spirits. They absorb some of this energy and, being creatures of light, will change it, resonate with it, and feed it back to you and to others. The energy is shared and a greater state of harmony and love is created. Most people are not conscious of these beings that coexist and work with you. Little children may know of them but may not speak of them, thinking they would be laughed at.

Positive thought forms generally allow etheric vibrations to strengthen into resonant patterns that are usually beneficial, and thus act as conduits for higher levels of information and understanding within people, the environment, and the Earth. These positive thought forms raise the overall general vibrations of the ethers and are quite healthy. They assist in many processes of spiritual and psychic growth.

There can be difficulties from any source of thought forms, negative or positive, but the difficulties among both types relate to karma. Karma involves energy that a person has already accumulated and brought into this lifetime. The difference is that the negative karma from the past is engendered unconsciously without the person's direct willingness by the negative thought forms and densification of the ethers. Positive thought forms bring greater conscious choice into this process, so people may understand the karma and choose it appropriately.

The energies of past karma, negative or positive, are always brought to the individual at some point in their lives. The forces of negativity may be elemental, energies of pure negative thought forms, or patterns of a morphogenetic field larger than the individual's own life. It does not matter. Indeed, these energies accelerate the individual's karma, and if these are of negative origin, they will resonate with the negative patterns of karma a person has already developed for himself. Thus, these are brought more quickly into the person's existence.

The homunculi theory of disease is the idea that disease organisms are available all over the planet at all times. Individuals who attune to a particular disease get that particular set of symptoms, perhaps because of an intervening energy of some intelligence. This homunculi or sentient being is created as a negative thought form. It is perhaps described as the negative thought form theory of disease, except that negative thought forms are not as well, or precisely, defined.

When people are diseased there are two sides to it. First there are the negative thought forms. Then there is the positive aspect—the inner lesson that the individual is seeking to learn. Thought forms interrelate with the physical level. The means by which this takes place must involve people. This includes the will, the spirit, the way the body and mind coordinate, and the inner patterns of an individual. This is where one has choice. Generally, however, such choices are made unconsciously very early for an individual in the current lifetime, and in some cases in past lifetimes, such as when a repeated debilitating tendency towards a particular thought form leading to a specific disease, is evidenced in the littlest baby throughout their life as it grows. This is a bit unusual. However, in many cases the essential thought forms associated with each disease get started quite early in life, around age two or three until about age ten or so, by which time many choices are already made by the individual.

This is why many remembrances of early childhood may come to the surface when working with emotional thought forms. These are generally held in check with regards to the relationship between the disease and the thought form by an emotion. If these emotions are not experienced, the message that created them in the first place cannot be fully understood by the person. The emotion holds the message in check.

For instance, to really feel what has happened, a little child might have to experience great anger and sadness at his parents. But this may not be permitted because the little boy has been told by his parents, friends, or his own thought forms that little boys do not cry. The difficulty may relate to the child having seen something that has created a deep sense of emotional pain. That he has seen this is important for his own self-development, but because of this other thought form—do not cry—that painful incident is not resolved. Under the influence of an herb or psychological process, that image and initial childhood experience may come back into consciousness, and this time a person may have a chance to cry, to release the emotion holding back the images, and then they would know the truth of that experience. These are two separate things that interfere with each other.

The emotions a person may release in working in these areas, be it through talking therapy, bonding therapy, or therapies of a body nature such as reiki, yield a new point of view. It is an ongoing process, so that as one goes deeper new emotions are released. At the bottom of the heap of these emotions will generally be found a sense of inner peace or quiet. This is a very good thing to be ready for.

With the release of the emotions, it is useful to ask the question, as if posing it to a little child, "Based on these feelings, what is your decision about these thought forms?" With cancer ask, "How do you feel about a particular loss, or direction, and about love." With AIDS, reflect on your attraction to people of the same and opposite sex. As one examines the reactions in the little child, one may be more able to forgive a similar reaction in oneself. The pivotal point to deeply understand the way a thought form creates disease, revolves again and again around forgiveness. If an individual experiences forgiveness in themselves, this often opens the door for them to finally release the thought form in its purest, most energized form. This is the most subtle form, the one that connects across the Earth, although it will not immediately have the effect on the physical body that one might wish.

However, with time, greater forgiveness, patience, and the use of vibrational remedies, electromagnetic healing techniques, and herbs, the person may bring this energy to greater consciousness and release it on the physical level as well. The difference is that once solved from the point of view of the thought form, it is likely never to return to the person in this or any other lifetime. This would seem obvious on the face of it, but when looked at from the soul's development it is ultimately more important than the person's survival in this lifetime, or of being free of a single disease in this lifetime. If one can understand the overall message, then their soul has made great progress. And this, ultimately, is why the soul even permits disease thought forms to manifest in the physical body. It is hoped that the person will understand experientially once and for all that thought form.

Negative thought forms are a much greater problem now. The influence of the mass media, the greater mixing of many societies, the interchange of diseases from one society to the next, and the movement of contaminated food substances across national boundaries are but resulting symptoms of negative thought forms. We see the cause of this to be on a much higher vibrational level.

These things support the reality of the Earth being a classroom with many lessons and of the enhanced probability of doing away with disease once and for all. Now is the time to be on the Earth. There is no greater or more important time for most souls. This is the time of greatest learning, and because there are so many souls here, there are more opportunities to meet with them, to work with the karma of balancing and understanding. There is no greater time or more powerful schoolhouse than the Earth right now.

At the same time, this means that many lessons from past lives, many thought forms, and many diseases also are manifest at this time. This is not an accident. It is part of the schooling. Many are here on the Earth to experience and move through these various negative thought forms and diseased states. It is as if some have come specifically to work with those patterns. The increased tendency of mutating viruses and more difficult negative thought forms and diseases are also here for mankind to apply the principles of holistic medicine and to understand that the Earth as a being is working with humanity. All of these things point at a greater solution. Gradually, one will no longer need negative thought forms to learn the lesson, nor the physical disease to understand oneself. Those incarnating now accelerate this process by contracting a disease, by communicating with it, and by working with negative thought forms in any way they choose. This increases the probability for a human race free of disease once and for all.

Holism taken to its ultimate conclusion, reveals that one is a part of the universe. It is a little paradoxical that something that would normally cause separation, a disease that might keep one separate from understanding if viewed in the traditional medical model, might still be a catapult to a deeper level of understanding. That is the paradox that individuals must under-stand and resolve for themselves. But indeed, if all parts do contribute to the whole, even the smallest disease or negative thought form must have its place in this greater evolution. That is the logical side. The feeling side of this is that as greater forgiveness, understanding, and love naturally en-genders this stronger sense of a connected whole, it becomes unnecessary for negative thought forms and diseases to manifest physically for the per-son to notice that something is out of balance. Assert a correcting force, so that you come back into balance, serving and working with the whole.

Microorganisms that cause diseases are also influenced by thought forms. Bacteria have a slightly higher innate degree of intelligence and therefore are vulnerable in a different way to negative thought forms than viruses. Bacteria invade an organism just as viruses do, but they will generally not move into a physical body as deeply. They harbor a bit more of their own thought forms and processes to learn from the person. This is not only related to death within a physical body, which is the normal reaction to invading microorganisms. Bacteria receive energies from a person more easily to assimilate this as information.

In many cases, bacteria change into viruses. This is not commonly accepted in current day medical practice, and has been termed the pleomorphic theory of disease.[2] However, it is likely that in the next ten years scientists will verify and publically acknowledge the pleomorphic principle, that various small organisms can change into a virus and bacteria. The changing from one form of microorganism into another has been well observed by those with the proper equipment, but is not generally discussed in scientific circles because it goes so much against the status quo. These organisms change their size, shape, colorations, and certain of their characteristics, and there are certain relationships between viruses and bacteria. It is a microcosm to what is happening in macrocosm to people, to processes of coming together in groups, learning together, splitting apart, and then forming again. This way the organisms learn about some of the basic functions of life. This relates to the law of permanence, the law of karma, and the law of reflection. They observe the way people work, understanding through their bodies different processes in a very elemental and basic way.

Negative thought forms pave the way for this learning. They open the door by which vibrations of a baser or more difficult characteristic in a person invite a microorganism to come into the physical body to share in the learning. A person may have the lesson brought to them by infection, by some difficulty associated with a specific body part because the lowered vibration at that body part is in resonance with the vibration of the virus or invading bacterium.

A bacterium is much easier to deal with, in general, because its innate higher intelligence will be much more affected by visualization or by a treatment to change certain characteristics of the physical body, even by antibiotics. Viruses are much more resistant because they are in essence, stupider. They do not respond to these levels of intelligence, yet, they still respond to the primary negative thought form energy. If that is dealt with directly, if it is fully released from the person, the virus cannot survive. Healing, sometimes called spontaneous remission as in the case of cancer, relates to the releasing of negative thought forms. This is also a key reason why visualization exercises and positive thinking sometimes cure people of various diseases.

It is also important to understand that by externally destroying and keeping in resonant condition various microorganisms, the life's lesson for the person is also stirred up. It is as if the viruses and bacteria, in continuing to hold open the doorway that is welcome to them by negative thought forms, allow some vibrational energy transfer from any technique that acts on them directly. Such a technique would be, for instance, the use of inert gas energy or the Rife ray, in which an energy is added to the etheric body of the virus or bacteria destroys it. But such an energy will not simply destroy the virus; it allows some of the message at a very basic, cellular level to be transmitted into the person. If the person can absorb it, learn from it, and work with it, they may grow in their own understanding. Yes, it is possible to be reinfected, and in the case of cancer, this can occur through the eating of pork, but generally, individuals will then be free of the virus and be given an open door to look at the purpose of disease and how they might change their characteristics that attracted the disease in the first place.

Insects have the capacity to absorb a negative thought form of a relatively low sentience. If an insect has attributes that are repugnant or repulsive to a human, a bridge is connected unconsciously between the person and that insect. The insect can, by this bridge of energy, absorb some of these negative thought forms. In many cases, this does not harm the insect at all. In fact, it may sustain it for a time. This is because the sentience level of the insect is below the threshold of permanence that the person has and is slightly below that of the negative thought form. Because some aspect of the personality of the person who is creating the negative thought form is transferred into the insect, its vibrational state is temporarily raised.

If you kill an insect, the negative thought form is liberated. This cannot always be seen or immediately noticed, but it may affect the person. In many cases, a negative thought form may have a sentience level sufficient to motivate the insect into annoying behavior. An example of this, of course, is the common housefly. It will often do whatever it is doing on your windows and your body in an annoying way, flying around in the room until you sit down and meditate. Then the vibration that is imparted from your being increases the sentience level of the negative thought form associated with the housefly that has taken on some of this negative thought form energy. This is perfectly in balance with karmic law, because you will be attempting to kill the insect.

You might ask, "What is to be done here?" If you kill the insect, there is no great karmic retribution. The negative thought form is retribution enough; as it is released, you will need to deal with it. That is one aspect of this perfect balance. However, if you resist the energy, if you seek to shut it out, this repression may lower your vibration. The insect may no longer annoy you, but you will not achieve the higher meditative state. If you manifest love towards the insect, the negative thought form may find it uncomfortable to be in its current state and may be dispersed. Under such a condition, a door has been opened by which the loving energy you emit is absorbed temporarily by the insect, raising its vibration into a harmonious state. If you create a shielding energy of any kind, it will be quite receptive to this and perhaps respond appropriately. It will leave your house, if you open a window for it, or be easily chased out of the room.

Garlic, particularly the flower essence, is quite effective in this process. The love that you manifest is supplemented by the devic order associated with garlic. Then the cleansing effect and shielding area is stronger. It may even be seen to expand from you like a sphere, moving from the heart outwards, perhaps to a diameter of five or ten feet.

Some individuals focus energy on negative thought forms in general. Anxiety, worry, and irritability are an important part of their way. Such individuals are sometimes termed neurotic in traditional psychotherapeutic jargon. It is wise for such individuals to realize that there is a purpose in this overall picture that allows them to keep moving and learning. It might be wise to look at the roots of this and see the purpose behind it and strike out in a new direction that does not require such irritability. You will see less of this pattern with flower essences of fruits. These focus on more spiritual properties, that will not necessarily draw attention to the overall disease negative thought forms.

Many gem elixirs have a potent effect in dealing with negative thought forms, particularly those that affect the crown chakra such as white diamond, various forms of opal, and tourmaline. Many gem elixirs have interesting effects upon the physical body and will also bring negative thought forms into greater perspective. These are general tendencies that affect the mineral kingdom even more than herbs or flower essences. The reason for this is that stones pre-date negative thought forms. They relate more directly to the Earth herself. They are part of the Earth in a much deeper way than are plants. Therefore, these inspire in individuals a greater sense of self-worth and a greater knowledge of the Earth. The entire picture of diseases as seemingly necessary begins to dissolve.

1 Rudolf Steiner, *The Cycle of the Year As A Breathing Process of the Earth* (London: Rudolf Steiner Press, 1956).
2 Barry Lynes and John Crane, *The Cancer Cure That Worked! Fifty Years of Suppression* (Toronto: Marcus Books, 1987).

CHAPTER V

TREATING AIDS

Few herbs match the efficiency of echinacea for strengthening the immune system to weaken AIDS in the body. A cleansing of the entire system is needed. Herbs such as juniper and comfrey are also excellent. Herbs that relieve stress, such as chamomile, and herbs that strengthen the blood, as do many Chinese herbs, stimulate an overall immune boosting response. That is good to recognize and work with. Indeed, most Chinese herbs are very helpful. And the sea vegetables have interesting capabilities for people with AIDS. The effects takes longer to work, but they are very important because releasing certain unconscious fears, tendencies, and misunderstandings about sexuality makes it much easier for people to deal with AIDS. The sea vegetables do not usually directly affect the immune system, but overall, do have a strengthening effect when used in the regular diet.

It is important to understand the karmic or soul lessons to be learned from many new diseases such as AIDS that involve the immune system. The immune system acts as the interface or boundary between the individual as they perceive the world as a threat, and the way they perceive and know the world as home, as loving, and as harmonious. Stemming from this essential conflict regarding the world as a dangerous or safe place lies the possibility for many different disorders. For instance, Epstein-Barr as an immune efficiency difficulty relates to accomplishment in the world. The level of burnout, the way an individual acts powerfully and strongly, overdoing things, makes them susceptible to this disease. The various immunodeficiency diseases involving the skin, such as lupus develop from mistreating animals in a past life. Or in the past a person was forced to work with animals and they disliked it; they had difficulty accepting the energies of animals. With AIDS and its many mutating forms, you see difficulty regarding sexuality, how the individual perceives intimacy, closeness, and acceptance of the sexual side, versus the way this is threatening and not whole or complete.

The immune system is now undergoing important changes, which is a positive aspect of AIDS. The immune system is now becoming more important in the overall function of the physical body. This is partly because of the constant influence of negative thought forms coming into the physical body in the form of viruses, pollutants, and stresses. While echinacea is certainly useful on a medicinal level to boost the immune system, it will also gradually be understood that this herb enables one to release negative energy and to accept the flow of life to raise one's vibration. This has a greater positive impact on the immune system than to just struggle with and resist negative influences. In battle after battle, the immune system is gradually weakened. Through greater love and less resistance, the deeper functions of the immune system are activated. The increased focus on the immune system has a deeper spiritual purpose—to reveal to people that there are better ways than constant resistance during life.

There are ways to work with the immune system to become more loving and lovable, to see the world as harmonious with one. Then the issues causing these diseases will gradually disappear because they are not very important. It is often seen that in states of deep meditation and relaxation the immune system is bolstered, while in states of greater depression and difficulty the immune system is suppressed. Under these conditions, the simpler lessons of health and disease appear more obvious to an individual. How they act upon these issues relates to their own personal karma and the way greater and vaster thought forms are available to change this planet. This is what we see right now in the case of AIDS. It is changing mankind's ability to relate to sexuality. This is even perceived to some extent through the heterosexual community, even though there is no clear and immediate threat of AIDS in that community.

Certain herbs help to understand the spiritual lesson of AIDS. Many herbs have been mentioned that awaken higher consciousness. Herbs an individual is drawn to sometimes just for the taste, or for some unique characteristic, are also helpful. In conjunction with aromatherapy, many herbs mentioned that have pungent odors are excellent for individuals to reach deeper states of meditation. But here it is more along the lines of individual choice, rather than overall patterns.

Certain flower essences are also of benefit in treating AIDS and to understand the deeper lessons of that disease. Pansy flower essence is generally indicated for dealing with most viral conditions, and, though this is not commonly used, echinacea flower essence is also beneficial. Those essences that stir up consciousness around sexuality, the squash family, watermelon, and zucchini will aid one in dealing with some of the higher issues around negative thought forms regarding sexuality. Banana is of benefit for men to release stress associated with attempting to incorporate new ideas about changing lifestyles, relationships, and intimacy. Banksia flower essences will be of benefit to individuals who feel attracted to them, especially when seeing their pictures.

Ginseng, lotus, and date palm flower essences, to name a few, will all have benefit. There will generally be one or two roses that people with AIDS attune to. Study the pictures of various roses. About 25 percent of those who do this, will be deeply attracted to one particular rose. This would be an excellent flower essence for that person to take, again to bring through a higher spiritual understanding and a sense of deeper love. Health practitioners and counselors helping those with AIDS should consider using certain herbs, flower essences, and gem elixirs to better understand AIDS from a point of consciousness.

Regarding gem elixirs, ruby is of some benefit because attuning to root chakra energy at a very deep level has some benefit in working with AIDS. Emerald releases grief when a loved one passes on. People, in reading about gem elixirs, may attune to certain ones more easily. The astrological mandala referred to in *Gem Elixirs and Vibrational Healing, Vol II* can be constructed based upon the natal chart, and this will help a person work with AIDS. There can be a strengthening of character.

All gem elixirs that stimulate higher consciousness will also assist, but here be a bit cautious. If there is a particular affinity to the more powerful gems, such as white diamond, jelly opal, or smoky quartz, for activating the spiritual nature, there may be reason to attune to these. But usually do not combine these and other powerful spiritual awakening tools. It could overload the person with too much energy, but this also depends on how advanced the illness is. If the immune system has not been too weakened and one is willing to work with lessons that come up, then use the more powerful gem elixirs. The tourmaline series, lapis lazuli, and clear quartz are better for most individuals working to bring higher facets of spiritual awakening into the process of releasing thought forms associated with AIDS.

We have seen many possibilities of curing AIDS, and we see orthodox medicine shut out of nearly all of them. There are many techniques that are now increasingly understood regarding morphogenetic thought forms on their most basic level that will likely have the most powerful impact. One technology is certainly that of vibrational remedies. Work in electromagnetic medicine in many different areas is also going on. The way this field is developing will present many possibilities for successfully treating AIDS, as well as cancer, but clearly we put the Rife work as front runner for having the greatest and most far reaching potential for success.

Indeed, the successful treatment of AIDS is already in the developmental stage. What Rife developed and used in the 1920s and 1930s, sending certain frequencies through the inert gas helium to people with cancer and other illnesses to cure them, is a powerful technique to heal AIDS. The trouble is that any technique used in a way the current establishment feels is significantly threatening can defeat itself. Therefore, gradual attention is necessary, and this is all. Otherwise private industry, the AMA, and possibly the government will step in to stop it. Because of current medical thinking, it may take around five years or more before the Rife work is fully perfected and released to the public. It is a matter of understanding by those prominent in research and science and of public acceptance.

The Rife work was developed in the 1920s and 1930s with a number of doctors quietly using it to cure people of cancer and a wide range of other diseases. Not only did Rife develop a treatment that cured many, but he also developed several highly sophisticated microscopes that in many ways are more advanced then the microscopes in use today. Unfortunately, there were political trials in 1939 and 1961. During each time period, a growing number of doctors around the United States successfully treated people, so the movement was perceived as a threat to the establishment. Government agents on the state and federal levels went out of the way to learn which doctors were using the Rife devices, and these doctors were threatened with loss of their license to practice medicine if the treatments continued.

I have been told that a prominent medical center is now using electromagnetic medical techniques related to but not identical with the Rife work, and they have been getting an 80-90 percent remission and possible cure rate with AIDS. The medical directors do not understand why the treatments are working, so they have decided to quietly continue their work for four years without going public. And several holistic clinics have been successfully using one of the several Rife treatment devices to bring about a clear remission and possible cure of AIDS and cancer. In fact, after the political trials in 1939 and 1961, some doctors quietly continued to use the Rife microscopes and treatment machines for many years, with many people being cured of cancer and other diseases. I am not involved in the Rife research, but people interested in exploring this work can read the book *The Cancer Cure That Worked! Fifty Years of Suppression* by Barry Lynes and John Crane. The book is not widely available but can be ordered for $12.00 including shipping from the publisher, Marcus Books P.O. Box 327 Queensville, Ontario, Canada L0G 1R0. The book is distributed by Bookpeople in the United States. Stores can order it. People can also write to this address for further information: Barry Lynes, P.O. Box 5564, Washington, D.C. 20016.

For all the suffering that AIDS is causing, it may provide enough of an impetus for a major medical breakthrough in the acceptance of the Rife technology in the coming years. Today, millions of Americans no longer automatically believe what people in the political or economic establishment say. Watergate and the Vietnam war have seen to that. There is also the increased power and influence that the media and investigative reporting exerts in our lives. It is no longer quite so easy to bury the truth. In addition, there is the growing concern over AIDS. Even many conservative doctors would be more open to a somewhat radical technology that actually healed people with AIDS.

The Rife research is really a primitive form of Atlantean technology. Some reading this may have had dreams or inner impressions or have read of a time when people entered a chamber and a certain frequency was sent through them. This was a common practice in Atlantis. The cleansing was sufficient so that for many years there was little or no disease in Atlantis. Unfortunately, people came to depend too much on these devices without also taking responsibility for their own health. And an inner spiritual attunement was forgotten. It is hoped in the coming years, as the Rife technology is widely used, that people understand and remember that true health in mind, body, and spirit requires acting in a reasonable manner and that an attunement to the inner being must always be maintained.

Beyond the immediate treatment of numerous serious diseases, the Rife technology also offers the opportunity for much spiritual growth, when used with various spiritual practices. The Rife ray can be used to discharge the miasms from the system, cleanse the subtle bodies, and open the chakras. This is more advanced work of great importance that will gradually be explored by serious researchers in the coming years.

In recent years, there has been a growing movement in congress to pressure the federal government to support research with more natural modalities in health care. People interested in seeing this develop should write to their congressional representatives to express such views.

Today, vibrational techniques to treat AIDS are quietly being developed in France and New Zealand. These interesting new devices use magnetic energy and various frequencies for balancing, polarization, and utilization of the physical body's biomagnetic field. There are also several interesting mushroom substances, reishi in particular, that have important effects in weakening the AIDS virus. It would be helpful to make the reishi mushroom into a homeopathic remedy for people with AIDS.

The action of most small life forms, we call them 'cell wall deficient,' can be weakened dramatically by the presence of ozone. What happens is a complicated process that also involves etheric energies. With many of these cell wall deficient diseases, including the AIDS, cancer, and syphilis viruses in particular, there is a dramatic reduction in the potency of these diseases. At the same time, the T cells are assisted. However, there also appears to be a point at which most of these cell wall deficient forms become deeply ingrained and affect the DNA structures of the body. Then ozone is of little utility. Other magnetic, electromagnetic, light, and, of course, vibrational therapies will still have a powerful effect. At such a point, ozone is still of some assistance, but is usually not a direct cure.

It is difficult to tell exactly when ozone will be less effective, but there may be a sense of inner hopelessness that is difficult to change. Also, a few treatments of ozone may produce no significant increase in physical energy or assistance in the person. Ozone will usually provide some assistance fairly quickly when the disease is not too deeply ingrained in the body. However, there is a possibility that with treatments such as ozone or other techniques that strengthen and oxygenate the body the physical body processes can reverse. Then certain processes that begin to repair the DNA structures will be set in motion. This will only happen in a small percentage of cases, but it is significant enough that most people should not rule out ozone therapy if their case of AIDS is quite developed.

It is also important to recognize that ozone in too large a quantity is quite poisonous; therefore, it must be used appropriately. What is usually done is injection, but introduction through the anal opening is of some use. The difficulty here is that there are many who will understand and work with this as an adjunct to other therapies, but there will also be some who will depend on it alone. We would not recommend such a path. When ozone therapy is used in conjunction with other natural therapies, such as herbs and vibrational remedies, it may be quite useful.

One key problem in treating AIDS is the mutation of these viral thought forms. As they change, the frequencies for treatment must be correctly adjusted. In the orthodox and holistic approaches to treating AIDS, mutations of the virus are usually not being sufficiently considered. This will cause a great deal of trouble as AIDS treatments develop. There are many forms of AIDS, and many more forms are likely to be found.

At the essential core frequency, the AIDS and cancer viruses are the same in the way they are created and transferred in the body. Body conditions generally dictate how they will be created on the physical level and how they will be transmitted from one person to the other. On the more physical level, AIDS is the generation of a more resistant strain, a contagious cancer, that has developed. AIDS has been buried in the genetic code for thousands of years as a part of the cancer miasm. Otherwise, no virus could be activated by a mere thought form. AIDS first appeared as a distinct virus separate from cancer in 1807, but this was not observed or worked with until much later. In fact, scientists will find traces of this virus in many areas of the world, including in various strains of monkey and other animals back to the 1930s. There was a recent article in *Time* magazine about a black youth who died of a mysterious disease in the late 1960s in Missouri. His blood was saved and recently analyzed. It was found that AIDS had been the cause of death.[1]

Mutation of the AIDS virus gradually took place during this century as pollution got worse, with particular emphasis as the ozone layer was depleted in the 1960s. Increased environmental pollution and radiation such as the depletion of the ozone layer contribute to the ability of viruses to mutate. This allowed increased ultraviolet radiation and the AIDS virus is fairly sensitive to this.

Increased ultraviolet radiation will continue to cause mutation of the AIDS virus, but this will also simplify the way the virus may be observed. Ultraviolet light modulated by visible light through certain microscopes, such as the Rife microscope, make use of the heterodyne principle, which involves using ultraviolet light modulated by visible light. This method will make the AIDS virus more visible and easier to work with.

The AIDS problem is happening now partly because many are being exposed as AIDS shifts from one person to another through sexual contact and exposure to contaminated fluid. Also, heavy vaccination, petrochemical contamination, and, of course, difficulty in the water supply is predisposing individuals to greater and greater states of disease. The continued reduction of the ozone layer in the atmosphere, increased environmental pollution from various chemicals, and more ultraviolet radiation is creating many interesting new life forms. Several new mutant viral strains will be observed. Certain drug treatments developed for AIDS will become ineffective when new strains manifest. This obviously calls for a much broader viewpoint, one that does not involve treating individual AIDS viruses just with specific drugs. This may require that some new frequencies be developed with the Rife ray to treat AIDS, but this will not be very difficult to do.

In the near future AIDS will also be spread by insects. This has already begun but only a few scientists have publicly suggested this. This will at first not affect the northern climates. It will initially affect people in more tropical climates, and the tsetse fly in Africa is a likely candidate for transmitting the AIDS virus. Presently, the main transmission of the AIDS virus that scientists do not yet recognize occurs through bovine leukemia. As insect transmission of AIDS becomes recognized, it will likely parallel new techniques of healing AIDS so this development will probably not cause great concern.

The intimate relationship of AIDS and cancer is not just channeled guidance. Cantwell, a prominent cancer researcher in 1984 stated that AIDS and cancer were the same viruses. His research is discussed in *AIDS The Mystery and the Solution* by Alan Cantwell, Jr., M.D. This book is not widely available but it can be ordered for $11.95 including postage from Aries Rising Press, P.O. Box 29532, Los Angeles, CA. 90029. Bookpeople distributes this book, so stores can easily order it.

The current increase of the AIDS virus in the populace is affecting the cancer miasm. AIDS is allowing it to stabilize deeper in individuals on the purely physical level because there are more individuals who are having their own processes altered by the AIDS negative thought form. This will concentrate the essential character of AIDS—which is a very simple virus almost identical to the causative virus of cancer. This concentration is multiplied by the intelligence in cells, the morphogenetic field. The morphogenetic field associated with cancer is strengthened because there are more cells that are dealing with the entire issue. The various ways the cancer virus can extend into the physical body is enhanced by the AIDS virus. It is as if the AIDS virus can predispose many cells to deal with cancer. This may sometimes first occur at subtle vibrational levels, but it is still an important part of recognizing the depth by which cancer penetrates into the body in the presence of AIDS.

One variant of looking at morphogenetic fields, is the miasm concept. The morphogenetic field concept is as deep and important to a holistic understanding of viruses, thought forms, and indeed many areas of health, as is the concept of the miasm. These two concepts are fundamentally different in certain areas, but have certain specifics that are exactly the same.

They are exactly the same in the way they appear to affect the human form. The miasm has created, as an overall thought form, an energy similar to a pattern or morphogenetic field, that is unformed until it interacts with a human. The person working with it in lifetime after lifetime begins to assimilate certain morphogenetic field constructs, certain patterns of energy that are developed around the way the miasm interacts with the person's own soul, existence on the Earth, karmic interaction with other people, and the decisions they make in life. Therefore, these concepts seem almost to be as one when they are worked with by people.

However, in an overall sense, miasms seem to affect things at a vibrational level that relates specifically to particular lessons, lessons that indeed may apply in many areas outside of those that occur only in people. A morphogenetic field is a superset, while a miasm is a subset. Morphogenetic fields relate to patterns of all types. The morphogenetic field, as an overall pattern-forming energy, applies to inanimate objects, to areas of the galaxy, and to things that have nothing specifically to do with the human form or human existence. A miasm is a pattern that is a subset of the entire concept of morphogenetic fields. However, it is also important to see that miasms are an important area for people to discover and work with.

The relationship of morphogenetic fields, AIDS, and the cancer miasm is an important consideration. Patterns are repeated over and over again, the way people allow negative thought forms to come into their lives. A particular example here might be in the gay community, which has permitted certain principles of sexuality and intimacy. Intimacy has often been rejected, while sexuality is embraced. These principles are also seen in what happens with the cancer miasm, when an individual holds onto something beyond the point at which it is necessary. The loss sustained by the movement of that thing out of their lives creates disharmony, difficulty, anxiety, and ultimately an emotional energy that is generally blocked from the person's conscious awareness. This energy can cause a miasm, such as the cancer miasm, to deeply ingrain in an individual without their conscious knowledge.

A similar relationship between AIDS and cancer exists. The way this happens regarding the change in attitudes concerning sexuality is an example. The morphogenetic field around these areas becomes a miasm. A miasm is a form of morphogenetic field, a greater pattern that humanity falls into. However, this greater pattern pre-dates many of the areas in which the miasms form specific areas of difficulty for humanity. Therefore, along with the initial creation of mankind is the idea of patterns, of morphogenetic fields because of thought. It is thought in itself that creates patterns over and over again. Individuals who think and work in areas to support their thoughts about fear, areas about the world that they do not understand, places in which they seek power or understanding, create patterns over and over. These overall patterns exist far beyond the soul stream of an individual, far beyond their own life, from one lifetime to the next. Their patterns coexist and mesh with others from other soul streams.

Sometimes it is necessary to learn life's lessons from others, to learn of group thought forms. An example of this dealing with AIDS is the way some individuals with a homosexual lifestyle may have gotten closely involved with other men who are unable to understand issues of intimacy versus sexuality. They are influenced powerfully by the thoughts of others. Thus, they begin a pleasure-seeking cycle in which the ability to understand intimacy, closeness, and commitment is clearly reduced. This is not simply due to the influence of the others they have worked with. It is also due to a pattern that has been established over a long period of time through other lifetimes and other areas of their lives so that intimacy is an overall thought form issue. The ability to understand and work with it may be reduced because of the willingness to attune to this overall crude thought form. At the same time, there is a positive aspect, as is already occurring now in gay communities in the United States and certain other places across the world. These men are establishing new forms of sexuality and new ways of relating men to men so that greater intimacy is embraced. The process as it is learned in a group will also be transmitted to the individuals involved.

To some extent, morphogenetic fields are even aided by people from other star systems who incarnate here or in any way act and work with people on this planet. This is because these energies are simply the energies of existence. As mankind seeks to understand existence, through the miasms, the physical body, through the greater patterns, these fields take form and shape that is specific to individuals in their lives. This is one important area in which the cancer miasm supplies energy, as if from the overall patterns, to individuals who are struggling in these areas.

The problem with AIDS is unique, in that with cancer there can at times be observed an immune response. It is perhaps not powerful enough to stop cancer, but it can be observed nevertheless. The nature of AIDS is that the immune response is so severely suppressed that the cells themselves broadcast the cancer miasm, the inner message. This gradually strengthens the cancer miasm throughout the planet. Thought forms and disease work hand in hand. This happens primarily the way a virus allows energy to be transmitted throughout the body. It converts in vibration a cell that it enters to a similar mode of its own vibration. The nourishing and sustaining energy, which is purely etheric energy, initially derives from thought from the miasm, morphogenetic field, or negative thought form aspect, and becomes concentrated through the etheric vibration into the virus. As the organism is converted, as many cells succumb to the virus, there is a strengthening of the etheric connection ultimately feeding the person's life force energy into the negative thought form. This is obvious when you see that people, as they become more afraid of their own death and of their own suffering, allow their life force energy to be more and more depleted.

The obvious question one would ask is, "If such life force energy comes from karma, the soul, the sun, food, and from the various things that nourish and sustain a person, where is it going?" The pattern creates this energy returning to the negative thought form, in many cases, to strengthen it. And again, this is reflected in a simple way on the Earth in which people who are first told about having AIDS, or having to deal with the antibodies in their body, may quickly tie-in to this negative thought form, thus reducing their own immune response, as if the fear of it is almost as bad as the disease and difficulty itself.

There is no direct evidence that presence of the antibody in the physical body means that the person is going to be sick with all the symptoms of AIDS. In fact, AIDS is perhaps the only disease where the generation of the antibody is supposed to be a symbol of the person's actual disease.

AIDS for ten years will cause a dramatic deepening of the cancer miasm, but over time the immune system will strengthen so that the cancer miasm will not penetrate so deeply into the physical body. This may peak in ten or fifteen years, but it is hoped that before then the technologies associated with the Rife work will again be understood and widely applied for the cure of AIDS and cancer. As various treatments that work with AIDS are developed, the cancer miasm will gradually be released from mankind.

Emotions are being confronted with AIDS, even more than they are dealt with through cancer. Individuals seeking to cure cancer in themselves should explore their emotions for a full understanding of the life lessons associated with cancer. With AIDS, because there are so few pathways available to achieve a cure, many more individuals approach and look at the deeper emotional issues. This will likely have a spillover effect into cancer itself. As a result of this process, the emotional body is a key factor. It is as if these inner lessons come closer to the surface for the people involved. This strengthens the link between the cancer miasm and the emotional body in all people.

You would think that, in most situations, because of the clear relationship between syphilis and AIDS, the syphilitic miasm would create the tendencies for a person to get AIDS. The AIDS virus more easily attacks the immune system, especially injured by already taking syphilis and therapeutic drugs which are immuno-suppressant. Drugs to suppress syphilis are often quite damaging to the immune system. That is basically true with certain exceptions. The AIDS virus has a fascinating plethora of mutations. In a majority of these, this syphilis piggy-back effect takes place. There are other varieties of AIDS that cause exceptions to this pattern.

Evidence contrary to this is the relatively recent development of AIDS from the cancer miasm. The essential mechanism, the AIDS virus, has a more direct link to cancer and to the cancer miasm than it does to syphilis. However, the syphilitic miasm is a strong tendency in many individuals currently on the planet, and because of this tendency, it is increasingly difficult to treat such individuals by traditional means for syphilis. This means that whenever they are treated by orthodox or even homeopathic techniques, unless they are fully tested and are fully aware of the release of syphilis from their bodies, they remain susceptible to cancer thought forms and to several others as well. This is because syphilis so weakens the immune system, and this weakening effect continues for a long time.[2]

As one awakens to negative thought forms of all types, one should try to understand the lessons involved. Sometimes those relating to cancer may be of some importance, even though the individual is primarily struggling with syphilis, and vice versa. They do not reach deeper levels, but with AIDS that is not necessary. For AIDS to have a devastating effect on the physical body, it need not reach very deep into the system. This is because of the opportunistic infections that surround people at the current time. There are many more opportunities for them to get sick simply because the immune system is not functioning properly.

Mafu, a popular spirit guide in California, said that one in three will have the AIDS virus in their system. This may occur by 1995 or so. Many people already have the cancer virus within them. It is said by various scientists that one in four people will contract cancer. This implies that one in four has the cancer virus. The way this virus metamorphoses to become that which you recognize as the AIDS virus often happens as a precursor to cancer. The person is able to change something in themselves through the immune system and perhaps move out of the dysfunctional state. This often takes place in the pancreas. Then the individual moves it from cancer to AIDS and perhaps into a state which is not harmful. It is a virus, remember, so it is very tiny and does not take very much to spread. Many individuals may have this virus but not spread it to others, and it will occur in the body at too subtle a level to be recognized through tests that measure AIDS antibodies. It is quite likely that the cancer virus will naturally shift to the AIDS type of cancer virus in the coming years for millions of people with cancer, even though most of these people have had no outside infection or contact with AIDS.

When people have cancer and the AIDS type of cancer develops, they will not necessarily develop actual AIDS with potentially fatal symptoms. There is this distinction in what often happens to people with AIDS because, for many individuals, the immune response still functions reasonably well. As the movement into the AIDS problem becomes stronger for them, they investigate the alternatives more readily than they would by other means. These alternatives provide them with higher vibration, greater immune response, and less stress, all the things that are necessary to slow the spread of this virus within the body. One positive benefit of AIDS is that it is inspiring more people to explore more natural and beneficial holistic medical techniques such as vibrational remedies and herbs. Without AIDS, it seems less likely that the right discoveries would again come to light.

There will probably not be an AIDS miasm; it is just basically the cancer miasm in a new form. But there is a small possibility of this defining itself more fully should AIDS not be cured, should the full understanding of viruses and disease thought forms not develop in the coming years. It is possible for an AIDS miasm to start in about 40 or 50 years. We do not see very much hope for humanity if many issues are not solved during this time period, however, so this is not very likely. We are most certainly optimistic. The probability of this happening is less than five percent.

The lessons associated with AIDS are more important than the virus. The main lesson to learn with AIDS concerns loving oneself and others, and the way sexuality is an intense, spiritual, and precious part of that process. It is time for humanity to better understand intimacy and love.

1 Christine Gorman, "Strange Trip Back to the Future," *Time Magazine* (Nov. 9, 1987), 83.
2 Harris Coulter, *AIDS and Syphilis, the Hidden Link* (Berkeley,CA: North Atlantic Books, 1987).

CHAPTER VI

PREPARING AND TAKING HERBS

There are various ways to prepare herbs to activate their spiritual properties. It is particularly wise to use a method that involves water because water has the ability to manifest many levels of pranic interchange. This is obvious to those who understand prana and work with water. Thus, placing herbs in boiling water is suggested; in some way, water should be part of the process. It is even of assistance to take extracts that are prepared by alcohol distillation for medicinal purposes. When you wish to release some of the spiritual properties more fully from the extract, even if it is one made with only pure alcohol, add a little water just before taking the herb. Always try to use very pure water.

Rain can be utilized for its energetic properties. Rain brings very interesting and beautiful qualities from sunlight energy that is already directly enmeshed in the vibration of water. Rain is the evaporation cycle in action, and water from the clouds has been exposed to sunlight energy at high altitudes. This energy is well transferred vibrationally for many different processes. In fact, simply being in the rain, and having the rain fall upon your skin, is a good healing technique as long as no chill or cold develops. Thus, having rain fall upon an herb can be useful, but if the herb is to remain dry, then a glass covering is necessary. This will generally still permit some of the energy to be transferred.

Unfortunately, rain on the Earth is often chemically contaminated, so it may not be wise to use rainwater directly to enhance herbs. One could put a glass bowl with herbs in it with a glass cover out in the rain. There would be benefit if rainwater flowed over it. Since rainwater still carries the vibration of sunlight energy, using the glass container prevents contamination and some of the Sun's beneficial properties are transferred to the herbs. All these natural forces concentrate energy in herbs.

It is also useful to invoke other natural forces such as sunlight in taking herbs to activate their spiritual properties. A sun tea is even better than one that is prepared by bringing water to a boil, putting the herb in, and then letting it sit for a while. This takes longer, of course, because for sun teas to be fully prepared, they must sit in the sun perhaps all day. But this has a greater impact because of the addition of the Sun's natural force. Herbs can also be dried in the Sun. Many times they are dried with devices called dehydrators that also concentrate sunlight energy. Solar dehydrators are the best ones to use. Herbs should be exposed to the open air for at least a few minutes. This is often not done because insects may infest the dehydrating plant substance, but if you stay with the herbs you can perhaps keep the insects away.

Other techniques that use natural forces are beneficial. You can put an herb in a glass container and bury it underneath the ground. This concentrates some of the earth's natural forces within it. It is best to place the glass container a few feet under the ground, but even a few inches is good. Beneficial effects from the earth will be concentrated in the herbs within three days. This process points to the added spiritual benefit of what is termed the root cellar, or a place where herbs and roots are sometimes stored. There is a natural coolness, which is the usual reason these places are created. But, in addition, some of the natural energy of the earth is more available to the herbs.

There is the obvious technique of burning an herb when it is used in a ritual process. And indeed, for many herbs and plants that can be burned, there is some benefit in doing this when you are taking an herb for its spiritual properties. You might take the tea, but you could also burn some of the herb just after taking the tea. The smell generates the fire element within a person, which brings greater insight to an individual.

It is important that individuals follow their intuition when drawn to particular techniques for preparing herbs. The intuitive process is sometimes overlooked when herbs are prepared. The more physical or even chemical techniques of working with solvents such as alcohol do concentrate various capabilities of the herbs. However, when the intuitive faculties are part of the process, there is a further enhancement. Vibrational attributes of people can be brought into herbal preparations. Water is best for this energy transfer, but many solvents have the capacity to absorb vibrations from both an herb and a person. If someone is conscious of this potential, they bring more of their conscious energy into the herbal preparation.

It is wise, at least at some point in the process, to stop the various techniques, such as brewing, and simply be with the herb. This may mean bringing light in by visualization, or bringing sound into the room as you do this process. This will, at different points in the process, assist in the way the energy is made closer in vibration and resonance to your inner being. Of course, it is better if the individual can use wildcrafted herbs. But sometimes there is a problem with this, if the herbs came from a place that is contaminated.

If people are working with plants of which the primary properties are in the root, they may wish to experiment with the stems, leaves, or flowers. There will often be a correspondence between the part of the plant usually used for medicinal purposes or for various other uses, even if it is just a flavor, and the concentration of spiritual effects most assimilable to individuals. But individuals who are growing herbs themselves should experiment with the flowers when possible.

It would be good for people to look at how they use herbs in their lives. People now generally act unconsciously, out of a reaction to older beverage techniques with coffee, black tea, and in Japan, green tea. Gradually, more individuals are seeking substitutes with various herbs. Choose an herb based on the activities that you are involved in when drinking herb teas. Do not be influenced just by the taste or smell. Make the choice also based on spiritual principles, on the way the herb affects you. Thus, when herbs that tend to affect groups are utilized, choose those herbs because you are going to be with a group. Herbs that are good for focusing and bringing into your awareness greater soul or spiritual energy should often be taken early in the morning when you are still quiet, before your day has begun. Similarly, herbs that affect the astral body in a more harmonizing manner should usually be taken before going to sleep at night.

Many individuals use herbs extensively in ways that they perhaps are not even aware of. Let us say that, in cooking, you are using herbs for their spiciness, for the flavor they impart, or for the odor or aroma that they give. Be aware of their spiritual properties as you prepare the herbs. When you have a choice of working with several herbs that could provide a similar effect, be aware of the herbs' spiritual properties in making such a choice. These spiritual properties will be present in the food as it is eaten.

Today, herbs are often found in many prepackaged products and one does not know what specifically is in these products. If you regularly work with such goods, it is wise, when possible, to develop the product yourself. If, for instance, you regularly eat ketchup, prepare your own mixture of tomatoes and choose what spices to add to the mixture. Gradually, individuals become aware that all they do affects their spirituality, the way they see things and how they come to know themselves and God. However, it is a big leap for people to understand that every word they say, everything they do impresses some aspect of God into their lives, if they are willing to look for it. Here is a place where this principle can be applied into something people are already doing but without much awareness. The ways the spiritual properties of herbs are a part of this will gradually be made clearer.

There are different ways to take herbs to activate their spiritual properties. Focus on the deeper message of the plant, the karmic purpose of the devic order bringing their message to you, and the energy of the signature. This is impressed upon the individual in addition to the gross physical or medicinal properties of the herb. Anything that encourages this is useful. If you are using a dried herb that has been chopped so that it appears indistinguishable, form a picture of the plant in your mind. Perhaps you can obtain an herb book that shows pictures of many of these herbs in their natural habitat.

Working with herbs as part of a ritual is very useful to activate the herb's spiritual properties. By strengthening the spiritual properties in herbs, you also strengthen those properties in yourself. Combine these techniques with meditation, creative visualization, and chanting. One beautiful technique is referred to as the Japanese tea ceremony. Various herb teas could easily be substituted here. There is a great deal in the philosophical and social literature about this as a time of introspection, honoring, and silence. These characteristics are useful in strengthening the spiritual effects of herbs. The nature of plants is silence and respect, which lead to introspection. These qualities are definitely enhanced in such a ritual.

CHAPTER VII

USING HERBS WITH GEM ELIXIRS, FLOWER ESSENCES, AND HOMEOPATHIC REMEDIES

The spiritual properties of herbs can be activated by mixing them with flower essences. The vibration of the flowers of herbs have a unity on the level of the thought form, the genetic character of the plant, and the life stream. Flowers usually concentrate and focalize spiritual properties to a more specific level than do the rest of the herb. This is because flowers have a very specific purpose. They are seeking to reproduce the plant, to attract insects, and they have been modified more powerfully by mankind's thought processes, especially in Lemurian times, for the purposes of flower essences. Therefore, what happens is a strengthening effect in which a particular flower essence will have its effect broadened as well as made deeper. If powerful energy is begun at a tiny point, it tends to expand outward with great force. There is a focalization and concentration of energy that is deepened and strengthened.

For instance, the herb comfrey has an important healing property of cleansing the physical body. This has been well known for some time; its aroma indicates this and is part of its signature. The comfrey flower portrays as its signature the ability to regenerate nerves in the body. If comfrey flower essence is taken at the same time as the herb comfrey, nerve regeneration is felt not only more deeply in the body, but in other areas of life—especially in areas where an individual needs to purify, awaken, and transform. On the spiritual level it becomes easier to understand what one needs, what one is willing to release, and what one needs to focus more attention upon. This would develop when comfrey is taken by itself, but it would not be as clearly focused by someone as when combined with the flower essence.

The difficulty here is that you are working with many levels of vibration all at once. An individual might seek to understand what was the contribution from the herb and from the flower essence. This is usually not wise to pursue because it can get too confusing. In most cases, it is best to take at least a small quantity of the herb, in combination with the flower essence. Then the herb and flower essence are amplified. The main exception to this rule is when the herb is harmful. For instance, when taking belladonna flower essence, do not consume any of the herb belladonna.

Many homeopathic remedies are prepared from the entire herb, not just from the flower. The homeopathic remedy, when taken from the overall plant, has a stronger effect. This principle is also true when an herb is taken from the overall plant. Here, however, it is the physical debilitating effect that is being focused upon by the homeopathic law of similars, so the individual is given assistance. However, when an individual taking a particular homeopathic remedy also wishes to experience the spiritual effects associated with it, take only the herb and not the flower essence, unless this herb is particularly difficult or damaging to the physical body. Then only the flower essence should be taken. If you take the homeopathic version, the flower essence, and the herb of the same plant, it usually has more impact than most people are able to work with. A future book in this series will more fully discuss the relationship between homeopathy and herbs.

There are many obvious ways to combine flower essences and herbs. When taking a flower essence associated with a particular spiritual property, an herb associated with that spiritual property can often be combined with no ill effects or difficulties. Generally, do not take these preparations at the same time. Separate taking each substance by at least a few minutes. Sometimes, with flower essences, it is wise to take them by themselves, and wait at least an hour before ingesting anything else, so the vibration is felt more deeply inside you. Some of the spiritual effects of vibrational remedies penetrate people in ways in which the physical vibrational effects caused by the herb may interfere. This time separation will usually avoid such difficulties.

If gem elixirs are chosen which are broadening in their effects and assist overall, such as with quartz, then one might be able to combine these appropriately with herbs and the flower essence of the herb. Gems which concentrate energy in a particular area such as white diamond, which concentrates energy strongly in the crown chakra, would often focalize too much energy to be combined with herbs. Caution is needed. Only individuals who feel particularly attracted to this should attempt it. This same principle also applies to taking an herb, its homeopathic preparation, and a gem elixir at the same time.

For most people, it is best not to take more then nine flower essences and gem elixirs internally at the same time. And most people can take up to nine vibrational essences with one or more herbs. There is no recommended maximum for herbs. However, to attune to a particular herb's properties, it is often wise not to take too many herbs at once. The one main limitation in merging herbs would be if their properties are not attuned. For instance, it would not be wise to take an herb that promotes loosening of the stool with one that promotes a hardening of the stool.

Taking nine flower essences at once combined with herbs will very rarely cause any problems. This is also true if someone takes nine gem elixirs with herbs, but there will be some exceptions with certain very powerful gem elixirs, such as opal or white diamond. It is important that people utilize their own judgment. In many cases, a maximum of three gem elixirs will be fairly effective when mixed with herbs.

As mentioned in *Flower Essences and Vibrational Healing*, it is often good to place flower essences in a bath. Again, there are many possible combinations of essences and herbs that can be effectively used in a bath. This is especially true with herbs that have a strong aroma. This is a good combination with flower essences because the aroma tends to focus the levels of the mind that are not conscious, both superconscious and unconscious, upon spiritual characteristics associated with what the individual is looking for. This means that there are rarely any contraindications for taking flower essences and herbs together. The capacities of a flower essence and the herb's spiritual properties will be well combined for most people when taking a bath, particularly when they feel attuned to the spiritual properties of the herb.

As for combining herbs, flower essences, and gem elixirs in a bath, it will sometimes be best to take one flower essence, one gem elixir, and one herb to not overload the system. One could usually use more herbs, particularly if looking for a particular combination of scents, as created by a potpourri or when adding herbs to a bath because of the odor they produce. There is not really a maximum in terms of effectiveness or a likelihood of creating harm for most people when taking herbs in a bath. As for mixing flower essences and gem elixirs in a bath, especially when herbs are also being taken, the maximum number of nine flower essences and gem elixirs should be observed for most people.

Certain patterns develop when individuals consume large quantities of herb teas. These relate to the herb's spiritual properties, but individuals may not be able to focus upon or understand them. Take the example of rosehips tea. This is fairly popular today. Some people take this combined with hibiscus flowers. When these two herbs are combined, they can open the crown and throat chakras. The signature, this red color, and utilization of Vitamin C are affected on the spiritual and physical levels. The energy pouring through the spine from the root chakra upwards may lodge in the throat as a result of extended use of this herbal combination. One could bring the spiritual energy of these herbs into focus by taking the flower essence of a rose that one has familiarity with, and, of course, of hibiscus. The flower essence should be taken especially when meditating and if there is any difficulty or blockage in the throat or crown chakras. This is one example of how an extended use of herbs, when there is not a physical need for them, can have spiritual effects but not in a way that an individual is always able to work with easily.

There is one other area in which flower essences can be very useful. Taking the essence associated with the herb can bring into greater consciousness some of the spiritual properties already transferred to the physical body by the herb. This is a longer term effect, but it can be of some importance.

It is important in working with gems that individuals recognize the vibrational changes that take place in the physical body. This permeates deep into the physical body, usually to the cellular level, and will remain as a vibration for the individual to tap into, usually for three days after wearing or having a gem near the body. It is similar with herbs. The way herbs are taken into the body has a resounding effect even three days afterwards on the spiritual level, because the transfer to the etheric body is extremely similar to the way the body reacts to gemstones.

The effects of vibrational remedies are felt at the subtle body levels and then often returned to the physical body. The nature of most physical substances found in herbs will stay in the physical body. They accumulate in various organs, in the circulatory system, and eventually are excreted. But this process generally takes about three days to complete itself. This is mostly a physical process. Over that three day period, there will be a continuous series of vibrations as if washing from the physical into the subtle body level, particularly the etheric body.

When a gem elixir is taken, there is generally an immediate effect as various vibrations move into the subtle bodies. The etheric body is quite affected but the impact then usually moves to the other subtle bodies, lodging there vibrationally. Over a period of three days or so, these vibrations generally penetrate from the other subtle bodies to the etheric body or, if lodged directly in the etheric body, begin to focus and strengthen there. Thus, the final result is that this energy by waves moves into the etheric body though the pathway is very different.

Physically present gemstones can be of some benefit in working with herbs. If there are certain gems you are particularly attuned to, use them while taking herbs. Gemstones make the process more physical for people. Gem elixirs can also be used with herbs, but a bit more caution is sometimes needed.

The colors associated with different vibrational remedies affect people due to various factors. This is something individuals should explore. Organic substances such as amber have particularly interesting properties with regards to herbs because of their more organic origins. Opal in all its forms has a special resonance with all herbs. This is because of its extremely high water content, which changes from time to time. Water is seen as a repository of the unconscious, a symbol for working with various levels of pranic force, and this is an important symbol. At the physical level, water has the ability to absorb and change vibrations. It has been called the universal solvent in chemistry, and this is indeed true for it attempts to capture and work with vibration. The unique construction of opal and its brilliance are directly related to water content and humidity. In fact, opal changes the way it looks and is extremely sensitive vibrationally to the way water is held. Water absorbs, by many interesting vibrational pathways, numerous characteristics associated with vibrational remedies and herbs. Herbs create a vibration which is amplified by the water within an opal.

These things affect the way herbs may be utilized. For instance, in spiritual work when one wishes to raise consciousness, particularly as focused in the crown chakra, there are certain herbs that are of some assistance. When ingesting these herbs you could coordinate this by placing an opal on the crown chakra. There is also some benefit in placing amber around you. Herbs and gems do not have to be taken at exactly the same time. You could take the herbs and within three days apply the gems. This would work equally well.

Regarding gem elixirs, there are more specific properties relating to various levels of healing on the physical level. Gem elixirs are very attuned to specific parts of the physical body. And many spiritual levels are activated, especially by the more important gemstones such as ruby, emerald, diamond, garnet, sapphire, and opal. Each of these as elixirs have powerful spiritual properties that focalize in certain levels of the individual, when taken in coordination with herbs that also stimulate similar spiritual properties. A certain synergism takes place. You must, of course, be careful, because elixirs can be partly nullified when more crude substance are taken at the very same time. Thus, do not take three drops of a gem elixir and put it into a cup of very hot herbal tea. Rather, you might wait five or ten minutes after taking the tea and then take a gem elixir, or take a gem elixir a few minutes before taking the tea. It does not matter if you take the herbs before or after the gem elixir. What matters is that they are not taken at the same time.

What is of even greater benefit is to take a cup of tea while in the bath, and to add one or more gem elixirs to the bath water. Then sip the tea while in the bath. The resulting synergism will not always be easily noted or understood because the results often take place on the higher subtle bodies. This process begins with the mental body, the astral body is somewhat activated, and the causal and soul bodies are particularly strengthened.

The time factor with herbs is extremely important. You also see this in the way herbs work on the physical level. They take their own time. Most herbalists cannot tell you precisely when a physical effect will take place as opposed to, for instance, antibiotics or other substances which are quite controlled in their physical effects. This is because the physical body's reaction to antibiotics and other drugs is the primary factor. But the physical body's reaction to herbs is not the primary factor. Healing with herbs is very much connected with the etheric body, and then the impact gradually enters the physical body depending on the unique situation. Antibiotics work more directly in the physical body, which is why their effect is more obvious.

As a gem elixir and various herb combinations or just an herb tea is taken, perhaps in the bath, what can take place often requires some time to resolve itself. Part of the reason for this is that the energy added on the spiritual level by the physical and emotional bodies is not fully applied in life. This assists the process more than anything else because mankind's purpose in working with spiritual energy is always to know it by applying it. It is not enough to have a wonderful meditation. Somehow the energy must be used; something must be done with it. To speed up this process and make it more conscious, when gem elixirs and herbs are combined, focus particularly over the next three days on examining the application of the spiritual principles for which you took these herbs and gem elixirs. This can be of some benefit over the next few months. Sometimes these effects, even from a single bath with a single cup of tea, can indeed be felt for some time. Because these are spiritual effects, they must be long-range. There is a similar pattern when just flower essences are taken with herbs.

With gemstones it is useful to realize that they resonate with certain physical centers of the body. Some herbs, when there is a place in the physical body that needs more physical help, will have a similar resonance. But generally, the spiritual properties will not resonate on the physical level. Vibrational properties are transmitted through the physical body to the subtle bodies by an herb differently than is the case with gemstones. Thus, herbs and gems can be quite complementary. This is true, in some cases, even more than with flower essences and herbs, simply because they are working on multiple levels simultaneously, and the two levels coordinate. This sometimes creates a polarity, and means that as you apply this spiritual understanding or as these new aspects come into your life, you would be required to resolve paradoxes or difficulties to understand the polarity. As herbs and gem elixirs are taken, you then have a chance for three days to examine what in your life is unbalanced, what is of a duality, and how you see paradox.

There is a simple technique of applying gem elixirs and herbs to the third eye center. They could be easily combined. If making a tea, let the water cool before placing the herbs and gem elixirs in it. Because the spiritual properties intermix with some of the physical properties, combine these two mixtures when they are below 70 degrees Fahrenheit, and not in boiling water, not even warm water. Then place the mixture in the sun or under a pyramid for two hours. This mixes the properties vibrationally. Then this substance could be applied to the third eye center with some direct benefits. These substances could also be applied separately to the third eye. The third eye center is quite sensitive to vibrations on such a level. This will not work as well if only herbs or only gem elixirs are applied to the third eye. The effect is much stronger when they are applied together.

CHAPTER VIII

HERBAL USE WITH
PLANTS AND ANIMALS

In ancient times, spiritual properties were important attributes of all plants. Today, this is largely lost. Indeed, many individuals who work with plants and develop a comraderie or what is termed a 'green thumb' or talent with plants, are tapping into a resonance. In such cases, the plants wish to teach the individuals about themselves. This is not so true with herbs. Herbs generally have very potent and powerful vibrational characteristics. These may relate to specific functions and unique characteristics, such as the signature or ways humans have worked with these plants in the past. It is as if they have a very specific message, but not a way of easily enlightening humans. But once this message has been transmitted, new pathways can open in which the herb can then be modified by a person and used appropriately. This is not generally done today. It is through this pathway of learning the specific messages and working directly with herbs that changes were made in the way herbs were used and grown in the past.

Many on the spiritual path explore herbs, just as herbs attune to people, and the herbs, with inner intelligence and knowingness, bring the person into greater resonance on a spiritual level. This is natural because their effects have not been diluted by extensive hybridization. When plant substances are not hybridized, they have more spiritual energy. Individuals working with such plants can more easily experience the plant's spiritual properties. For instance, nonhybridized corn contains a stronger inner sense than hybridized corn. And it usually has more minerals and vitamins that act as carriers for physical substances that eventually bring a vibrational shift in individuals. Individuals exploring their own spirituality and who are farmers growing food crops, would be wise to occasionally ingest nonhybridized forms of plants to awaken some of these deep spiritual properties that are being impressed upon them all the time.

The spiritual presence in plants is strongest in the spring, especially during germination. Individuals are able to feel and know this spiritual awakening in themselves. It is wise to meditate around germinating plants. Then the devic orders can more easily work with, change, and resonate with the energy that the individual is producing. This allows plants, which are also in resonance with the individual, to have this energy transferred to them, and plants become more resistant to disease and negative thought forms.

Purer and less hybridized forms of plants can be used to provide a spiritual effect by intermingling hybridized and nonhybridized plants. Some of the characteristics of each can be merged, so that the higher properties of each are combined into a new plant.

Companion planting, the placing of one plant next to another, is of benefit not only because the plants shade each other in the early growth period and because insects are repelled by the odors coming from the companion plant, but because spiritually the life force associated with the companion plant is very strong. It is in such a similar state of vibration to that of the plant it is working with that some of that property is transferred, and the plants to which it is transferred need this added energy. This process can be enhanced by meditation and by pouring love into the plant. Companion planting is a way individuals find resonance and ask deeper questions.

Individuals learning about food substances and agriculture are sometimes relatively young souls. They have come onto the planet to learn many things, and this often starts with the Earth itself. They are building a very good foundation. We do not wish by this to imply any degree of intelligence as associated with the youthfulness or age of a soul. It is simply the number of lifetimes that one has had on the planet and the paths one has explored. There are also exceptions here. Some people return to the foundation to again grow and learn of the Earth. By and large, these individuals will be well served by herbs that increase the spiritual understanding of their own foundation level. This refers to what they are constructing in their lives, what they bring in on the level of family, what they seek to know in pure relationship, and how they work with the Earth. In working with such herbs, they become better farmers, which often increases their comraderie and attunement with the devic orders. Indeed, those who come to know herbs might use them for deeper states of meditation to assist in agricultural development. This is their primary focus.

Plants have their own life stream which relates to the plant's purpose and its willingness to join with humanity. Plants are influenced by people in many different ways, but the most important way is the path of love. It is a path by which one honors all principals in the plant. This is not done by just the mind or curiosity, but indeed, is the way the beauty of a plant is received and the way a person understands or sees directly the devic order and cares for it out of this experience of wanting to love. As these things are provided, plants grow and there is more resistance to insects and diseases.

This process relates to the will function in people. As a person wills love into a plant, and utilizing the powerful nature of being a human in accepting nature, the natural kingdoms, and the Earth herself, the energies for the plant multiply. This in itself engenders a resonant vibration between the overall thought forms associated with the plant, the plant's devic order, the various karmic purposes of the plant, and the information about its signature. All these things are made more assimilable to people, to their minds and hearts. It is as if they understand in a loving way what the plant is saying, what its purpose is, how it interacts with animals, with other plants, and with the environment. The difficulty with this now for many plants is environmental pollution. Open your heart to attune to these plants, to learn these lessons, and waves of sadness must sometimes be experienced. How mankind has abused or harmed these plants may be the first thing that is received. Therefore, opening the heart may be difficult at first, but it is the key to truly understanding plants.

Plants do not create their conceptions of understanding in scientific, rational, or written form, but by the energies of love. Plants should be loved, cared for, and worked with, not for the purpose of making money, but because of the will function, because of a willingness to work with them simply because of their beauty. This enhances all the important properties that relate to a plant's growth. The proper use of will involves love.

How this is accomplished is no longer an easy matter. There may be great sadness when initially opening the heart to plants because of an inability to understand the way the will works. Too many individuals work with plants and herbs for monetary gain and not for a deep understanding of plants. In addition, the etheric density on the planet makes it harder to receive the inner messages generated from plants and to understand their purpose and the devic order associated with the plant.

It is the devic kingdom that provides much energy when attuning to plants. If an individual is working with particular herbs or plants and wishes to explore and apply their own spirituality, there is some chance of success. The application should include a spiritual understanding of the devic kingdom. Simplify what you have learned of your own life and reveal it in some way to an unseen, but often felt, spiritual presence with your plants. Your thought forms become an issue here. If thought forms in your life and what you have learned relate to love, share this with the plant's devic order, not just with the plant, then they may learn from this and reflect it to you.

This can be done in many ways such as sleeping by the plant, inviting a dream state, moving into states of meditation, or focusing on the third eye and opening the eyes gently to gaze at the devas. Then the energies are received at the level which is important, the spiritual level. The devic order is well-associated with this, and can indeed transmit images, ideas, and love back to the person. These will be very modified by the devic order's karmic purpose, by their love for the plants, and their particular affiliation with the Earth. This will change the person's thought forms and enable them to perhaps understand a little more of themselves.

Negative thought forms [1] also need to be examined with disease and the problem of insect infestation in agriculture. Here the intervening factor is the petrochemical miasm and the great difficulties with largely petrochemical or synthetically derived substances that are used for pesticides and herbicides. Occasionally, these products are herbally derived. This causes changes and mutations in plants. The way these substances are applied allows the devic orders far less communication with plants. These problems take place on many different levels. Substances that are extremely enervating, that remove life force energy, will coat the plant, affecting the tiniest molecular systems of interchange with water. This occurs especially through the roots and leaves of plants and in the way water transmits the vibrations and love of the devic orders. Then the devic orders are cut off from plants, and it is difficult for them to continue influencing the plants. This influence is often necessary to create germination. Thus, continued use of pesticides can sometimes lead to mutation, and germination becomes very difficult.

Negative thought forms will generally be ungrounded, in that they will not manifest in physical form unless given a specific pathway. These pathways are now being provided for mankind by the insect kingdom, particularly insects that are injurious to people, plants, or to the the Earth itself. If you look at this, you can understand why it is necessary for such an intervening factor to be present. Thought forms do not have a specific form or way of embodying these energies. They cannot directly transmit their energies to the environment for people to feel and experience how the results relate to plants, animals, and to their own bodies. Insects are an intermediating force because they are basically without much overall guidance. It is as if they are automatons without intelligence, simply able to work with these thought forms.

This pattern positively affects the overall creation of the insect kingdom. Insects, especially when not of a hive-like nature, are assisted by negative thought forms. They come into a fuller existence. They come to know themselves better and to experience life and themselves more deeply, even though they experience life through these negative thought forms.

The petrochemicals currently used destroy the insect's physical body, so that the vehicle to capture the negative thought form is lost. The negative thought forms then find another pathway. The most obvious pathway is for negative thought forms of similar vibrations to concentrate together to promote a rapid physical mutation of insects. Thus, new insect forms can be created fairly rapidly under the influence of various petrochemicals, and one must use stronger petrochemicals to destroy them. This is the spiritual side of evolution and mutation with regard to petrochemicals.

What is also happening here is that the petrochemical miasm is strengthening. Petrochemicals affect the physical processes of plants, animals, and people. These physical processes take energy away from the creation of positive thought forms. Such positive thought forms act in direct ways to influence, mitigate, and balance negative thought forms. Thus, negative thought forms, as personified by the insect kingdom, are affected by petrochemicals in two ways. First, the energy of petrochemicals as utilized in pesticides and other physical processes, works directly on the insect kingdom and the plants they feed on. But, in another way, these petrochemicals affect and weaken the production of positive thought forms, those things that balance, assist, and even change insects.

This process is just now reaching the point by which intelligence is transferred into petrochemicals which are essentially inert substances. Until recently petrochemicals could not directly receive and work with negative thought forms. An entire new breed of insects is just forming that are based upon certain petrochemicals, actually incorporating them into their bodies and feeding upon them. This is now taking place in countries with a strong sun and active petrochemical industry such as Saudi Arabia. This would seem to be a natural result when looked at from an evolutionary perspective. This is a bad thing for mankind because it will solidify the petrochemical miasm in people. More new diseases will develop. The ability of insects to spread diseases is already an important factor. Disease is the spreading of a negative thought form, an energy that paves the way for a particular virus or microorganism to get started in individuals. While these insects have just begun to form, it will be at least ten or fifteen years before scientists begin to isolate and study these new life forms. This may sound strange but scientists have already isolated a new microorganism that thrives on high doses of radiation.[2]

The ability to destroy more and more insects, the hatred felt, and the war that starts by using greater and greater pesticides in larger and larger quantities with newer and newer chemicals interferes with humanity's consciousness. The ultimate way to deal with this problem is through awareness and understanding. Deal with the energies that create the difficulty in the first place. An overemphasis on making money from plants or owning land to overcome economical and political barriers that others have created will not create an attunement with nature. All these things have nothing to do with the natural kingdoms. Understanding negative thought forms assists in relieving some of the stress they create. But this awareness and understanding will not have much effect with land that has been over saturated with pesticides until such land has been cleared, cleansed, and in some cases, had plants grown on it that draw these chemicals out of the soil. Then these plants should be burned.

Most plants that are conventionally considered ground cover such as certain beans and grasses could be used. When there is more time for plants to grow on reclaimed land, plants with even deeper roots such as dandelion can also be employed. The ability of certain plants to remove specific pesticides was not a talent created in Lemuria, but the Lemurians did, as a general tendency, imbue certain plants with an ability to work over large areas to cleanse the soil.

It is also important to understand that the petrochemical miasm is getting established more deeply in people who work around pesticides partly because they are exposed to negative thought forms that are associated with the insect kingdom. The insect kingdom is quite numerous and is growing every day. There is a direct correlation between the allowance of stronger, wider spread, and deeper negative thought forms and the insect kingdom. This understanding can be of special help to someone if they are opened to this when they kill an insect. You may notice that there is a brief moment of what might be called psychic babble, a great deal of chatter, as if there is a whole string of sounds and inner noises that the inner person may experience. This may be experienced visually as a great light, many different colors flashing. Some may experience a gnawing sensation of uncomfortableness that has many waves of energy within it.

It would be wise for individuals to recognize that this is the negative thought form of the insect, now escaping into the ethers. Sometimes this negative thought form will naturally recombine and come back to the person. Whether or not this occurs often depends upon the negative thought form, upon the person's understanding, and upon the willingness of the person to deal with this particular issue. If a person learns to understand negative thought forms, as well as to appreciate what he is dealing with in himself, and love and appreciation develops for the insect, the insect is much less likely to bother a person. It tends to move to another location so that negative thought forms are not transmitted.

When stuck in a pattern by which insects must be killed in large quantities, then deal with this in a very gradual way. But when the problem involves something like capturing an insect in your house and taking it outside, a sense of love can be engendered, strengthened, and sent towards these creatures. This can assist greatly because negative thought forms begin to be replaced with loving thought forms. This is not going to change the character of the insect, but it will definitely be retransmitted to the overall negative thought forms associated with the insect. It will change and show its purpose, but do not attempt to just love the insect for its beauty, appearance, or particular function. Ask why it might be around you, what your negative thought forms are, what you are dealing with in your life, and see how this might be changed. Then project this loving attitude to the insect. This can indeed cause a difference in understanding how negative thought forms work. It is far more important for people to have the experience of this in working with insects, than to simply take the word of channeled guidance. To experience this in your heart is very important.

Animals work primarily with herbs as a food substance. An animal needs a certain food so it seeks out the herb. Often this is by smell. However, this is lost when an animal is in contact with human beings for too long. This is not well known. You might, for instance, see your dog chewing grass. Because domesticated animals often lose the ability to differentiate between different kinds of herbs to enhance their health, disease may result. The spiritual properties activated by herbs are important for the animal's self-understanding, but animals mainly seek herbs for their medicinal properties to heal specific diseases or to maintain health. Sometimes, if you are taking an herb the same time a pet does, it becomes easier for the herb's spiritual properties to be transferred to the animal.

When you take an herb, your animal should often be offered a little of the same herb so it will not be imbalanced by the effect you experience from the herb. But the animal must be allowed to choose it in such cases. Offer the herb to the animal at least once a week, if you are working with the herb over an extended period of time. If you use the herb only once or twice, provide it to the animal at least once when you first take the herb. Sometimes the animal will recognize the necessity for the herb and choose it.

The way people respond to inner changes is mirrored by pets. If you use herbs that affect the crown chakra, your animals may stare into space, or do things that are quite touching but are done at the wrong time, like in the middle of the night or in the middle of a meal. Such attributes should be recognized as mirroring something in yourself. This is because the vibration of herbs will be directly absorbed by the animals.

With wild animals, there life stream is quite well set and knows which herbs to take and when and how they should be taken. But this is forgotten by caged wild animals. Occasionally, caged wild animals, not domesticated ones, should be released for a time in an herb garden. They will tear it up a little, but they will consume some of the plants that are good for them, and that is a good thing to allow. They should be given this choice.

Pets get the usual diseases associated with man. This is why more and more animals suffer from cancer, venereal diseases, and urinary infections. Yet curiously, you will see that there is not so much scientific literature about these difficulties, even 20 years ago. This problem has gotten worse partly because domesticated animals have lost some of their natural ability to utilize the plant kingdom for healing, and partly because they absorb the negative thought forms associated with disease. People need to learn that animals are around and always receiving from them.

Alice Bailey also spoke of the importance of thought forms in our lives.[3] Negative thought forms are contagious. As an individual attunes to you, negative thought forms may also be received by that individual. Some individuals who live and grow together may begin to take on each other's negative thought forms. This could even be a relationship that is not very close, like roommates or a work situation. When struggling in a certain area, such as trying to receive money, though the other individual has never dealt with this, they may also begin to struggle with it. This often happens on an unconscious level because you care for the person in some way.

When the caring is unconscious and you do not understand the energetic process involved, a link develops between the negative thought forms that the other person is dealing with and your own love for them and willingness to help. This draws some of that energy to you. You may also not welcome that energy or resist it in some way. This can be beneficial for the other person. For instance, if you understand lessons about money and explain it to your friend, it will help them. But in many cases, you will perceive that unless you show how it actually works for you, the individual will not gain much merely from your relieving them of certain negative thoughts, which you would do by an explanation.

Negative thought forms are not always a major problem with people. Many learn from each other, regardless of how they deal with any thought forms, positive or negative. If consciousness is involved share love, empathy, and caring for the roommates or business associates. Then one may more easily see the purpose of negative thought forms and find a way to reveal it to them in love.

With the animal kingdom there are difficulties with negative thought forms. Animals may be unconscious of this process, and there may be little you can do to assist them. They work with the negative thought forms of individuals who are near them, in an unconscious fashion. However, some assistance is provided to animals by loving them. This is particularly true when you find in your own life some release, acknowledgment, or assistance with your negative thought forms and the things you struggle with in life. If you make that as clear and simple as possible, it may be provided in love and caring directly to the animal. For instance, if someone struggles with understanding money, a cat in the house may experience physical difficulties and be unable to fully absorb food. When the individual, who is dealing with negative thought forms regarding money makes some progress and sees themself as lovable, they can bring this love into action in their heart and pour it into the cat. This will directly assist the animal.

Scientists have long been aware that animals are instinctively drawn to specific plants, but the reason for this is not understood.[4] Animals have a particular kinship at extremely high vibrational levels relating to their own souls with certain herbs. It is a way to simply know the vibration of the plant. This explains many things, such as how an animal can be taken from its local habitat and still recognize an herb that is healthful and useful for that animal. It is as if some higher aspect of the animal attunes to the essential vibration of the herb. This is provided by the natural kingdom in very beautiful ways. One of these is with the devic order that brings interesting and loving energies to animals, thus drawing attraction to certain plants.

In addition, many animals have a well-developed sense of smell. This helps an animal recognize an inner understanding of the natural way an herb grows and creates their own vibration. It is as if in smelling it, the animal is changed slightly. The vibration of the animal shifts, and the effect is known within the animal. As a result of this, the animal feels good and any pain may dissolve. This draws it closer to the herb so that it may begin to eat it. The taste of the herb also affects an animal, rekindling the instinctual eye. But it is primarily through the smell that this takes place. Even for people, some of this is relevant because the aroma of an herb is very important.

At higher levels, it is important to see that the overall soul of the animal, the joint soul across animal species that is within a given species, is very linked. The group soul of a given species allows animals to interrelate and share their lessons obtained on the Earth and to understand their development alongside humanity, other animal, and plant life. This soul vibration may attune to particular vibrations of certain plants.[5]

This has come about for many different reasons, but most of them are historical. Animals were fed these plants for many centuries, and certain plants were used repeatedly for healing and assistance. But most importantly, animals by choice have sought out certain plants in the natural kingdom. You have the wonderful example of cats and catnip and the way these two species have gotten together and been associated for so long. The overall soul the joined thought form or morphogenetic field of a particular plant species and certain animals may intermesh over long periods of time. This gives the animal an instinctual understanding of the plant that transcends the usual keynotes of vibration, physical appearance, and even odor. This enables an animal to seek out varieties of a plant it has never seen or even smelled.

1 Hilarion, *The Nature of Reality* (Toronto: Marcus Books, 1980), p. 29, 31, 38.
_____, *Symbols* (Toronto: Marcus Books, 1982), p. 39, 40, 70, 87.
Max Heindel, *Occult Principles of Health and Healing* (Oceanside, CA: The Rosicrucian Fellowship, 1938).
2 Louis C. Kervran, *Biological Transmutations* (Binghamton, NY: Swan House, 1972).
3 Alice Bailey, *A Treatise On Cosmic Fire* (NY: Lucis Publishing Co., 1977), p. 557-600, 975.
_____, *Esoteric Healing* (NY: Lucis Publishing Co., 1975).
_____, *Esoteric Psychology* (NY: Lucis Publishing Co., 1980).
4 William H. Lee, Ph.D., "Herbal Medicine: Its Properties Are Instinctively Sought By the Animal Kingdom," *Let's Live*, (August, 1988), 66-67.
5 Rudolf Steiner, "Group Souls of Animals Plants and Minerals,"(Feb., 2,1908).

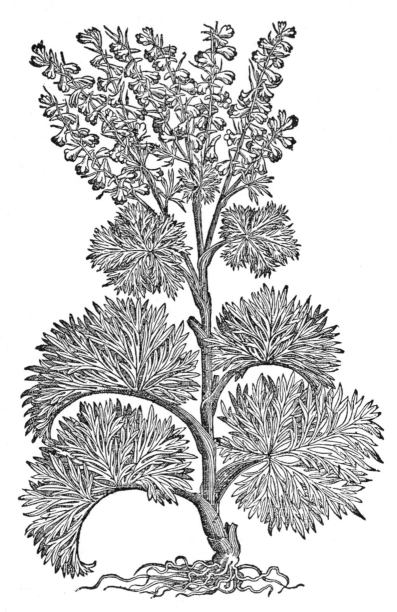

LARKSPUR

CHAPTER IX

INFORMATION TO BE
DISCUSSED WITH EACH HERB

This text discusses 108 individual herbs, with up to 15 points relating to each herb. These include common and obscure herbs, Chinese herbs, tropical fruits, and trees. While some of these herbs are quite obscure, I have generally avoided listing herbs that are unobtainable. With so many herbs in use I decided to list basic ones that are available.

An herb's spiritual properties will usually be activated in whatever manner the herb is applied. However, in a few instances a specific application is best. For instance, pine is best applied as a salve to the third eye. This information is always provided with these herbs.

Usually any part of an herb can be used with a similar effect. And, by and large, plants tend to maintain a certain signature and overall impact on a person. This is generally carried into all parts of the plant. With some plants there is a special concentration in certain parts of the plant. When this occurs with the herbs described in this book it is noted such as with raspberry and its leaf. Generally, the herb's spiritual properties are readily available when the plant is utilized in its most convenient form. However, since people often buy herbs in stores, the obtainable part of the plant may not be the best part to use. Environmental pollutants and even negative thought forms from people handling the herbs—may have weakened the plants' spiritual properties. Therefore it is always good to purchase organically grown or wildcrafted herbs—or grow herbs yourself.

There are systems of thought which directly associate various parts of a plant with different responses in the body. The root tends to affect the more physical and medicinal properties; the leaf or stem are more for conscious everyday work, communication, and interrelationships; while flowers attune to higher spiritual levels regarding the consciousness specifically associated with God and the spiritual path. The seeds are associated with concentrated energy as it is transmitted into past, present, and future generations. We find that in some cases this symbolism is useful.

As a general principle, more of an herb's spiritual properties are concentrated in the flower. However, the rest of a plant always contains the spiritual properties stored in that plant. And sometimes it is easier for a person to assimilate a plant's spiritual lessons from parts of the plant other than the flowers. This is especially true with the roots because of their connection with the Earth. Sometimes the plant's evolution, the concentration of spiritual properties in the roots or another part of the plant, corresponds to mankind's evolution. That is the level that people are best able to receive.

For instance, the ginseng flower contains much spiritual energy. However, this powerful energy will not be assimilated by a human unless it is captured by a technique such as preparing a flower essence. The ginseng flower itself will have very little spiritual impact upon a person. Of course, it is wise to combine the flower essence with the ginseng root at various times to amplify the spiritual properties; but mankind, having a similar vibration in many ways to the power of the spiritual vibration within the ginseng root, will gain much more from the root than from the flower. Thus, you see that all parts of a plant can have important spiritual properties for people, not just the flowers. This principle especially applies with Chinese herbs, because they have for thousands of years been directly influenced by positive thought forms of people using them for healing and spiritual growth.

Initially, some botanical information is provided about each herb. Readers can refer to numerous herb books to learn more about the botanical aspect of these plants.

Next, there is a detailed discussion of the herbs' spiritual, psychological, and psychic property. Psychological property refers to attitudes of the mind, the ability to work with attitudes and behavior patterns, and the ability to understand one's own methods and ways of being. The psychic patterns relate to abilities that are not generally accepted or understood, and therefore may seem mystical or magical. These abilities relate to extensions beyond the traditional five senses. Spiritual abilities activate higher understanding, wisdom, knowledge, and vibrational shifts by acknowledging God's energy in people and in their work.

I have chosen not to include how these herbs can be used medicinally. The medicinal properties of herbs has been well researched. There is an occasional exception when an herb has important medicinal properties that are not yet understood. For instance, olive has strong cleansing properties for the liver and gall bladder that modern medicine does not yet understand. Such information is provided in the hope that it will be researched in the coming years.

A particular plant species has a subdivision of the entire devic order associated with it. This order has no specific name and is sometimes referred to as the devic order of that species—such as the pomegranate devic order. This understanding sometimes enhances the preparation and clinical effectiveness of herbs. While sometimes referring to the nature spirits or devas, this book does not present a detailed discussion of the role of the nature spirits with each plant.

The properties discussed with these herbs usually extend to all species of that plant. As previously discussed in *Flower Essence and Vibrational Healing*, the exact species is usually very important with flower essences. The reason for this distinction with herbs and flower essences is that with herbs the whole plant is often used. The herb has numerous properties more directly related to its life stream than to the specific attributes engendered in the flower. However, there are some exceptions, which are noted when individual herbs are discussed. Occasionally it would be helpful to combine a number of different species of a plant to merge the plant's spiritual properties. Walnut exemplifies this pattern.

Some flowers are especially short or long lasting. Generally this refers to an impact of energy. This often relates to the mental body if the flower is short, and to the etheric and emotional bodies if it is longer. The size of the flower may also be influenced by other characteristics of the plant. When it is exceptionally short, it can relate to aspects of quickness or rapid change in an individual. This can mean rapid thought, or be the catalyst for great dramatic change in life, as in a sudden shift in perspective. This is often associated with the planet Uranus.

The shape, color, odor, make-up, taste, and nutrient qualities of many plants are associated with the human body. This relationship is known as the doctrine of signature and offers clues as to how herbs can be used in healing and spiritual work. It is important to see that herbs are blessings upon the planet. To fully resolve and work with the signature of plants, you might imagine the Lemurian frame of mind, the joyousness of herbs, their beauty, what in them is striking and unique, and what is there in nature as you view an herb growing that you praise and love. If this is difficult, imagine beaming love at another person you care for dearly, and then focus that same beam of energy upon this image of the plant in your mind. Gradually what emerges is a picture of these higher and more beautiful properties.

The doctrine of signatures is simply looking at these attributes as they affect people on the spiritual level. However, in reading these words and knowing this information, you as a person may also find this in yourself. This is an important thing to realize. The doctrine of signatures is not to be laid down in stone. It is something instead for all to discover in themselves as they work with and understand plants on the level of love and joyousness.

You may see certain unusual characteristics in a plant. Perhaps it sends roots very deep, or grows in conditions of extreme acidity or alkalinity. Or it may grow after a fire or heavy rains. All of these traits are processed characteristics that imply a certain level of uniqueness. As you view this uniqueness, experience joy and praise within yourself. See and know that energy, and you will know the signature.

There are also unusual attributes relating to color. Certain colors vibrate with specific chakras. This is obvious. But at the same time, ask in looking at the plant: what here is special? It is not only the color or shading, but the way it appears on the plant. Most plants will not be one color. There is usually an emphasis in this coloration in what would be described in artistic terms as a movement—the emphasis upward or downward as if the tips of the leaves, for instance, have an extra brightness and color. The ways a plant grows manifest some of these colors in certain patterns. That is a most beautiful and useful thing.

The way herbs have been used over the centuries also affects them. Sometimes this influences a plant's particular name, which can aid in identifying the signature. But one must be careful here, because sometimes the name translated into other languages is extremely different. The energies associated with a plant's way of reproduction and its particular health benefits are also clues to a plant's signature. It is wise to approach these things with a joyous resonance rather than with preconceived ideas.

There are also etheric nonphysical signatures not visible on the physical level. The energies associated with a plant are especially concentrated in the plant's etheric body. This is because over a long period of time the energy that is transmitted to a human by a plant must only take the path of the etheric level. The devic order associated with this level provides the energy and concentration into the etheric body. It works primarily on the etheric level. This means that as you connect to the devic order more clearly, the etheric level of the plant is more easily transmitted.

Feelings of joy and love can attune one more deeply to these signatures. This is difficult when you simply read that "This plant has an etheric signature that looks like such and such." But the energy is available if you can resonate with the plant, for that is what is created by this joyousness and love.

As the signature of a plant develops, it is known and felt in love and joy by human beings. In ancient times this joy often changed the plant. Just loving plants makes them grow larger and stronger. The experiences at the Findhorn community in Scotland affirm this pattern today.

Regarding the origins of these herbs—many plants and trees were created in Lemuria and Atlantis through the use of meditation, mental energy, and creative visualization to learn specific lessons for conscious growth, to help shape the body, and to manifest healing in mind, body, and spirit. It is important to understand the origins and karmic purpose of herbs because they still affect people today.

Chakras are centers of energy situated in the subtle anatomy. Spiritual information and the life force is channeled into the body through the chakras. Traditional esoteric literature generally states that there are seven chakras. In a few instances twelve chakras are described. These other main chakras are on the two hands, the two feet, and the medulla oblongata coordinated with the midbrain. Unfortunately, only a handful understand that there are just over 360 chakras in the human body. These chakras are about evenly divided between the physical and subtle bodies and aura. There is generally a direct relationship or polarity between a specific chakra in the physical body and one in the subtle bodies. The exact number of chakras varies according to various ancient religious traditions. These many chakras are described in great technical detail in some of the ancient religious scriptures in India, such as in some of the Upanishads, and in ancient Egyptian, Mayan, and Atlantean texts. Although the information could be channeled, because it has existed in some of the Indian scriptures for thousands of years, it would be better if it were translated into several western languages. Alice Bailey and several others have described some of these minor chakras. Practitioners of acupuncture, jin shin, and jyutsu will find this information especially helpful in their work. How various herbs affect the minor chakras may be described in a later text.

There are also five very important chakras above the crown chakra. When I note the eighth, ninth, tenth, eleventh, or twelfth chakras, I am referring to these chakras above the head. The eighth chakra must open for a person to directly experience the higher realms. This chakra also aligns the etheric and emotional bodies. The ninth chakra unites the emotional and mental bodies, the tenth chakra unifies the mental and astral bodies, the eleventh chakra coordinates the astral and causal bodies, and the twelfth chakra unites the causal and integrated spiritual bodies. This is one way the subtle bodies are joined together. The top three chakras are intersecting points for all the subtle bodies. In *Gem Elixirs and Vibrational Healing, Vol I*, I discussed the attributes of the seven main chakras as well as other material on the chakras.

The nadis are petals inside the chakras that distribute the life force and energy of each chakra into the physical and subtle bodies. There are approximately 72,000 nadis or ethereal channels of energy in the subtle anatomy, which are interwoven with the nervous system. The nadis are like an ethereal nervous system.

The meridians are passageways for the life force to enter the body. They lie between the etheric and physical bodies and have a direct association with the circulatory and nervous systems. The meridians also connect the different acupuncture points in the body. As with the miasms, many herbs affect the miasms but the meridians are not mentioned unless a specific herb especially influences them.

The subtle bodies are also referred to with these herbs. There is the etheric body, emotional body, mental body, astral body, causal body, soul body, and integrated spiritual body. The integrated spiritual body represents a combination of the spiritual qualities of the other subtle bodies and the physical body. These subtle bodies usually spread out from the physical body in the above order, respectively. There is also the aura, the ethereal fluidium, and the thermal body, which are connected to the subtle bodies. These bodies are aligned with each other in various patterns. I provided a detailed discussion of these subtle bodies in my text, *Gem Elixirs and Vibrational Healing, Vol I*.

The miasms are inherited energy patterns that contribute to causing all chronic and many acute diseases. A detailed discussion of the miasms has been presented in my previous books. Traditional homeopathic literature also provides much information on the miasms.

With any miasm there are many ways of utilizing what is essentially an out-of-harmony condition. However, the miasm as demonstrating an out-of-harmony condition runs very deep in an individual. It could be aligned with life purpose, deep lessons in life, and the reason for incarnation. This is why these are long standing conditions difficult to understand, work with, and remove from the entire being. This means that life lessons and the spiritual side of the miasms are brought into much greater clarity and understanding as the miasms are examined.

In learning about the miasms, individuals will recognize certain similarities between their own chronic health and spiritual difficulties, and which aspects of God's essentials laws, for instance, one is out of harmony with. The spiritual properties of herbs ease and remove miasms by dislodging certain aspects of past life karma and facets of one's personality affected by the miasms. As a miasm is eased, certain life lessons associated with it are dislodged and more easy to work with. This is extremely beneficial in a spiritual sense, because it more deeply shows individuals their own paths and allows them true growth. True growth must include that which is new in your own pattern, in your own life stream, and in your sequence of lifetimes. This is where the miasms are extremely important, because they prevent such growth. As they are eased, deeper growth is permitted.

While people often feel that there are seven rays there are really twelve main rays. These rays are subtle incoming energy that create potential within a person. A detailed discussion of the 12 rays is presented in *Gem Elixirs and Vibrational Healing, Vol II.*

Today, individuals are coming more into resonance, awareness, and knowledge of their own purposes and therefore of the rays. This is because the rays are an incoming energy that assists in people's development. This also extends to plants. There are plants that are associated with certain rays, although in general the primary spiritual properties of plants do not associate so directly with specific rays as usually happens with people. When you take a particular herb it may assist in working with one ray or another. It does not mean the herb specifically relates to that ray. It is the effect on people that is being developed. There are many plants that assist individuals in developing their own potential. This is mainly because the vibrational and spiritual effects come not only from the plant but from the devic order, the changes within the plant, and the soul energy it may tap into.

To a degree, plants particularly associated with the rays are slated for genetic change. Changes reflected in mankind's society will eventually be reflected in various plants. Herbs that have been noted for their healing qualities for the last hundred years or so will especially undergo changes. Each of the rays, having characteristics associated with it, will effect a plant associated with that ray. This development of plants parallels that of humanity.

With spiritual development, one comes more closely into harmony with the purpose of one's being with the ray energy itself. For this reason, all the plants' substances and all the herbs' spiritual properties assist in developing the twelve rays within an individual. The rays are indicative of potential. Herbs are taken partly to develop potential within people. Sometimes this is created by a new vibration, sometimes by emphasis on something you are already familiar with, but in all cases it is the development of this potential.

There is also a discussion how herbs are influenced by various astrological configurations. The spiritual effects of herbs are often amplified because of the movement of different planets. And how herbs aid the consciousness of various plants and animals is discussed in detail.

Test points are also recommended for individual plants. A test point is a particular part of the body to which an individual herb is attuned. If the herb eases heart problems, the heart might be the test point for that herb. When a particular area is pressed, a person's outstretched arm will initially weaken rapidly when you press it down, if the person needs treatment in that area of the anatomy. If the person then holds the herb you are considering prescribing, the individual may sharply resist when you again press the arm down. This suggests that the herb could ease the problem. If the arm still noticeably weakens when the person holds the plant, that remedy will probably not be of much help.

The test point is often different for the herb's spiritual properties in contrast to the medicinal effects of the same herb. The test point for an herb as it provides particular medicinal effects for the body usually relates to whatever part of the body is affected. To illustrate, when taking licorice root to supplement the adrenals, the test points on the abdominal region corresponding to the adrenals would be indicated. But licorice root in its spiritual ability to increase the awareness and ability to see into other dimensional levels, will be enhanced by the test points at the third eye and base of the throat.

An herb's spiritual properties may deviate remarkably and powerfully from the medicinal properties. In such cases a differentiation as to its action and effectiveness on the chakra level is important. The spiritual properties of the flower essence may relate to areas that are far different than those of the spiritual properties of the herb. When these differ, as in the more powerful plants, sometimes it is important that these be differentiated as test points. In this book the test point for the herb's spiritual properties is always given. If the test point is different for the herb's flower essence or medicinal properties, that information is not provided.

LAVENDER

CHAPTER X

INDIVIDUAL HERBS

Adder's Tongue

This perennial plant has drooping yellow flowers that appear in the spring. It is traditionally used as an emetic, emollient, and poultice.

Certain ideas that an individual may know are true but are difficult to work with may be assimilated more easily. The ability to express such understanding to others is also assisted. The signature of the tongue-like shape is of some benefit, and the ability of the individual to use the energy is enhanced. The will and the sense of expression develop. If an understanding of spiritual principles is important, but an individual is struggling with some of them, this herb may be useful.

There is an enhanced ability to assist others struggling to understand God's laws. New psychic material, new techniques, and new ideas become easier to assimilate. The herb is also useful for people to share what they have learned, to write it down as they perceive it. The ability to express this new understanding is enhanced.

In Lemuria, the plant was utilized to enhance tastefulness when another plant, herb, or food substance was ingested that had a strong or distasteful effect to the physical body. There was a certain cleansing noticed with this. This cleansing was a key for the Lemurians to see that these aspects of expression might be shifted if they put their energy into the plant. It was chosen for such a purpose, and was useful to the Lemurians. In Atlantis the plant was not often recognized for these capacities, and it is only in recent times that its karmic purpose may again be brought into light for mankind.

The fifth and ninth chakras are stimulated by this herb, and there is some strengthening of the nadis in the throat and jaw. There is some release of energies that may be stuck in the meridians moving through the throat and jaw. As a result, a number of meridians may receive increased energy; this is especially true with the stomach meridian. The mental body is strengthened, the causal body is cleansed, and the emotional body becomes more relaxed. The cancer miasm is slightly eased, and the test point is the jaw at the tip of the chin.

Amaranthus

This ancient Aztec plant is again becoming a popular grain. It coordinates the root and crown chakra energies so that what you wish accomplished on the physical level is known on the spiritual level; its inner purpose is revealed. What you wish to accomplish is felt deeply in the individual. This means that there will be a great deal of added energy in the activities of the world. This can be useful for those who see that what they do in the world is closely tied to their own spirituality and the way they are seen by others. This application has many implications such as in working with groups of people who are coordinating their efforts to create a particular project. This is why this plant is now being presented to mankind again.

The psychic abilities can be quite potent and powerful; one may see exactly where energy can be applied to make a positive change. This is indeed a psychic property. It is a way of knowing the right time and right thing to say. It is a strengthened intuition that shows you how your goals may resonate with someone else's.

Amaranthus is on the Earth to bring action of a beautiful and high purpose. This is what it was bred for initially, and this quality remains within it and is again being discovered. Moreover, the plant has a high degree of protein and has not been hybridized. In ancient times, this was seen as an important trait. This was true not only in the Aztec world, but even long before this in Lemuria. As to the signature, there is strength in the way the grain is produced. The plant has a certain heartiness, and its timing for mankind's applicability is perfect for today. Until a few years ago, no one outside of certain agricultural circles had even heard of amaranthus.

The root and crown chakras are activated. When these energies achieve resonance, the third chakra moves into a higher level of vibration. All the meridians are strengthened, especially all of the yang meridians. The etheric and emotional bodies are enhanced, the petrochemical miasm is significantly eased, and the fourth and fifth rays are energized.

Those struggling with the influence of Saturn in their lives, can be greatly aided by taking amaranthus. It can be of some benefit to feed amaranthus to animals one is having a power struggle with. It could be a large dog, but more often it is a caged wild animal that is having some difficulty with people, such as in a circus. The test points are the very top of the head and the base of the spine.

Balm (Lemon)

This popular culinary herb is commonly found in the Mediterranean region. Medically, this herb is used as an anti-spasmodic, and it eases common female complaints, insomnia, and melancholy.

The odor which is part of the plant's signature is quite strong and at times penetrates deeply into an individual. If the plant is bruised, it smells like a lemon. This aligns a person more deeply with a past life purpose. This is useful for past-life regression and for understanding the current life to fulfill and balance one's karma. Psychic properties relating to what was learned in a past life will be amplified. Lifetimes lived in Atlantis or other civilizations where greater knowledge and wisdom were developed will be more firmly felt in the individual. Telepathy develops especially when individuals wish to join together and work towards a particular goal. In addition, this herb can be a relaxant to release tension and achieve spiritual growth. Therefore, it is of some benefit in meditation, especially when individuals meditate in a group and the group energy is aligned to a common spiritual purpose.

This herb has been on the planet for a long time. It was used in Lemuria to bring peace to individuals. Its use was gradually expanded to reveal some of its other properties. Its karmic lesson is to help individuals relax, to release tensions, and to remember and understand lessons from the past.

The third and heart chakras are energized, and energy is diffused from them into the other chakras. The kidney meridian is strengthened, while the astral and mental bodies are activated. Taking this herb may help when negative aspects with Pluto exist. This herb may be indicated for individuals who have allergies to specific animals, in particular cats or dogs, because often this is related to past life difficulties. But this herb is not generally indicated to work directly with animals. The test points are the center of the chest and the sternum area.

Basil

Sweet basil is an annual that grows to three feet with red or white flowers appearing during the summer. This aromatic kitchen herb is an appetizer that is good for cramps and digestion.

Enthusiasm develops when this herb is used. This enthusiasm is put to good use when it is directed into spiritual awakening, deeper meditation, or states in which energy is expended, as in chanting, dancing, or to help others. This can also be useful in emotional states, such as anger, that may develop when you are in a state of greater spiritual awareness or meditation. The anger is not released or blocked but is transformed by allowing enthusiasm to be felt more strongly.

Basil grows under many conditions, and the aroma stimulates an emotional response in individuals as if they then wish to achieve more growth. This herb enables individuals to know their emotional selves better, to make better choices. These choices are then applied in situations in which intuitive knowledge is needed to make the correct decision. As an example, when you have sudden doubts about a project, using this herb assists you to understand the source of the doubts, trust yourself more deeply, and convert the energy associated with doubt and worry into what you are seeking to decide. This is not precisely a psychic ability, but it relates to the intuitive side by which these processes occur. Intuition for better decision making is enhanced.

The plant has been used extensively by mankind for aromatic and cooking purposes. Its use in enhancing the appetite has gradually created in the morphogenetic fields, in the genetic structure of mankind, an appetite for life. There is no one specific area in which this has been engendered, rather it has been gradual throughout history.

The first, second, and third chakras, and the minor chakras in the feet and hands, are given added energy and strength. And the current, or sushumna channel, in the spinal column from these chakras upwards is opened. The governing vessel meridian is strengthened, and all of the nadis are energized. The connection between the etheric and physical bodies is enhanced slightly. The obvious connection here is that the emotional body is brought into a greater state of clarity. It is more focused. The syphilitic and gonorrhea miasms are eased, and there is some influence with the planet Jupiter, but this is primarily symbolic. Fifth ray energy is more revealed, and an individual has greater purpose in their life, approaching this understanding, not as a burden, but as a gift. The test point is the medulla oblongata.

Beechdrops

A native American plant twelve to eighteen inches tall, the entire plant is a dull red color. It is used externally for wounds and some skin problems.

There is an increased ability to properly utilize kundalini, pranic force, and the connection between the feet and Earth. Individuals have an energy that focuses in the throat region. This is Earth energy. Beechdrops is useful in expressing Earth energy in art. Many individuals who are artistically inclined may find that using this herb enhances an understanding of the media they are working in. We refer to people working with stone, pigments, or various forms of sculpture. The way the Earth as an energy is willing to speak to people may be more easily felt.

The red color of the entire plant reflects its impact on root chakra energy. The spiritual energy that accumulates as the herb is taken tends to focus in the root chakra for a short time. It is wise, when using this herb, to be aware of this. About fifteen minutes after using the herb, consciously visualize the energy pouring into the legs down to the Earth and from the root chakra up the spine and to the throat in particular. Those who are not artistically inclined may wish to use this herb for chanting purposes. They may find that they can chant for longer periods than they had previously. The expressiveness of such essentially physical energy is the overriding pattern here.

There is greater inspiration in communion with the Earth, in the way it is available and expressed to others. This inspiration may create a temporary psychic link between those who view art work and the artist. This is what is often unconsciously desired by those who seek to give their art to the world, that they may know humanity and humanity know them. This is enhanced, but more importantly, the process itself is enhanced for a person. Indeed, this is exactly in alignment with what the Earth is doing—that she wishes her lessons to be known by humanity and to learn humanity's lessons herself.

In Lemuria, the plant was seen as sacred because of the way Earth energy throbbed and moved within it. This was understood to be beneficial and useful. All that was needed for its use to be continued was to alert the nature kingdom associated with this plant that mankind might forget about the Earth. At first this possibility was not taken seriously by the Lemurians, but in the later phase it was recognized.

The governing vessel meridian is significantly strengthened, and there is some assistance in the bladder meridian. The nadis at the root chakra and in the throat are stimulated, while the emotional, etheric, and causal bodies are cleansed. The tubercular miasm is eased, and the first, second, and third rays are brought into clearer focus. The test point is the base of spine.

Birch

The several varieties of this tree are found in North America and Europe. White birch has slightly stronger properties than other types. Birch is used as an astringent, diuretic, and diaphoretic.

With birch, people are better able to appreciate beauty, to understand it, to experience it, and then not judge it. Those who judge beauty should take this herb from time to time. Often these individuals feel, deep inside of themselves, that they do not measure up to the beauty they observe. An excellent example here is about half of the world's population associated with the Sun sign Virgo. Indeed, all people associated with Virgo may find some assistance in using this herb from time to time. Secondly, the beauty of the tree imparts a certain calmness. Those struggling with patterns of speech—seeking to change their modes of expression or perhaps overcome stuttering, or seeking ways to change their speech patterns—should consider using birch. Again, this is one aspect of the judgment qualities activated by birch, but it is also because birch imparts a certain calmness as one views it.

There is some confluence with the flower essence of birch in its ability to work with male energies. But what actually happens is that, on a psychic level, you see through another's eyes. This is how the judgment process is eased, because in knowing that you see through another, you accept them and their view of yourself. Thus, self-judgment is lessened. The ability to see through another's eyes is one form of telepathy that is not formed by mental words but rather more purely by pictures and sensations. These processes are enhanced by this tree.

The tree originated in Lemuria but much later increased in height. Part of this was encouraged by the devic order. The idea was to impart a quiet and deep beauty for individuals. The tree has the ability to release its bark from time to time, and its bark is the principle part that should be used. It is as if birch is showing a way to release patterns. This ability to throw off the skin of judgment is the karmic lesson for the tree. There is a quiet beauty imparted as one views this tree. Also, the bark has a slight odor that can also bring individuals to a place of inner quiet. Because of birch's beauty, attitudes of judgment can be exposed when one pours love into this tree.

The heart chakra and heart meridian are energized, the heavy metal miasm is eased, and the emotional and etheric bodies are slightly energized. The test point is the roof of the mouth.

Bird's Tongue

This is a European tree, over a hundred feet high. It is used to remove intestinal worms.

The signature of its name and how it is derived from the odd leaf shape and its attraction to birds has been noted for quite some time. The energy associated with the plant can be used by individuals seeking to understand freedom. It serves to reduce states of emotional repression and leads to a greater sense of freedom. Freedom involves many levels of responsibility, and this can cause fear. In the meditative state, these fear-producing responsibilities are released more easily for an individual. They may see clearly where they have held themselves back causing their own inner jail. Teenagers developing a sense of freedom and responsibility should sometimes use this herb.

The way individuals can use this herb in meditation is rather interesting. Imagine yourself as a bird, or see the energy of the wind moving through you. If possible, meditate outdoors when there is some wind or it can be heard. An individual may gradually acquire an ability to leave the physical body in these periods of meditation, using the astral body, but journeying specifically upward. Begin a chant immediately after taking it, as you move gradually into the meditative states. Use any chant that evokes the chakras from the first to the seventh, in that order, and with the imagination allow yourself to move out the top of your head. Various syllables have been proposed for this.

This energy, as it is strengthened, allows a sense of freedom. Individuals must make choices about freedom. This is extremely important right now because there are so many people on the Earth who do not understand this principle of freedom versus responsibility. Some will suffer and some will prosper, determined partly by how they apply freedom and responsibility. These techniques can take an individual into new levels of understanding this aspect of humanity's purpose.

There is an ability to experience another person's point of view. There is also the ability to understand the karmic purpose for an entire country, region, or people who are struggling towards personal freedom. Political systems and their inner purpose for spiritual awakening or change of a people may be appreciated more. Individuals in political power may be forgiven for their errors or mistakes. Individuals involving themselves in the political process may find more energy to continue by using this herb.

There was an association in Lemuria with the strengthening bird forms. Birds have come to this planet from many different parts of the galaxy. Each has been added to the various genetic strains of others and sometimes it is difficult for the birds to get fully rooted and awakened here on Earth. They have also been combined with reptilian forms, which is obvious when you look at some of the structures of dinosaurs that flew. Some of this genetic merging required psychic strengthening, and indeed this was provided by the Lemurians for the evolving bird forms.

The Lemurians understood birds in ways in which the birds never truly understood the Earth. The properties of freedom and the options available to the birds were not fully understood by birds. The Lemurians attempted as much as was possible to transfer this understanding to the birds through their love. However, even today birds do not yet understand these things. The plant has the karmic purpose of bridging the human and bird life streams.

Those who work with or breed birds will better understand those life streams by using this herb. There is within the entire life stream of all birds a burning question. This is particularly true now as more and more varieties of bird become extinct upon the Earth. That question is, "What is mankind's purpose? Why are they here? What is it that they are all about, and what are they doing?" An individual contemplating this in the presence of birds who are aware of the individual's presence may indeed assist the bird life form to understand its own struggles with freedom and territorial rights much more easily. This is useful for mankind because this energy is then shared with those who also struggle with territoriality and the issues of freedom and repression worldwide.

There is a strengthening of the fifth and sixth chakras, and the nadis in the hands, feet, and wrists are stimulated. There is accelerated movement of energy between the spleen and stomach meridians. The astral body is strengthened and given more connection to the mental body so that journeys can be understood better. The gonorrhea miasm is slightly eased. The tenth and eleventh rays are strengthened so an individual can perceive and work with them more clearly. When Mercury is in negative aspect to any natal aspects in a person's chart, there is some benefit in using this herb. The test point is the medulla oblongata.

Birthroot

This small herb produces red, white, or yellow flowers in the late spring. Traditionally, it has been used as a poultice, antiseptic, and tonic.

There is a deeper understanding of life purpose and the way Earth energy affects a person. This is a stimulating aspect, so what may occur is that the spiritual path is questioned, and a person understands their relationship to the Earth better. They may be able to then manifest more energy. This activated energy sometimes affects the lung area, so energy in the lungs is more easily released. If one is already on a spiritual path, lung difficulties are more likely to be eased than might otherwise be the case.

There is an enhanced ability to perceive future events, particularly when relating to relationships, such as the energy that people share in an enterprise or when networking. The way people can work together, share information, and pool resources is enhanced with birthroot. As ideas in a group project become more focused, this herb is especially indicated. When you interact with many people and you perceive many possibilities and there is some confusion, birthroot aids in bringing focus to the enterprise. Birthroot also helps one understand the potential of large groups, what they might be able to accomplish together. The singular focus of that group is what would emerge psychically to the individual.

Birthroot was used in Lemuria for the development of many ideas and in rituals. The herb might be shared among a number of individuals before they focused on a given project. This did not affect the energy associated with the project, but it gave increased ability for one-pointed focus. As people again recognize this potential, they will seek this herb and use it in such fashion. However, as its karmic purpose has largely been fulfilled, it is not seen in such capacity anymore. The way individuals join their creative energy has an intrinsic lesson associated with it which mankind has already understood. This has not always been understood in the highest sense. In the past, working with others has too often been seen as patriotism or some way of excluding other groups or individuals. But the essential growth experience achieved when people work together to accomplish set goals is a lesson that mankind has learned today.

The singular focus on the flower and its wide effect on the human body is the signature that indicates the way it transmits Earth energy to a person. It is like a funnel of energy being concentrated and focused into the Earth and into a person.

There is increased energy in the heart and third eye chakras, the lung meridian is stimulated, and there can be some energy released in the chest area through the nadis. There is a strengthening of the mental body, while the causal body is purified and brought into an energetic state temporarily, perhaps half an hour or so after consuming a tea of this herb. There is some release of the radiation miasm, and there is greater clarity with the seventh and eighth rays. When Mars or Mercury are in square or opposition, birthroot will ease any resulting difficulties. The test point is the third eye.

Bistort

This small herb is found in high mountain regions of the United States and Europe. Bistort is used as a diuretic, a mouthwash, and to ease diarrhea.

With bistort, the lessons learned working in the world are applied to greater spiritual awareness. This is partly expressed in the signature, the way bistort grows in higher regions, but it is also shown by the way individuals, in loving and knowing the plant, may feel that something must be done with what they have learned. Ultimately, this spiritual application permeates all facets of one's being and spiritual integration is encouraged. This means that concepts from a religious doctrine or philosophy are merged, and a person may more easily absorb and work with those facets they find most true and important.

The ability to know quickly whether what someone is saying is the truth or not is enhanced. This is because there is an alignment with the higher truth. When this is simply a matter of judgment, the conscious mind is too involved, and it is not what is meant here. Rather there is the ability to know that what someone is saying is in harmony and aligned with what you feel to be the truth.

The plant has been through several interesting changes. In ancient times, especially in the early Lemurian phase, it was found only in the very highest mountain peaks. It was treasured, and then at the appropriate time it was forgotten. As its thought form became more rarefied, it was not seen much on the Earth for quite some time. It has now again become more common as the time draws near when mankind must learn from spiritual and physical experiences and use these for greater awareness on the spiritual level.

The fifth chakra is particularly energized, and the mental body is strengthened. Although no specific ray is activated, the entire investigation into which rays one works with is enhanced. It is wise to use bistort in certain forms of agriculture, such as when growing herbs in a greenhouse. A mist made from this herb may be of some benefit. Bistort is especially valuable when the plants grown are rare or are difficult to grow. Ginseng exemplifies this because it is difficult to create the correct conditions for its growth. The test point is the area at the top of the sternum and base of the throat.

Blackberry

This bush produces white flowers each summer. Long used to treat bleeding gums, blackberry is also considered to be a tonic and astringent.

Blackberry stimulates the ability to awaken love and sweetness. One also develops persistence and patience. This not only means patience in love, but also patience with the loving aspects of a spiritual discipline, religious pursuit, or anytime you judge yourself or when someone judges you. Greater forgiveness also develops. However, this is not a forgiveness that occurs in a moment, rather it is the ability to persist, to remain, even though there are difficulties, because one is aware of the sweetness and love that lie ahead. The thorns in this plant are important too because they symbolize that which slows down the process of gratification. Because of these thorns, blackberry exists, grows, and persists even when someone cuts it back. The signature is obvious here—the persistence and sweetness of the berries. These two aspects combined provide the key to its spiritual properties.

With blackberry there is the ability to recognize a kindred soul and to perceive a path upon which you feel love is available. This is often a long and patient path. When the berries fully ripen they are sweetest. The individual also becomes more tenacious to pursue a goal that involves patience. This added strength allows the conscious mind to be quieter in certain states of meditation, for one is not so anxious about the results, but is patient and willing to wait for them to occur.

The plant in its original form was much less persistent and was cultivated even more easily than it is today. This is because there was little reason for it to protect itself. However, it was seen that in growing thorns and making it easier to run rampant something would be gained for humanity as a symbol. The plant accepted this willingly, and these traits were added at the end of the Lemurian phase. This ability of blackberry to persist and fend off all who might interfere, but also experience sweetness at the end of persistence, symbolizes the lessons the plant wishes to teach so that its beingness will be felt and its patience will be well received.

The astral body is stretched, which is useful in astral travel experiences so that no harm comes to the astral body. When one journeys, for instance, to a very emotional area there can be much fear engendered. That is when the astral body tends to collapse in on itself. Problems that occur during astral projection are generally of an emotional nature, but they can also be accidental. For instance, there may be a moving object, physical or astral in nature, that affects the astral body. If the individual, in the astral state, begins to recognize the concept of weight and falls from a great height, or if a stone should accidentally dislodge and come down upon you while you are exploring an area, the astral body will not be directly affected as if a physical stone landed on the physical body. However, there will be an emotional impact. Just as if a physical stone were to strike the physical body, a number of protective mechanisms will be activated. The astral body may shrink in size or collapse in on itself. This pattern can occur in many different ways. Sometimes the shrinkage may occur immediately after the person leaves the physical body. This usually occurs because of extreme fear. The person may then snap back into the physical body and awaken with a start.

The third chakra and bladder meridian are strengthened. When there is any difficulty with the planet Saturn, even if it is only in a square, opposition, or conjunction with the Moon, there is benefit in taking this herb. As an animal approaches old age, there is some benefit in providing this herb. It allows the animal to be more patient in old age. The test point is the medulla oblongata.

Blazing Star

The name of this North American perennial comes from the flowers that seem to burst forth. It is used as a gargle and diuretic.

There is inherent in this plant the ability for the most humble to change into something quite magnificent and wonderful, especially in a spiritual sense. It is found in many places and it is fairly common, yet it has the beautiful property of the flowers bursting forth. This is part of the plant's signature. Astrologically, there is a direct relation to the planet Uranus, which is slow-moving, yet, when positively aspected at the correct time with other areas of the chart, can indicate a great blossoming forth, a great change in the individual. Individuals may experience changes in their lives not knowing from whence it came. With Uranus what is unknown often suddenly becomes known. This new energy is more easily understood and assimilated if one uses blazing star. An example is the individual who perhaps has had a mild interest in psychic phenomena and suddenly finds himself channeling or doing powerful work of an energetic nature with people. This is more easily understood and applied with blazing star.

What actually happens is that the blockages to this new energy are easily dissolved in the emotional body. This herb works primarily on the emotional body. The individual no longer stands in their own way. This is not usually perceived by the person, however. Instead, they simply put less attention on the questions and more attention on new points of view, developing new ideas or talents.

Many psychic abilities that are dormant in the individual, are enhanced. When this is timed with the individual's own blossoming forth and allowing these newfound abilities deep into their lives, then there can be a direct enhancement. The plant allows a deeper integration because what is placed in the way can be moved out of the way. This can be especially important when new points of view acquired because the new psychic gifts are in conflict with what has been previously learned.

This plant was seeded into mankind to symbolize the very aspects of this surprise nature. At many times in the past it was rarely seen. Currently, its reminder on the subtle level is necessary, because so many have these psychic gifts. In Lemuria, it was seen that it was important that this underpinning be placed with all plants, but especially this one, so that humanity would be reminded of these possibilities at various junctures in its future history. Its karmic purpose is to remind mankind of this when it is needed.

The heart and crown chakras are enhanced. Several of the chakras above the head may come into a temporary state of energy transfer and alignment, but this will depend on the individual and what psychic gifts they are working with. There is a strengthening of the spleen meridian, as if the receptacle of this new found energy is found more easily on the physical level. The emotional body is cleansed and augmented, there is some release of the cancer miasm, and the eighth and fourth rays are brought into clearer focus. There can occasionally be a similar pattern in animals when there is a difficult change that they go through. This may occur, for instance, with a dog about one year after birth and a cat for about nine months after birth. This often has to do with certain psychic properties. Around that time there is some wisdom in providing this herb for the animal to eat if it chooses. The test point is the top of the head.

Buckthorn

Buckthorn is found in damp places throughout the United States and Europe. It is a prominent purgative. Excessive amounts of the berries or fresh bark can cause poisoning. Do not take this plant when pregnant.

There is a strengthening of the will. This is often because what is in the way is released. When buckthorn syrup is taken, there is a strengthening of will because of a desire within the person to fulfill the original purpose of their incarnation. There may therefore be a rejection of things that stand in the way. There is a danger in this because too much resistance clouds your understanding of what these actual obstacles are. However, the strengthening effect can be quite profound. It gives the will an ability to almost force feed spiritual knowledge so that, for instance, you might awaken in the morning wanting to go to a particular bookstore or library and explore a particular avenue. With the strengthening effect of the herb in the syrup form one might then take a particular task to completion. There is within the person a willingness to continue working on spiritual projects. This does not guarantee completion, but takes them another step.

On the higher spiritual levels, a certain fear may be released. This is because of the cleansing effect this syrup has on the emotional body. The individual, in facing the possible future, one's potential and God nature, is less afraid and is more able to work with that energy, accepting only the highest and releasing that which is not of the highest level.

There is an enhancement of telepathic ability. Part of this is because the will is stimulated, and there is a great deal of fear associated with telepathy today for most people. There is good reason for this, of course. When opening the mind to receive impressions and thoughts, it is sometimes difficult to be one-directional. You usually open to all the thoughts that are around you, and there is good reason to fear some of this. But as the will is strengthened, focusing of telepathic ability will become easier. When you are ready, then allow it; when you are not, allow that also.

This plant keeps away those who might invade it, but it also has the capacity, when taken for medicinal purposes, to cause vomiting, to eject what is not needed. There is a certain power present throughout this plant. This is seen in its physical form and in its root structure. This strengthening runs deeply throughout the plant and is its signature.

The plant was quite different in Lemuria. It was much smaller and not nearly as developed. Then the will, as externalized, was unnecessary. However, it was also seen then that the Atlanteans might need a stronger will. Thus, more will was brought into this plant. The devic order associated with buckthorn was trained. There was energy associated with the will, as if an introspection of the entire Lemurian culture took place to personify will as this devic order. This was not entirely successful. The Atlanteans did not work with this plant, or even recognize many of its properties, and it fell into dormancy. However, it was recognized for some of its interesting properties early in this century, partly through the work of Rudolf Steiner. Today, the Steiner-oriented Weleda pharmacies sell buckthorn syrup in many countries, and it is available in a growing number of health food stores. The willingness to manifest spiritual ideas is again coming into action. This is the fulfillment of its karmic purpose.

The third chakra is strengthened, but there is also an opening on the heart level. Individuals must be able to choose whether to use such energy. Those who do chakra meditation would be wise to see energy moving from the third to the fourth chakra. The emotional body is cleansed, and the governing vessel, liver, and stomach meridians are strengthened. The tubercular miasm is eased, and the third, fourth, and fifth rays are activated. Individuals may repeatedly need buckthorn syrup when the Earth is negatively aspected in the natal chart. The test point is the midback.

Occasionally, animals need buckthorn for physical purposes, particularly when ingestion of poor foods has taken place. But spiritually there is rarely a need. An individual who works with wild animals may benefit from this herb at times.

Environmental pollution problems often run deeper with plants. This is because the will sometimes needs to be strengthened in a plant or crop that you are growing. This is a very subtle thing, but can be important, particularly when you are growing a plant that you are not familiar with, or one that does not usually grow in your area. Prepare a homeopathic preparation of buckthorn syrup at a 2x potency. Then mix this with water at seven drops to one gallon of water. This should be sufficient to assist with these types of plants.

Environmental pollutants often create disturbing vibrations with the devic orders. For instance, when certain plants or herbs grow near a freeway, the devic orders are quite disturbed by this. The devas transmit this disharmonious energy to plants, making it more difficult to grow them under these conditions. It is important that the devic orders transmit their vibrations to plants. This is not the same as environmental pollutants directly affecting the growing conditions of plants. That involves the absorption of various pollutants and the difficulty absorbing substances from the soil that are normally nourishing, such as various minerals and fertilizers.

There are many ways environmental pollutants interfere with plants, but this takes place primarily at the vibrational level. This includes the ways people relate to the devic orders associated with plants, the ways plants grow, and the ways they understand nature. The will in its highest form is usually brought to a place of greater consciousness. For instance, in observing the plant you may recognize a similarity in your own life to the way plants grow and interact in their environment. By applying this information, you may find your own will working better.

The will of the plant is nurtured powerfully by the devic order but this begins in the seed, in the genetic structure of the plant itself. Environmental pollution has for some time interfered with the way will within the plant acts to fulfill its karmic destiny, to grow in certain patterns, and to interact with other plant species and with mankind. This interference has been assisted also by the devic order—not just in regard to karmic purpose, but also in regard to mankind's creative pollutants. With all this, there is a focusing of will in individuals as they understand this process. That is, the way environmental pollutants affect the will and the working of the devic order with the plants themselves.

A similar and parallel effect happens with humans. It is important to recognize that there is choice in these matters. Mankind often choses the profit motive over harmonious coexistence with the environment. This is a willful choice, so the ability to use the will must be understood better. The ability of one's own will to be in harmony with divine will is interfered with by environmental pollutants. This happens in a similar way to plants. The interesting thing here is that those who have the will to work with plants, a strong 'green thumb effect' and comraderie with nature, may understand this more powerfully even than the devic orders. Thus, their protective yet human energies assist greatly with reducing the effect of environmental pollutants on plants.

Individuals not in alignment with the profit motive or with the creation of environmental pollutants, and who wish to be in harmony with their environment, are also affected by these difficulties, these shared thought forms. Until the will within each individual fully commits itself to understanding God's creation and divine will as manifested in the natural kingdoms, difficulties with environmental pollutants will not be resolved. This means that forgiveness, as well as a deeper appreciation of the natural order, is necessary for mankind.

Buttercup

Yellow to gold flowers appear in this perennial found in various parts of the United States. The juice of buttercup is used to remove warts and to treat other skin problems.

With buttercup there is enhanced ability to attune to the fairy kingdom. This is partly expressed by the plant's pretty shape and its ability to grow in the wildest places, far from civilization. People exploring wooded regions and areas away from civilization may suddenly come upon this plant and perhaps find it in great profusion and beauty. The fairy kingdom has for quite some time been out of touch with humanity. Though the fairy kingdom exists and is available to many, few wish to acknowledge it or communicate with it. The properties of this kingdom include the ability, with a childlike frame of reference, to gain vast amounts of knowledge in the childish way of doing things, to play, enjoy, have fun, and at the same time attain greater attunement and awareness with all you are doing. The ability for long life and assistance even towards immortality is enhanced by this herb. This is because the fairies, though youthful in appearance, have existed for long periods of time.

The ability to see the fairy kingdom increases. Likewise, the way childlike attitudes bring new knowledge in an individual are enhanced. These are psychic abilities, for those who approach things with a fully open mind approach them from a truly childlike point of view. If one explores the various nature kingdoms, such as botany or geology, the fairies may bring questions into one's mind. Deep questions about nature are not easily answered except with a childlike attitude. Therefore, the ability to let these questions resonate, to then understand the natural sciences by the intuitive process is enhanced.

The origin of this plant actually did not occur on Earth. It was brought into action and used by the Lemurians for the specific purpose of greater comradeship with the lovely fairy kingdom. The devic order associated with it is on the fairy level, but these energies existed on an etheric level first. These beings shaped the plant and brought it into existence. The karmic purpose of this plant is to act as a psychic tie between the fairy kingdom and mankind.

The third eye chakra and all five chakras above the head are stimulated, although the fifth chakra above the head is slightly less activated. An understanding of the twelfth house can be easier for people when this herb is ingested. This is one of the final houses of transition in which the understanding of these other kingdoms becomes easier.

When animals are influenced and assisted in the wild by fairies, there is some benefit if they eat buttercup. When buttercup is eaten as an herb, it is then easier for an individual to make contact with wild animals, especially those quite shy of humans. The devic order associated with this plant is given added energy, as if the energies of the fairy kingdom are made more available. In the seed germination process, buttercup could be applied in the soil as a companion plant, but it could also be added to the soil as a tincture almost on a vibrational level. A proper ratio would be one drop of tincture to about twenty gallons of water. The test point is the medulla oblongata.

Carrot   (Queen Anne's Lace)

Carrot is a widely cultivated vegetable. The original wild form of carrot is called Queen Anne's lace. Carrot is a carminative, diuretic, and stimulant.

With carrot we are dealing with mankind's influence because of the continued genetic selection to emphasize carrot over Queen Anne's lace. This has led to a differentiation in the properties of the two plants. Carrot, as a food substance, has obvious benefits of vitamin A and a good balance of minerals. This is quite enough to open third eye vision, greater understanding, and the willingness to see greater balance in life. However, these properties are greatly intensified by Queen Anne's lace. This herb should not be taken in large quantities because there can be some difficulty, but as an occasional tea it is of some benefit. A particular focus on the third eye region takes place, and an individual gains much greater clarity on many levels. There is greater intuition, clairvoyance, and sometimes even the ability to see into other dimensions. The ability to create energy is also enhanced. This is useful when small and subtle motions are needed or when you are seeking to heal another individual who is extremely deficient in energy. Therefore, after using this herb one might focus a ball of light or some powerful energy inside the body of another person with some positive effect.

However, on the spiritual level, one is confronted with the question of what to do with such energy. The understanding of your purpose is brought more clearly into focus, as is the ability to see the truth of religious pathways as applied to yourself. One comes to better appreciate what they have already gained from various religious studies. What is also awakened is an understanding of another's point of view. This is not the same thing as a childlike viewpoint; rather, it is a way in which you understand someone else's point of view as if you created it. Indeed, the aspects of manifestation as thought forms are created is enhanced by Queen Anne's lace.

With the signature, there is again a differentiation between the two plants. The beauty of Queen Anne's lace and the sense of delicacy that develops inside an individual in loving this plant may give rise to an awakening in the third eye. In seeing through Queen Anne's lace, one may see what is hidden on the other side. Carrot, with its deep roots and orange color, symbolizes the light changed by the physical level pulled from the lower areas upwards in the physical body, its shape pointing up.

Queen Anne's lace was utilized by the devic kingdom even before the full understanding of this kingdom developed in Lemuria. In Lemuria, Queen Anne's lace was greatly praised and honored for its ability to enhance certain attributes of the third eye. However, this plant was modified until much of its karmic purpose has been differentiated into carrot and Queen Anne's lace, so that some of its original intent has been modified by mankind. Thus, as more focus is placed on carrot, a differentiation karmically will increasingly take place with Queen Anne's lace. Ultimately, Queen Anne's lace is likely to present its karmic picture to mankind as purely the willingness to see and know, while carrot is more likely to affect one on the purely physical level.

The sixth chakra is energized, the gall bladder meridian is balanced, and all the nadis in the head are stimulated. The mental body is given added energy, and the syphilitic, gonorrhea, and heavy metal miasms are eased. The fifth and sixth rays are brought into greater focus for an individual. The test point is the third eye.

Cayenne

Native to tropical America, cayenne has yellow or white flowers that appear from April until the fall. Cayenne has long been used as an appetizer and stimulant.

There is a transference of the heating ability of cayenne onto the spiritual level. It speeds up all levels of action on the spiritual plane. Meditation towards a specific end will be speeded up. Or if you are attempting to focus energy for healing, this will be accelerated. Because of this heating effect, the heart opens more. This is under the direction of will, so an individual may choose to use such a heart opening in ways that are appropriate to them. The heat of cayenne is part of the signature. This heat effect can be smelled by some, and sometimes it can even be seen on the etheric level as a fire around the plant.

The inner lesson of cayenne is to provoke choice. In fact, this is the karmic lesson of cayenne. Choice on the level of the heart is extremely difficult for most individuals. When you have this loving feeling, you have the opportunity to share it with many individuals or with only one person. Even the scent of cayenne allows individuals to understand this heating deep within themselves. This acceleration can be extremely important when an individual is involved in spiritual studies, when they are seeking to combine mental energy and the energy of meditation, or when involved in healing. This combination is often slowed by the blockages a person creates. One is better able to perceive, understand, and remove such obstacles in one's life.

The development of all psychic gifts is greatly accelerated. There is, of course, a point of diminishing returns. When sufficient cayenne is taken into the physical body, with great cleansing taking place, the cycle tends to reverse itself after a point and there is a weakening of cayenne's functions. This is why, when taking cayenne for these spiritual purposes, one should take small quantities rather than a large amount.

The Lemurians saw that cayenne could assist the Atlantean civilization in many different ways. Cayenne works on the herbal or medicinal level to cleanse, and it purifies on a spiritual level to speed up processes by which the Atlanteans came to know themselves better. However, the spiciness of the plant and its impact on the tongue and palate did not come into existence until the end of the Atlantean phase. This was because some of the thought forms associated with the plant became somewhat bitter to take. It is characteristic of the great blockages and resistances that were found at the end of the Atlantean phase.

The fourth chakra is especially opened. The pericardium meridian is accelerated greatly and the bladder and governing vessel meridians are enhanced. The nadis in the feet and lower legs are especially stimulated, and the emotional body is relaxed. The heavy metal and petrochemical miasms are eased.

With plants, there are certain climatic changes in which there is a great deal of stress. This is sometimes called root stress. Adding cayenne to the water or spraying it in the air, transfers some of cayenne's healing qualities, so that extra growth of rootlet hairs again takes place. This often pushes the plant through this difficult stage. The test point is the top of the head.

Chamomile

Yellow flowers appear during the summer in this European native. This popular herb and homeopathic remedy calms children. It is used as a tonic, carminative, and stomach balancer.

There is a tendency here for deeper states of relaxation to reveal to an individual many levels of existence. This can be useful in past life regression work, especially when one is seeking greater spiritual understanding from the past. It is very useful for an individual to acknowledge fully and understand the power and force within the body. This is not always easily understood. Sometimes deeper relaxation leads to lethargy, but with chamomile this tendency is usually shifted. An individual feels more energy for a while after chamomile is taken. Energy directed towards a particular spiritual purpose is affirmed. The individual feels more inner peace. This is not simply because of its relaxing properties. There is greater clarity in current relationships, what you are doing with your life, and your inner spiritual purpose. On the higher spiritual level, there is a relaxation in viewing and working with energies that are seen to stem directly from God. This means that the psora miasm is eased, the understanding of God's laws is more acceptable, and the way these laws may be assimilated and worked with are enhanced.

It would be wise not to take this herb before activities involving extreme mental stress. One may decide it is more important for the physical body simply to leave these highly stressful situations. Indeed, in many cases this is accurate. In forming a business, when there is great potential for individuals to work together, chamomile is recommended. This is not simply because of its calming effects, but because there is a tendency for these potentials to be felt as real in the shared individual and group thought forms that move between individuals as they work together.

There is an enhanced trancelike state, so channeling may be assisted. There is a feeling within the individual of accomplishment in whatever area they may wish to involve their psychic abilities. Specifically, telepathy is enhanced as is the ability to see through another's eyes, to know what it is to be in their life for a moment. This is empathy and transference. Similarly, in a relationship there is benefit in taking chamomile, especially between individuals who are committed to each other but struggle with that commitment. A closer understanding and empathy can develop between couples.

This is an herb that we do not recommended taking in intense emotional, psychiatric, or psychological processes. This applies to the therapist as well as the client. Chamomile has a sedative effect which can mask the discussion of emotions, symptoms, and information that would be shared. However, as chamomile is also popular for its taste as an herbal tea this might occur, and we caution against it, if possible. What is transferred between two people is not seen or expressed easily. It is masked by the effect of chamomile.

The plant has a certain rate of growth associated with it that individuals in meditating with the plant for a while would perceive as a different frequency than that of most plants. It tends to be a little slower, or a little stronger, as if Earth energy is building the plant more deeply than the life force of the plant. In Lemuria, this growth pattern was noted, and the greater ability of the plant to receive Lemurian thought form energy was also understood. This deep and powerful calming effect could be brought into the plant most easily. The Lemurians understood that chamomile is especially influenced by thought forms, so it was one of the early plants they worked with. The herb was taken by Lemurians in later Lemuria as the worries and troubles associated with the budding Atlantean civilization became clearer to the Lemurians. The plant was seen to create joy through ritual, and its devic order had the ability to work with such emotion. Indeed, the devic order associated with this plant often assisted the Lemurians in experiencing great joy, and the potential for this to continue still exists today.

The heart chakra is opened, the fifth and sixth chakras are strengthened, and there is added energy in the root and third chakras. The gall bladder meridian is slightly strengthened, and the nadis in the buttocks and abdomen are energized. The etheric, mental, and astral bodies are strengthened. There is a deeper appreciation of the added energy on an emotional level. In fact, the emotional body can open, with some practice, to absorb this energy from the etheric body. Then a unique and powerful interchange of energy can take place that will last for a number of hours.

Be aware of the connection between the emotional and etheric bodies shortly after taking the herb.

The cancer miasm is slightly eased, and the second and third rays are strengthened. Certain negative aspects of Mars may be eased by this herb. The ways in which the Sun is in conjunction, opposition, or square to Mars may be eased and assisted by this herb. The test point is the center of the chest.

Chickweed

This weed, which is found all over the world, is a demulcent, expectorant, and laxative.

It is used for joining together harmonious thought forms to be shared worldwide. This involves the generation of religious movements, the creation of societies, and the enhancement of larger sociological functions. Individuals who use this herb from time to time will be in increased communication with kindred souls worldwide who may have a spiritual involvement similar to their own. These individuals may not all be using the herb. This is largely an unconscious contact, but it is a way individuals may simply know each other. In recent years, people throughout the world have joined together to pray for world peace. It would be of benefit for some of these people to take chickweed at times.

The signature relates to the fact that the plant is found all over the planet. In fact, this pattern has gone on for a long time, even before the Lemurian civilization fully developed. While the flower was modified by the Lemurians, the plant from Lemuria has remained otherwise unchanged. The karmic lesson of the plant is, of course, to show worldwide that mankind is one, just as the plant is one. Even though chickweed is very old and has been through many civilizations, her name is even today largely unchanged.

The ability to know one's brother and thus ease racial prejudices takes place with chickweed. This is forgiveness, a way an individual can merge and release from another's energy field. This also means that the manipulation and understanding of energy fields as feelings can be enhanced by this herb.

The third, fourth, and fifth chakras are brought into a state of temporary resonance whenever the herb is taken. This rebalances the higher and lower levels and creates more energy in the heart. But this is an energy that is available for balance all over the physical body. The astral body is energized, and there is assistance with the psora miasm. When there are difficulties with the planet Neptune, there is benefit in taking this herb. The test point is the heart center.

Cinquefoil

Also called five leaf grass, cinquefoil has bright-yellow flowers that grow through the summer. It is used to relieve cramps, fever, and to stop bleeding.

Congestion or compacted energy that may manifest spiritually affects a person in many ways. Sometimes this may be a blind spot, when it gathers as powerfully compacted energy in the emotional or mental bodies. Sometimes individuals will not be able to see that which is right in front of them. A simple example of this is what has been termed by some 'the aha effect' or AHA. When someone brings you an interesting revelation about your life, an important truth, you hear them say the words, you know it makes sense, but you do not understand what they said. You may ask them to repeat this several times. This is a good indication that there is a blind spot.

Frequently, for individuals not on a spiritual path, this energy will be compacted in the emotional body. The effect of this herb is to balance that energy. It disperses it into the rest of the emotional body; it will not destroy it. You see through that blocked energy and then do something with the information you receive. This is actually more important when you are seeking to understand spiritual principles than with emotional cleansing. This 'aha effect' may often happen when you are reading a spiritual book. You will notice that you have read one paragraph nine or ten times without fully understanding what it means, even though the words may be quite simple to someone else. The tea form is good for taking this herb. This easing or dispersing of energy takes place in a self-governing manner that is also transferred into the plant as it is used medicinally. It has a self-regulating effect on the blood. This is why it works in relieving cramps.

As for the signature, you see in the runner the way the energy of the plant compacts, strengthens, and then moves out in all directions gently and easily to restart itself in many different places. The medicinal aspects of this are also important, the way cramps are eased. A cramp is compacted energy too.

There may be greater sight, which can directly affect the third eye. It may be easier to see auras because, when you must view another's aura, you are looking through your own. Therefore, if you are more aware of it as a filter, you will understand it better and not be block from seeing beyond it. It also becomes easier to work with clairvoyance. This clearer seeing which is retained as an internal message for a person may be enhanced. And individuals on a spiritual path have greater ability to absorb new information, new teachings, and new points of view.

The plant was not fully developed in Lemuria. The Atlanteans gradually contributed to its thought form. This was not a conscious effort. It was clear, towards the end of the Atlantean phase, that there were many things to be learned that were unable to be seen. It was as if, in seeking to assist, thought forms of Lemurians who had not incarnated because of the gross density of physical matter at that time began to influence this plant to take on the aspect of purging or destruction of blockages. Its use in the Atlantean civilization for medicinal purposes was widespread, especially to relieve cramps. However, the energy of this plant did not fulfill its karmic purpose—that of enabling civilization to see what blocked them. This involved the ability to work with nature, with the Earth herself, with a full coordination of spiritual development and will. Therefore, the plant's purpose remains unfulfilled. As humans use it now, greater spiritual awareness may fulfill the plant's purpose. And it then may be that which is used in greater harmony with humanity.

There is strengthening in the throat chakra, resulting in willingness to express and a strengthening of the third eye chakra. The kidney and bladder meridians are enhanced, so transfer of energy from the bladder meridian into the physical body is enhanced. The nadis associated with the back are stimulated, and there is a slightly thinning effect to the etheric, mental, and emotional bodies. However, its primary effect is to focus energy in one part of one of these bodies, usually the emotional or mental body. This focusing of energy allows greater energy transfer and dispersal. There is some relief of the cancer and gonorrhea miasms, and the ninth, tenth, and eleventh rays are made clearer. The test point is the center of the bicep.

Clover   (Red)

This perennial plant grows in meadows all over North America and Europe. Clover eases problems with the liver, gall bladder, and circulatory system.

Clover's spiritual properties can run deep within an individual. This can sometimes last for a fairly long period. The blood cleansing effects will usually last for as long as three weeks, but the spiritual effects may be noted as long as two and a half months after a single use of clover. Emotions can be made more conscious, so that a person has a deeper sense of the purpose of their emotions. In love or a relationship, there is a possibility for greater expansion. There is also a deep sense of relaxation and release of how an individual might understand the emotions. Thus, when one has struggled over an emotional issue for some time, red clover tea could be quite beneficial. The feeling of letting go may run deep within an individual.

People involved in any kind of counseling, especially around emotional issues, may benefit from this herb. Indeed, if a client is dealing with an emotional issue or they are having trouble resolving something and the therapist cannot seem to understand, take this tea after a session with the client. You may be able to create a dream state more easily when falling asleep in which there is clearer insight. Easier meditation may develop to resolve some of these problems. Often this lack of understanding exists with the therapist because the therapist cannot understand the same lesson that the client is working with. There is a similar karma and particularly emotional blockage. The therapist may also experience increased inner clarity by using clover. This creates a bond between the client and the therapist. The spirit guide working with the client and therapist may find it much easier to assist in the creative and healing process. The relationship will be enhanced and the client's need for transference, or for seeing the therapist as mother or father, will be reduced.

The odor of red clover is quite strong. You can imagine yourself, as the Lemurians often did, lying in a field of clover, inhaling it to know it. There is a deep sense of letting go that often results directly from this odor. There is an emotional content associated with the plant.

In Lemuria, clover was utilized primarily for the aroma to create deeper states of meditation. It was understood that in the future resolving emotional difficulties could take place when such deeper states of meditation were experienced. However, the Lemurians could not understand the densified ether that mankind is currently subjected to and that mankind actually creates. Clover did not come into actual use for these capacities until about 5,000 years ago, when the etheric density became a particular problem. Then assistance in relaxation and letting go of the emotions was a task taken on readily and willingly as the purpose of this plant. Meditation and the inert gases are about all that can currently ease the etheric density on the Earth.

Regarding the chakras, an energy is released in the throat center. There is some assistance in the sixth chakra, and there is added energy in the ninth chakra. Clover temporarily focuses more energy in the root chakra because of the red color. This vibration will likely move through the second and third chakras, liberating new expressions of energy regarding the emotions. The gall bladder and liver meridians are brought into a temporary state of alignment with energy built within them and then released. This energy is often released into the kidney meridian, when it is necessary, but more often it is simply released throughout the body with increased feelings of energy and peacefulness. Moreover, the nadis in the fingers are stimulated, and the emotional body is particularly cleansed. The cancer miasm is eased, and the third and fourth rays are strengthened. When the natal chart shows negative aspects to Venus, there is some benefit in regularly using this herb.

When an animal keeper has a past history of cruelty to animals, clover may activate a deeper sense of oneness with the animals. This develops by the 'letting go' process. There is also some benefit to using this plant in agriculture. Some feel agriculture is successful through fate or good luck. However, it is often the karma and emotional state of the person. When this deeper state of release and a greater realization of the purpose of the emotions take place, there is a vibration created which can be incorporated into the plants. Those concerned about this should drink a tea made from

clover and apply a spray to the crops they are working with. The spray
should be fairly diluted, perhaps three drops of a clover tincture to ten gallons of water. The test point is the center of the chest.

Cohosh (Black or Blue)

Cohosh is found in wooded regions in much of the United States. It
has traditionally been used as an antispasmodic, diuretic, and sedative.

The easing of cyclical patterns, especially ones that are difficult for an
individual to handle, occurs with cohosh. People may find themselves periodically moving into states of difficulty in understanding life. The obvious example here is manic-depressive states on psychological levels, but
spiritually this happens too. People sometimes go through periods of rejection and acceptance, bringing closer a spiritual oneness and then reject-
ing it for a time. At the same time, there is an easing on the emotional level
of the things that block an individual from a deep understanding of these
cycles. Emotionally, you usually find reasons not to do things, like keep a
diary of the cycles you are following, or come to know these habits more
easily. These emotional reasons, whatever they are, are eased.

This herb may also be good for those who learn in spurts. When they
are learning, they are learning from only one area, and then they wish to
withdraw from it and put their attention on something else. Cohosh allows
an easier focus to develop. It does not force the focus; it simply allows it to
develop more readily.

The ability to comprehend patterns is enhanced. One better understands the way in which growth is made in spurts, and how this growth is
taken deep within to be acknowledged more easily. One develops greater
sympathy for individuals who are also struggling on such levels. The energies associated with this are released so the emotional body is cleansed,
while the mental body is strengthened. This balance on a psychic level
leads to greater intuition, especially when the law of cycles is affected. On
subtler levels, the plant has the effect of acting like a diverging lens to ease
the energies of a pattern, to spread them out so they may be seen more
easily.

The plant has existed since Lemurian times, and it is a benefit for
many. The purpose of it originally was strictly for cleansing the blood and
for certain emotional states. This was even necessary at times in Lemuria,
because the blood was able to take on certain attributes of feelings, even to
the physical level. This did no harm, but ultimately blockages developed,
and an individual did not always understand things well. Gradually, the
ability to cleanse the blood was transferred to other, more powerful herbs,
such as red clover and chaparral. Moreover, the cyclical nature of the
emotional body and of feelings was better understood, so that the blood
was not so effected. This is what was left by the Lemurians. The karmic
lesson of the plant is to work with this understanding, so that people may

appreciate their cycles.

The timing and energy patterns flowing among all the chakras is brought more clearly into focus. Suppose an individual brings energy first into the heart, and then they notice a few days later that these energies affect the throat so that it is sore or perhaps digestion is affected. Most individuals will not fully understand this process; they will not even see a linkage between these points. They are not expressing the love they have felt, they are not activating their will in the world with this love, and they are not absorbing new teachings that are being shared with them. Cohosh may ease this problem and make the energy pattern more sensible, understandable, and therefore knowable in the physical body. Individuals may be more aware of the energy they take into the heart that moves into these other chakras, and the pattern becomes known to the individual more clearly.

All the meridians and nadis transfer energy more easily, the emotional body is calmed and given an inner strength, and the petrochemical miasm is eased. The fourth ray is brought more clearly into focus. The understanding of the law of cycles as it applies to astrological bodies is brought into greater clarity. An understanding of the seasons is of some importance. Thus, those who come to know planets better on a seasonal level, the way they move through their various cycles, will find some assistance with cohosh. Farmers should often use this herb, especially those who plant out of season such as with a greenhouse. The test point is the third eye.

Comfrey

Commonly found throughout the United States, comfrey produces white or purple flowers during the summer. This popular herb is used to ease digestive and menstrual problems.

Comfrey has a tendency to segment the individual, so that various aspects of the inner being that you wish to know better may be temporarily compartmentalized and then integrated. This cycle allows one to understand better by compartmentalizing and then bring these aspects together. This is a very important understanding for most people in the west. The oriental way is not usually to compartmentalize and analyze quite so much as is done in the west. Comfrey aids this process; one does not simply compartmentalize but does so knowing what the future brings in reintegration on a spiritual level. This allows various parts of a being to be recognized and honored, with individual attention paid to each of them. For instance, if in meditative states one sees difficulty, one can separate this from the states in which one is dreaming or imagining or when wishful thinking is going on. Ultimately, the focus on meditation is enhanced, and when combined with states of reverie, dreams, and astral travel, these things are seen in their true light and are integrated in a constructive manner. This also enables you to release aspects of the personality you do not need.

Because the western path of compartmentalization and the bringing together of energy for an inner integration can be a powerful route for individuals to take, it can give one greater clarity and focus for developing all psychic abilities. Comfrey assists in releasing things that stand in the way of developing any psychic ability.

The plant originated in Lemuria and was seen as one that could have many possible uses, but it was not allowed to be specialized for quite some time. The idea of it was that it would eventually unite civilizations worldwide. This would seem a bold task to give to a mere plant, but people worldwide have recognized comfrey's powerful healing abilities. Thus, they have a common base from which to begin sharing their own experiences of the herb kingdom. This worldwide sharing is the karmic lesson of comfrey.

Comfrey was developed in Lemurian times, but it did not fully develop these properties until the foundation of western civilization, about the time of Christ. This is because the herb previously was not as necessary for its inner cleansing abilities or its ability to balance and heal. Before the time of Christ, comfrey was grown, revered, and loved, but its karmic purpose has only developed recently.

As for the signature, the plant tends to compartmentalize the way it germinates. This can be seen in its physical as well as etheric patterns. This compartmentalization can also be experienced in the color, flavor, and touch of the plant. Most individuals feel a resonance with the plant because of its herbal or medicinal properties. This is because the human life stream, for the last few thousand years, has benefited so much from this plant.

The crown chakra is opened, and all the subtle bodies are temporarily brought into alignment. This pattern then tends to break apart, and energy is placed more clearly on the chakra that most needs energy. Comfrey is self-balancing in this respect. When an individual is seeking healing on the physical level, such as blood cleansing or using a poultice with a wound, there is extra assistance when an individual is willing to meditate on the spiritual consequences of what is going on, the lessons to be learned. During such a time, it is often beneficial to also take silversword or lotus flower essence.

The gonorrhea miasm is eased, and for those particularly associated with the tenth and eleventh rays, there is some benefit. Comfrey is quite useful for most animals that get worms or many physical complaints. There is tendency for the animal to bring behavioral problems more clearly into view for the owner to work with. Thus, in working with your pets, if comfrey is to be used, look for this behavioral property as well and it may assist. The test point is the base of the spine.

Currant

Currant is a shrub with green-yellow flowers and black or red berries. Conditions eased by this herb include respiratory and kidney problems.

This plant has many interesting properties. We see the greatest focus of spiritual properties in the fruit. This appears to have a direct relationship to the harboring of deep-seated fear regarding the spiritual path. One might not think that fear is of great importance in dealing with the spirit, but indeed it is. Sooner or later, one comes face to face with one's self. Yes, there is the facing of God and the understanding of divinity and of divine purpose, which is often forgotten on this planet. But this fear is nothing compared to facing one's self. In the journey towards the spirit you must sooner or later contend with the mirroring energy—that which you have created and that which stands as if in resistance or opposition to your self. Most individuals approach this and fear it so deeply that they are not willing to be with such an energy knowingly.

For example, if you are in a state of telepathy with another person, you see through their eyes a little of yourself, and you may see this in a complete and whole manner. You usually have a picture of yourself or a self-image that is fractured, that is not the entire picture. The fear of this realization is not, as you might imagine, that of stopping your progress, but rather it is an open doorway. Currant helps here; the energy available from it raises the vibration of your courage center.

Many associate this center with the third chakra, and there is some truth to this, but we see the association more with the deepest, darkest black, with that of facing the idea that you are nothing. There is in all human beings this inner fear that they are truly alone or that in some way what they face when they truly know themselves is emptiness or nothing. Thus, there is the dark color of the fruit. The black is preferred for facing fear, but many of the properties will be transferred, though to a lesser extent, into the red-colored fruit.

There is a direct association with the kidneys, because of currant's shape and because the energy of currant begins to release fear that often lodges within the kidneys. The spiritual effects do trickle down into the physical body. Of course, release of fear is useful in many different ways, but on the highest level, currant is often recommended to those who are on a spiritual quest or journey. If you are only eating fruit, and you are regularly moving into states of deeper meditation, currant is highly recommended.

There is a tendency for clearer sight and increased opening of the third eye. Seeing the future for other people, as well as for yourself, can develop. There is also an ability to merge with other aspects of nature, particularly the wind. The wind on many levels provides intrinsically a symbol of fear. Those who meditate on the wind might work with currant. Some should also purchase a wind chime, especially one made of quartz crystals. (I have placed several wind chimes about my home and find them to be most enjoyable.)

Many other psychic faculties open in the head region. This can include healing by remote means, which involves bringing into action a powerful energy, like a ball of light pouring from one part of your head, then moving outward from you to reach another being. Many who would do this might be afraid—not that the healing would not work, but that it would. Then they would have to face the fact that they have such an energy deep within them. Facing this fact creates an unconscious fear which currant alleviates.

Currant was utilized as food by the Lemurians and the Atlanteans. However, in the past, the plant's full spiritual properties were not fully understood, nor were they even a part of this plant. The Chinese influenced the gradual development of these properties. This has nothing to do with geological or geographical location. Rather, it was the idea of the relationship between the kidneys and understanding fear deep within a person. There is today housed within the energy of currant the possibility for mankind to release overall fear. This possibility is very important for the fulfillment of currant's overall thought pattern or karmic thought form. The red fruit personifies some of the fears regarding sexuality. In Atlantean times, this was largely dealt with, which is the main reason why the black fruit is today of greater importance.

There is a strengthening of the second chakra, which spills over into the third chakra. The kidney, bladder, and liver meridians are strengthened, and the nadis in the arms and chest are activated. There may be some assistance in the heart meridian. The emotional body is deeply strengthened. There is some easing of energy in the mental body as the vibrations within that body change slightly. The stellar miasm is eased, and the eleventh and twelfth rays are made more easily available and understandable. The action of Neptune is more harmonized with a person. Those who repeatedly show difficulty that corresponds to negative aspects of Neptune in the chart would be advised to use currant regularly. There is no specific animal use except for that of black currant oil. Animals who are constantly nervous may benefit from this oil. The test point is the navel.

Daisy

As is usually the case with these herbs, the several varieties of daisy are equally good to use. English daisy alleviates jaundice, skin problems, and intestinal disorders.

There is an accentuation and enhancement of a solitary childlike state of joy. This occurs for individuals when they are alone. Children have several modes by which they experience joy in the world. For instance, when playing, the child may be entirely separated as if they are in a world in and of themselves. Adults sometimes find this disturbing, perhaps considering it a variant of autism or emotional withdrawal. In fact, however, when the child is questioned they will leave this state and speak to you from a place of greater joy, deep understanding, and happiness. At any age, it is beneficial to return to this state. It is a place in which there is a sense of self, but this self is closer to the life force incarnating motivation. We refer to what your soul created to put you here in the first place. It is this energy that is being contacted.

In the quest for higher spiritual purpose and deeper understanding, there are many levels of energy to work with. Some of these levels are purely mental; others are entirely nonverbal, necessitating the childlike state so this energy can be fully felt. This state of being can appear trancelike, and there are some psychic properties associated with it. But it primarily allows an individual a sense of aloneness that is not lonely. The emotions associated with this state of being are joy, peace, and a greater sense of overall well-being. Certainly it is helpful with children, but this herb is more useful with adults. The reduction of stiffness not only occurs on the medicinal level; it is also vibrational. When one is stiff or has trouble in movement and flexibility, the childlike state is of great benefit. It enhances the energy to attempt new projects, to move in new directions, and to see new ways.

There is an activation of the trancelike state in which there is an inner strengthening of the being. However, in such states, it is not often possible to pose a question. Daisy enhances the ability to ask a question over and over again in the mind, like a mantra to yield a large number of answers. It is like a combination of hypnosis and mantra meditation. When working in psychic areas, there is a relaxation of the necessity for results. The process is focused on more than the answer or result. One becomes more at home and at peace with what happens in the process itself.

The solitary nature and its strong ability to exist in all kinds of interesting environments are two characteristics of daisy. However, it has an extremely simple look to it and is quite similar to certain mandala patterns. Its archetype draws the viewer in to its center. One becomes aware of this mandalic nature, as well as of an inner joy in just viewing it. It is almost like an emotional child to those who view it with an open and joyous frame of mind.

In Lemuria, the plant was utilized to train children in the relationship to the devic order. In making the initial contact, there was sometimes some fear. Daisy was quite useful simply to be around. It was rarely killed or used in the herbal forms. Rather, it was kept for its beautiful vibration and loving association with the devic order. Gradually, it was seen that it would be necessary for mankind to lose some of these childlike abilities earlier in life. This occurred in Atlantis. Some of the energies associated with the devic order are now lost at about six months of age. The karmic purpose of the plant is to make these childlike properties available wherever possible to anyone who opens to it.

The chakras are balanced, particularly the root, third, and sixth chakras, and the spleen and stomach meridians are also balanced. The energy in the shoulder areas becomes more relaxed, and the nadis become warmed and energy is released. There is a strengthening of the emotional body, and a deeper sense of peace may permeate through the mental, emotional, and etheric bodies. The soul body is stimulated, the tubercular miasm is eased, and the fourth and eighth rays are clarified. Use daisy when Venus and the Moon are in conjunction, or when Venus moves into the sign Aries. The test point is the back of the knees.

Dill

This short herb produces yellow flowers during the summer. Dill is often added to food to stimulate the appetite and to alleviate stomach problems.

You can focalize intentions powerfully, as if bringing them into separate existence for an individual to know. This is partly due to the signature—the singularity of the plant's growth, the way it grows by itself. The smell of dill enabled certain people in Lemuria to focalize these particular abilities into the plant. These spiritual capacities to focalize spiritual ambitions can have a negative effect, if an individual is feeling quite frustrated or having difficulty understanding or perhaps is misunderstanding how spiritual abilities are used in the world. That is when other herbs, amaranthus for instance, would be of greater benefit. But if an individual wishes to know this focalization clearly and to understand their path on the purely spiritual level, there is some assistance in taking this herb.

One of the spiritual properties associated with this is a singularity of purpose that other people will notice. It is a way of taking what is inside outside. For this reason there is a direct astrological association with the ascendant. Others see you more clearly regarding your spiritual aspirations, exactly what you wish to create in the world for others, for the purpose of love and for understanding God. What is also enhanced here is a clarity of vision. Any visions one is working with can be brought into clearer focus with the herb, but it does not produce visions itself.

In Lemuria, the plant was cultivated partly because of its odor. This allowed individuals working with it a mode of expression. A specific sound associated with this plant was often chanted, so that a vibration was activated between the Earth, the Lemurians, and the plant. The smell gradually changed as a result of this until it has become very recognizable and one-pointed. That was its potential, and that is what is now its karmic lesson—to bring this one-pointedness into action for any individual.

This specific sound would be difficult to project with the voice today. However, a close parallel to this sound is 'vah.' This would activate the chakras and could be experimented with today.

The third and fifth chakras are better able to exchange energy to bring greater clarity of expression and motivation. The nadis in the hands and feet are strengthened, and the emotional, mental, and causal bodies are brought into greater harmony. The heavy metal miasm is eased. The understanding of this one-pointedness can lead certain astrologers to a place where they understand more of the ascendant. The ascendant is often misunderstood in astrology, as was already discussed in *Gem Elixirs and Vibrational Healing, Vol. II*. Astrologers who seek to understand the ascendant of another person will find some benefit in the aroma of dill or by taking it as a tea. But the ascendant will not be easily revealed to an individual unless one is also an astrologer. The test point is the third eye.

Dogwood

This tree is found in Eastern China, Japan, and Korea. The Chinese variety of dogwood has slightly stronger spiritual properties than the American version. This is mainly because Chinese dogwood has been interfered with less by the use of pesticides. It has long been used as an astringent and as a tonic for the liver and kidneys.

The herb has a tendency to increase certain healing abilities, especially those associated with new ideas, new techniques, and new modes of expression. This newness is symbolized by the bursting forth of dogwood in the spring and the way it quickly comes into bloom. Because this plant also instills a degree of patience with new ideas, it is of some benefit spiritually.

In Lemuria, the plant was quite praised and loved for the beauty of its blossoms, and many varieties were then available. Because of its appearance, rapid change, and persistence, it was loved and cared for and even cultivated into much larger forms. These are the blooms that are available today. Over time, in working with new techniques and new ideas, individuals can again change the shape of dogwood flowers. The karmic lesson of the plant is to allow this newness and individuality to blossom in people.

The fourth and fifth chakras are energized, which can be of assistance in healing. The bladder meridian and the emotional and etheric bodies are strengthened. All the miasms are eased, although this is a subtle effect. All the water signs and planets associated with water are brought into a greater state of awareness for individuals. The test point is the palm of either hand.

Dong Quai (Angelica)

This prominent Chinese herb is also commonly used in the west. The roots from the Chinese variety should be used because they activate more of the plant's spiritual properties. In Chinese medicine dong quai, or angelica, is a tonic for the blood and is used in a wide variety of circulation, female, and rheumatic disorders.

This herb has a strong ability to bring one to several levels of consciousness in alignment with Christ by understanding what stands between you and the Christlike principle. This often means emotional release, for one who is working towards Christ consciousness, but it is important to realize that as spiritual properties are activated there is a release of blockages. Such blockages are more clearly seen and understood as a result of this herb. This attunement to Christ consciousness is characteristic of the upward reaching of this plant, which is part of its signature. There is also greater attunement to angels with this herb.

Several psychic properties are stimulated. One is the ability to see your path more clearly, to know what is coming in the future. This is not the same as seeing into the future for someone else, but rather it is to know what is specifically coming into your life. In working with what you see as developing in your life, it is beneficial to focus loving energy on these areas. Then there will be some increase in the psychic ability to manifest those specific states in harmony with your highest path.

The plant has existed for some time even before Lemuria. The karmic lesson of this plant is to teach mankind that reaching upwards is always a part of mankind's life. In knowing this as the purpose for being, there is an inner harmony.

The sixth, seventh, and eighth chakras are brought into a greater sense of unity. The astral and causal bodies are brought into harmony as well. The psora miasm is slightly eased, while the test points are the medulla oblongata and the third eye. When Chiron or Jupiter is in conjunction or in trine there will be an added effect in using this herb.

Echinacea

Native to the United States, echinacea has large purple rayed flowers that appear in the summer and fall. This common herb has long been used as a digestive aid and blood purifier.

There are qualities of swiftness, protection, and purification associated with this plant. These properties have changed since the plant was initially used in Lemuria. Today, the plant is undergoing a change on the subtle vibrational level. This is making it more effective to assist the immune system, and this is likely to continue for some years.

The immune system, which protects you from potential harm, is being given more energy, so that you do not need to focus on protecting yourself. This relates to unconscious fears and hatreds. But deeper than this is simply the ability to welcome change. Spiritually, this is very important; in welcoming change, one helps others to change. This is characteristic of echinacea because it is useful in combination with other herbs. Moreover, the disc shape of the flowers symbolizes the way the color patterns move in circles yet are unchanged.

The ability to allow and welcome change is useful in healing and in developing psychic abilities. You cannot develop psychically without radical change. Society forces one to accept many attitudes that do not really make sense as reality shifts into a more spiritual perspective. Echinacea makes it easier to accept new changes, new abilities, and new ways of seeing things. Then the changes you undergo become more acceptable to yourself and to society. This is of great assistance as psychic abilities develop and change. Psychic abilities indeed never disappear, they simply change into another form.

In Lemuria, this plant was used extensively, but for different purposes than current usage. Instead of being connected with the immune system, it was associated with those who wished to have a change for the better in directions that they did not yet understand. This eventually became the Atlantean civilization. The herb was useful then because the devic order associated with it became one that could act independently of the Lemurian civilization. It gradually learned to lead the Lemurian civilization into what ultimately became Atlantis. This herb, and its devic order goes ahead of mankind's difficulties, paving the way or providing assistance even before it is fully recognized that there is need for new direction.

All the upper chakras are brought into higher states of energy, and the etheric body is strengthened. The cancer miasm is significantly assisted, and the fourth, fifth, and seventh rays are brought more clearly into a person's awareness. Sometimes, this enables one to release old patterns, to develop new methods that truly work. There is some confluence with the positive aspects of Pluto, so there will be additional benefit in taking this herb when Pluto is in trine or conjunction to any of the major planets in an individual's natal chart. The test point is the medulla oblongata.

Elecampane

Bright yellow flowers appear on this attractive plant during the summer. Elecampane is traditionally used as a diuretic, stimulant, and tonic.

It promotes a sense of inner confidence and an awareness of beauty. This is a very spiritual property that is entirely nonverbal. It creates in the individual an appreciation of self, and it assists in ego development so that the ego is no longer the dominating factor. When you deal with the ego from the level of the ego and there is plenty of work to do on oneself, there is no outside context or way to view the situation. But when elecampane is taken and inner beauty is enhanced, the individual knows internally that the voice of the ego means nothing. That is how it works for developing and spiritualizing the ego. The ability to persist and continue in such self-development is enhanced by the herb. As for the signature, its persistence and beautiful shape remind an individual of this inner beauty.

One better appreciates elegance, strength, and beauty in other people. This is useful psychically when you wish to soothe another person, to speak to someone so they know that they are appreciated. Thus, when used in hypnosis there is some benefit if the practitioner and the person to be hypnotised take a small quantity of this herb. When this is done, increased appreciation for each other leads to a nonverbal trust. Hypnotic abilities develop in the hypnotist and the patient.

In ancient times, the plant was used medicinally to purify the blood and parts of the skin and hair. However, other substances have come into greater use to treat these parts of the body. It was always seen to reflect an inner beauty, and as it evolved and grew over the ages, more people have gradually come to appreciate this property. The American Indians have used elecampane to feel more connected to the Earth. Because the plant has largely achieved its life cycle purpose, in another few thousand year it is likely of its own accord to disappear from the planet.

The sixth and seventh chakras are aided slightly, and the lung meridian is energized. This is sometimes associated with experiencing beauty. The astral and causal bodies are slightly stimulated, and the third and fourth rays are brought more clearly into focus. There is no longer a direct effect on the miasms. About four or five thousand years ago, the cancer and gonorrhea miasms were eased. Miasms often reflect mankind's spiritual development. If more and more people have increased difficulty in repeated lifetimes with a miasm, then the miasms will penetrate into deeper levels. Then some herbs that were effective in treating a miasm will no longer be effective.

This herb has a direct association with the planet Venus. This is not only for the inner beauty that is activated, but for the unconscious association that individuals have for nonverbal communication and inner respect as Venus moves through their charts. This reflects on all aspects of the planet, whether positive or negative.

There is some assistance when an animal is depressed. Such depression may occur when confinement or difficulty associated with domestication of the animal has left it with low self-esteem. There is no way to give self-esteem to an animal as you would a human, with techniques of verbal communication or nurturing. Loving the animal helps, as does giving it elecampane. The test point is at the base of the sternum.

Everlasting

Found in the United States and Canada, everlasting produces brown, white, and yellow flowers. It is an astringent, diuretic, and mouthwash.

There is a gentle persistence, from which the plant's name is taken. The plant tends to recur in certain areas and it spreads quite easily, yet some also see it as a weed. There is an inner persistence in this plant that can be transferred in the herbal form to many people. The idea is not as profound as other herbs discussed, nor is it an energy that can be powerful enough to change you deeply. However, it gives you extra patience and a willingness to stick to it a little longer than has previously been the case.

There is also an inner balancing effect from this herb. This takes place on many different levels simultaneously, and will help a person stick with a particular problem, be it a mental or spiritual concern, for a longer period of time. This is because they are willing to see new ways to approach the problem, new points of view, and new possibilities for energy. The herb makes itself available by allowing a gentler balance; an inner strength is discovered by the person.

In properly using this herb, you might meditate and ask deeper questions, "How might I gain a little more patience towards this project or this spiritual endeavor by means of a new point of view, another possibility, or a new relationship?" The contextual shift is welcomed, and this is enhanced greatly by this herb. On many levels, this can be a powerful and long lasting effect. But you would not see it as if imposed from outside. Instead, you would be aware of it as if you created it. This has the important attribute of that which you can accept readily. It can have a long lasting effect and can be of great benefit for those on any spiritual path who are learning new things or exploring new areas. It can be taken once or twice a month over long periods of time with good effect.

An inner willingness to let go of what does not fit the new pictures also develops with everlasting. This is not so much because you see it was wrong, but because you are able to hold paradox within your mind and within your heart for a bit longer. Many times, in confronting spiritual wisdom, you must hold two ideas simultaneously within your being for a period of time. This can make a person quite restless. The herb may ease this. The result of this is that psychically they are able to grow in these new paths without worry about the past. This allows greater acceptance and, conversely, powerful energy available for that which you are exploring anew. This will be particularly applicable in areas where you receive intuitive information that does not fit the current world view. You may receive information about a person, or a place, or an idea that is a bigger picture of something that simply does not fit what you already know or what others are telling you. With this herb, such an awareness and an ability may be enhanced simply because you now hold it in the context of possibility for a little longer.

Some ancient Lemurian energy lies within this herb. It goes back even to the beginning of Lemurian times. Then the thought form associated with the plant was not as well developed as it is now. However, the essence was there, a willingness to continue alongside mankind, to learn from mankind, and to be with it. The nature of this thought form is a great and beautiful gift to mankind. The Lemurians recognized this and saw that it could be further developed; they spent a great deal of time imparting a sense of wisdom and joy into this plant. This persistence quality has developed in a much subtler form, one which is not readily apparent but which works gently and slowly. Thus, it fulfills its karmic purpose whenever this attitude is utilized in humans.

The energy of the throat chakra is strengthened. A great opening gradually takes place in the heart. The heart continues to open as long as the herb is used. This is a gentle opening, but it is powerful nevertheless. And the heart and liver meridians are enhanced. The nadis in the throat open, and the mental, emotional, and astral bodies are stimulated. The syphilitic and gonorrhea miasms are eased, and the sixth ray is made more available. There is some connection to the positive aspects of planet Neptune. There is the slow motion and willingness to allow a deeper state of intuitive knowledge within a person, as if the more patient side of Neptune becomes available. People with the planet Neptune only aspected positively in their chart will have a greater tendency to receive the energy of this herb. The test point is the top of the head.

Eyebright

This short annual produces white or purple flowers during the summer. Alleviating a wide range of eye problems has been the main use of eyebright by herbalists.

The plant represents the eyes of God and on a spiritual level actually assists individuals to view the eyes of God, to be in the presence of the light that they might imagine as the most powerful that they would come to know truly and understand. Individuals plagued with difficulties of conscience, particularly if born under the sign of Sagittarius, benefit from using eyebright. This energy is distinct from the Virgo conscience which generally relates to self-judgment. Here it is judgment in the eyes of God in which there is some difficulty.

The ability to behold the truth through the eyes of God is also enhanced. This means that as you look at another, you see them and the truth and love they present. You understand and absorb this without judgment and without seeking to block what you experience. You truly allow this clearer sight. For thousands of years, those who have appreciated eyebright for its herbal value have continued to focus their positive thought forms upon it. Every time somebody benefits from eyebright, there is great praise because this clarity of sight is like a thankfulness to God for the ability to see oneself. This energy has created a continued momentum with the plant and has allowed its energies to become stronger and stronger. We see no end to this. In fact, those who care for and raise eyebright, especially under conditions that are organic and helpful to the plant, may find that over the next few years the potency and ability to heal will become even stronger with the various herbs that they grow.

There is some stimulation of the third eye center which can easily lead to auric sight and the ability to see and distinguish various colors and rays. However, there is also a release of energy in the eye region. Difficulty with the physical eyes is often related to negative thought forms, because someone is unwilling to see a particular aspect of their life. An inner knowledge is resisted. As these are relieved, the difficulty is sometimes lessened or removed. Then what occurs for the individual is greater auric vision, but at the same time there is more energy in the eyes. Sometimes, in this process by which the negative thought form is fully understood, a great deal of energy is unleashed and trouble may result. An unbalanced state may develop in looking at auras or into other dimensions. These things may occur when the third eye opens too powerfully, too soon. Eyebright provides a balancing effect to the third eye center by balancing the release of these powerful energies. There is also a tendency for a lingering effect with eyebright. Even many months after it has been used, there can be positive and beneficial effects to the psychic abilities associated with the third eye.

There are several aspects to the signature. It is not only the ability of the plant to merge in consciousness with human beings. Some say that they can see the eyes of God shining through the plant, and they realize, in viewing the plant in joy, that on an ocular level, it is actually looking back and visualizing or receiving them. In ancient times, the etheric vision of a glowing, central shape at the place where the stem splits on this plant was viewed. Gradually, as karmic purpose was given to this plant, this etheric entity was diffused more deeply into the plant.

In Lemuria, eyebright was understood for many of its interesting abilities, so it was used in ritual. The Lemurians saw that it was necessary for mankind to have spiritual sight, and this open door was seen as something that might be lost for humanity. Thus, the assistance of devic spirits was necessary. With eyebright, this was a rather complicated process. The devic spirits worked with eyebright and were allowed a clearer insight into the Lemurian civilization to understand fully the Lemurian people and their connection with the Earth and the ability to manifest joy. The plant and devic spirits associated with it responded to this connection by creating a light within the plant that gave it the ability to receive light from higher vibrational levels. This capacity to receive light continues today and is that which imparts increased light and capacity to experience visions by working with eyebright. The Lemurians aided this process through love, to assist future generations.

In the past, it was seen over and over again that the intermingling of negative thought forms, which prevented deeper spiritual vision, would ultimately be released for mankind; at that time, the acceleration of energy within the eye region would take place. Since ancient Grecian times, in the understanding of eyebright, this energy has gathered greater and greater momentum. It is a grand opportunity for this particular life stream associated with humanity to have a most important balancing and healing effect. Its ultimate karmic purpose is to allow mankind to view and to know God. Then the plant will have fulfilled its mission and will be released from its current physical form. It will likely then move through several levels of transition in which its intelligence and strength will be greatly magnified.

All the minor chakras and nadis associated with the ears, face, top of the head, and back of the neck are strengthened. The third eye center and nadis moving in and out of the eyes are especially strengthened. There is extra energy available in the gall bladder meridian, and the mental body is strengthened and balanced so that blockages are released. This balances the emotional body, with buried emotions being confronted and released. The gonorrhea miasm is eased, and the fifth ray is particularly energized.

There is some assistance for those having negative aspects relating to Jupiter. Individuals working with Sagittarius as a sign whether positive or negative, being born under it, or having the Moon in it will have added vibration on a symbolic level in association with eyebright and may be assisted by taking it throughout their lives. Sometimes animals may demonstrate characteristics of eye problems such as nearsightedness, farsightedness, or cataracts. Each of these states have their own unique symbols representing certain blockages, as with humans. If eyebright is included in the animal's food, the animal questions some of these blockages and begins to examine them more deeply. If the owner can assist and know that this is taking place, there is benefit. The test point for individuals involved in a spiritual path is the corners of the eyes. For others the test point is the third eye.

Fennel

Fennel is a wild flower that grows in the Mediterranean region. Commonly used in food, fennel is an aromatic, carminative, and diuretic.

Its primary property is to allow a greater sense of grounding for an individual. This can be especially useful in certain healing states when a person needs to feel connected to the Earth to continue such work. There is greater Earth energy available. At a certain point, while using fennel, the individual is likely to move through several transitional phases in which there is deep introspection. That is when fennel is particularly helpful. As you attune to the Earth's energy, you will naturally look upon the Earth and see a great deal of difficulty and suffering. As you see this, you must move through a transition phase to accept and work with this suffering. Otherwise, the energy from the Earth is naturally cut off from the physical body. Then you focus on physical body complaints instead of the spiritual understanding that all people on the Earth deserve love. This is a current message. There have been times on the Earth when much less suffering took place. Then the message of fennel related more to pure Earth energy and ways it could be redirected in joy and happiness without such transitional phases being necessary.

The ability of the heart to open in a very grounded way is enhanced. Blockages between the healer and the person being healed are released. The released energy does not enter the Earth. Rather, the Earth energy reminds you that you will not be harmed by this process; thus, such energy may willingly pass through your body. The signature is the shape of the roots and the way they connect to the Earth.

Each time the plant was used in the past, the Earth energy that moved through it had a different effect. In Lemuria, it was used purely for joy, as if the plant was an antenna to project specific properties of the Earth into a ritual or a dance. For instance, when the Moon was full, a great light poured from the Earth through fennel. When the Moon was new, there was awareness in the Earth that anything was possible, and the light of many possibilities would pour forth through this plant. This ability of the plant to light up etherically has largely fallen into disuse, because the ability of the Earth to move through mankind in joyousness has also fallen into disuse. Its karmic lesson is eventually to bring mankind back to such a place, by moving through the transitions that will be necessary to experience joy again.

The first, second, and third chakras and all the chakras in the abdominal region including the kidney, liver, and pancreas are stimulated. However, this is secondary to the stimulation of the chakras in the soles of the feet. With this herb, there is some benefit in placing fennel oil directly upon the soles of the feet. The nadis in the feet are also stimulated. All the meridians that move through the feet and the kidney, liver, bladder, and spleen meridians are given additional energy. The etheric body is strengthened, the cancer and heavy metal miasms are eased slightly, and the second and third rays are assisted.

There is a minor association with the Sun and this herb. Astrologers working with the heliocentric system with the Sun as the center may find some association with the planet Earth. In working with a chart where the planet Earth is making negative aspects with any other planet, there is some benefit for the individual in using this herb. The test point is the soles of the feet.

Figwort

Purple flowers appear during the summer and fall on this perennial plant. Figwort is generally used to treat various skin problems.

There is a tendency for this plant to awaken the crown chakra, so that the individual will be drawn almost unconsciously to various people. It can enhance relationships on the purely spiritual level. There is a cleansing effect in relationships as well. This is partly seen in the signature, the purplish coloration indicating the higher spiritual properties. Also, there is a tendency for the plant to retain moisture in a most unique way. For individuals, this means that the emotional body can be viewed and understood more easily when they take this herb. They can see its purpose from a spiritual perspective. This is quite beneficial in relationships. As a relationship on a spiritual level develops, it is sometimes wise for both partners to take figwort.

The ability to love in a relationship in spite of fighting and difficulties is sometimes based on the psychic intuition that what lies ahead is worth the trouble. It may be worth the trouble because an individual is likely to learn and grow if they are willing.

In Atlantis, the herb was used more than in Lemuria; relationships were not then understood; the physical nature of a relationship was not seen in its full light. This is not even clear today, because a relationship is often begun on a physical level. In Atlantis, it was begun on the purely spiritual level. However, a relationship must begin on all levels to be successful. Human beings must learn about all parts of the other being. In Lemuria, this was understood, so the plant's use was not perceived as necessary until the beginning of the Atlantean phase. A fairly rapid focus of remaining Lemurian energy, in some cases from beyond the physical level, was necessary to gradually bring this lesson to figwort. Its activity now is simply to enhance relationships. That is its karmic purpose.

The second chakra functions more quickly and easily, the petrochemical miasm is eased, and the emotional body releases blocked energy. The more balanced emotional body can work closer with the physical and mental bodies.

One might think that the planet Venus would be involved here because of the impact that figwort has on relationships. However, it is the way in which both Venus and Uranus interact, such as when they are in conjunction or opposition, that are good times for this herb to be used. The action of these planets together reveals aspects of a relationship that had not previously been dealt with or even considered. This new context is brought much more easily into focus. These can be both negative and positive aspects; it does not matter. It is the contextual shift that Uranus brings to the action of a relationship governed by Venus. The test point is the nape of the neck.

Frank

This tree is found in South Arabia. As a prominent essential oil and incense, frank has long been used in many religious ceremonies.

Energy is concentrated within the third eye center when frank is used. This focuses upon the psychic level that two people are creating together. One awakens to psychic gifts that are in alignment with God's purpose. This means that life purpose, understanding relationships, and developing psychic abilities, particularly energies associated with the third eye, may be utilized for spiritual purposes. Deeper states of meditation may result, for instance, or one may develop easier ways to speak what you perceive as the truth. This focusing of energy is an extremely rarefied form of third eye energy. Third eye energy moves in many different levels as it works with individuals; most would call this pattern a more subtle, rarefied, or higher vibrational level. This is because frank links this center more with spiritual force and purpose.

When frank is used, the devic order associated with the herb may be called into action. This is not entirely up to mankind. Sometimes periods of fasting, chanting, and ways of purifying the physical body assist so that this devic order is called closer to an individual. As this energy is liberated, it allows one to see God's purpose in bestowing psychic gifts of vision, intuition, clairvoyance, clearsightedness, understanding the future, greater perception of the aura, and understanding one's path.

All the psychic gifts associated with the third eye center are brought into clarity. Some may have guilt or difficulty regarding the use of these abilities and their association with God, with understanding the deeper meaning of their use. There can be a diminution of psychic abilities if the spiritual side of a person is not also explored. Frank resin, when applied to the third eye, has a stimulating effect. This is due to its etheric, glowing properties, which comes from within the plant. Those with some opening of the third eye center may see this glow.

Frank resin could be applied to the forehead once a day for a few weeks or so to become acquainted with it. There might be a tendency for headaches. If an individual already has such a tendency, use it less frequently. However, if little tension is felt except for a slight pressure near the skin, then it is having an activating effect and could be applied more often. Frank could also be applied at each part of the skin opposite any of the major or minor chakras with positive effects. Someone could also chew the frank resin, but no more than twice a week.

In Lemuria, the sacredness of the plant was understood, and it was used in ritual. The rituals gradually brought into the plant a vibration by which the abilities that were natural to the Lemurians were transferred. The devic order and kingdom associated with frank became more closely enmeshed in Lemurian society. It was seen towards the end of the Lemurian phase that this devic order would have to disengage itself as the Lemurian culture began dispersing. Thus, it was given the task of carrying on the naturalness of these psychic abilities. For an individual to understand this naturalness, one must be aligned with God's purpose. That is the karmic lesson of the plant.

The third eye chakra is stimulated, the fifth and crown chakras are aligned, and the eighth, ninth, and tenth chakras are united. There is a balancing effect as a result of the alignment of these chakras. The gall bladder and bladder meridians are relaxed, and the nadis in the forehead are stimulated. The emotional, mental, and astral bodies also are stimulated, and the rays from the seventh upward are brought more clearly into focus. It is often wise to use frank when there are negative aspects of the planetoid Chiron, especially with the various inner planets, including Venus and Mars. There may be a square or opposition to Pluto. The key to the negative aspect is that there is some holding back or blockage of energy associated with Christ consciousness. The test point is the third eye.

Fraxinella   (Gas Plant)

This plant is a diuretic, expectorant, and tonic. In Chinese medicine, this herb is used to treat various skin problems such as eczema and scabies. Fraxinella produces a flammable substance in the summer which ignites with a flash over the whole plant without harming it.

The spiritual property here is to assist in most levels of kundalini energy work. That is obvious from the signature. What happens as the plant's inner processes produce various liquids, gases, and substances is that a gathering of energy takes place. When the temperature reaches a certain level and the plant is ready, the energy bursts forth. This is somewhat similar to the kundalini yoga process of building up energy by the 'breath of fire' or by certain exercises and techniques.

What often happens with an individual as a result of this process is that the energy moves into places in the body that are blocked or where there is difficulty. That is an excellent time for this herb to be used in small quantities, particularly as a tea. The herb can be useful spiritually in balancing kundalini, to bring the energy through the body, or for those who are simply studying this energy moving within them. This may happen for some people who experience certain imbalances of kundalini energy, even though they have not been doing kundalini yoga. There may be a spasm near the spine, or energy may move through the body during meditation without conscious control.

It is also important to note the way this energy is utilized in the aura. As kundalini energy moves through the body, it reaches the heart and pours into the higher chakras. This energy is now available as a potential in the aura to be utilized for healing and learning. This is the crowning achievement of kundalini yoga work that can also lead to more psychic abilities.

The enhancement of energy fields is important in the development of various psychic abilities. Fraxinella will enhance extending oneself into the near future or near past, some form of healing work, or even psychokinesis. The herb's effect on kundalini naturally affects psychic development. If there is a strong rise in energy that lodges in the third eye, for instance, the herb may be useful to nullify or balance that energy.

The kundalini awakening can have an important effect on developing psychic abilities. Released kundalini energy tends to focus in certain body centers. Depending on the state of consciousness at each chakra level, there will be positive or negative effects as the awakened kundalini energy passes through each chakra. A detailed discussion of the properties associated with each chakra is presented in my earlier work *Gem Elixirs and Vibrational Healing, Vol I*. The center in which the kundalini focuses tends to develop certain psychic abilities associated with that center. If there are problems, this is always caused by resistance to the energy in that chakra. Using creative visualization to see the energy moving upward in a positive fashion can be of some benefit. People interested in learning more about how kundalini works in the body should read the material by Gabriel Cousens and Gopi Krishna.[1]

For most individuals, there is not much problem with this process if the center is the second or third chakra in the body. This is because the world teaches you how to deal on an emotional level with people, even sexually to some extent, and certainly how to gather and use power. This does not mean that the energy is particularly beneficial or positive for mankind, but it does not harm an individual because they are able to use such energy.

Kundalini energy lodging in the heart may develop psychic abilities on a nonverbal, loving, and close knit relationship level that can be difficult. It can bring an intensity into a relationship. At the same time it can awaken much deeper states of empathy and can yield excellent healing capabilities.

Kundalini as it lodges in the throat chakra, can be quite beneficial when utilized properly for singing, chanting, and healing. However, the energy of the throat chakra can cause difficulty if the energy lodged there brings constriction because there is resistance to it. For instance, you may not see yourself singing in harmony with what you hold as your highest values. If you see God in your private life but are singing songs relating only to sex in your night club life, there will be disharmony and difficulty.

At the third eye level, the energy can lead to many psychic abilities, including enhancement of auric vision and a deeper understanding of life. However, it can also yield several difficulties in which there are headaches, constriction of the blood vessels in the head region, and problems that can affect the physical eyes and cause poor sight. This often creates nearsightedness or farsightedness, depending on the individual's attitudes.

At the crown chakra level, the energy may affect several physical body functions such as growth hormone production, proper understanding and working with pain in the physical body, and several difficulties relating to existence. This can be confused for energy in the root chakra center concerning survival. An individual who recognizes Christ consciousness as a strong possibility but turns away from it, creates resistance that involves physical body functioning. On the positive side, the goal is to bring kundalini energy to the crown chakra. What happens is a great unfolding of many energies, an automatic alignment of all the subtle bodies, and an energy that pours through the entire physical body energizing and healing it.

In Lemuria, the plant was bred, and almost by accident, it was discovered that the aura occasionally got very bright. The devic spirits wished to bring to the Lemurians a powerful energy, as if to bring them light in a dance. The Lemurians recognized and honored this, and then were able to make it more physical. This was done because it was felt that at some point in mankind's future the ability to see into the subtler dimensions, to see the beautiful display around the plant on the etheric level, would be lost to mankind. Thus, something needed to be left on the physical level that would help people to admire the plant. In ancient Greece, as the ability to see with the third eye was lost, it was necessary for these physical properties to be fully activated within the plant. Its karmic lesson is to remind humanity of the miracles of the plant kingdom and of the ability within people to change energy.

The astrological association here is very clear and strong with the planet Uranus. There is the element of surprise and an energy moving from within outward to be known. This connection is so strong at times that even the inflaming of the plant can occur in coordination with conjunctions of the Sun and Uranus. The third chakra is given more energy, and all the chakras are brought into a greater state of temporary balance. The etheric, emotional, and mental bodies are energized, the petrochemical miasm is eased, and the test point is at the base of the spine.

Garlic

White flowers grow on this popular herb. Garlic is used for a wide range of digestive, circulation, and heart problems.

Its spiritual properties are interesting in that mankind has somewhat misunderstood them, which is apparent from the legends regarding vampires and garlic. Garlic helps in the transition time during death. One becomes more relaxed and acquainted with the dimension that one moves to after leaving the physical body, which is essentially a level of the ethers. In rejoining and connecting with the soul, one feels an energy which is quite strong. Human beings stand next to this energy at all times, but they resist, filter, or change it so they may go on with their lives. The filter is lowered by using garlic. This is one way it has been mythologized, as if to protect an individual from the spirits of the dead. True protection does not involve shielding oneself but means understanding life after death, recognizing potentials, and seeing the possibilities while passing from the physical plane. These processes are assisted with garlic.

Garlic is often used in many cultures with food. Today, there is greater acceptance of death. Mankind is not now so afraid of death as it has been in the past, and part of the reason for this is the widespread use of this herb. There are many ramifications to this. To become more aware of garlic's spiritual properties, place a small quantity, perhaps a thin slice of one clove of garlic, in a glass of warm water for two hours. Then filter the water, and there will be very little left of a garlic scent or smell. Next, place the water in the sun for about two hours, and then drink it. This will enhance some of garlic's spiritual properties while at the same time not fully bringing it into a pure flower essence.

The plant's signature exhibits some of mankind's influence. The plant above ground might die before it is ready to be harvested. There is a trusting that the bulbs are ready and ripe to be taken from within the ground.

That which is deeply imbedded within the unconscious is allowed to remain there until one choses to remove it. It is usually necessary that an inner cleansing move through several phases. This relates in many ways to the insect kingdom and negative thought forms and to the purifying ability of the simple idea of surrender and of release.

The ability to make contact with individuals beyond the grave is enhanced slightly by garlic. It is also easier to understand negative thought forms, to see their purpose and thus to change your vibration so they are transcended. Some individuals are still afraid of this, and garlic eases this fear. You see this on an even higher vibrational level with garlic flower essence. Negative thought forms, which are partly expressed through the actions and very existence of insects, are often repelled by the flower essence.

In Lemuria, the plant was not fully understood in the current form. It was then largely a decorative flower. Towards the end of the Lemurian phase, it was understood that death was to become an extremely important part of existence on the planet. During almost the entire Lemurian phase, people lived for thousands of years and left the physical body when they decided it was time to do so. At that time, garlic in its current form was created, but even then its full herbal properties were not complete. This development took place in the mid-Atlantean phase.

The process was one in which a vibrational matching was made between mankind's fear of death, the beyond death experience, and the garlic devas. The devic spirits associated with garlic completed their task in Atlantis, which is why this plant has been largely unchanged since then. Today, new discoveries are being made with garlic. This is primarily because the increased intelligence of the devic spirit is here to assist mankind with this plant. New discoveries, such as the ability of garlic to change body chemistry and to assist in fat absorption, are the direct influence of a very intelligent devic spirit. Today, the plant's karmic purpose is to connect this devic spirit to scientists and to those who study plants and herbs.

The heart chakra is opened, and all the nadis are cleansed. As a result of this, all the chakras in the body will be affected, but that is a secondary result. The liver and kidney meridians and the astral body are cleansed. The psora and gonorrhea miasms are eased. Use garlic when Pluto is in negative aspects to Saturn or Mars.

Animals develop a greater appreciation of the life force. As animals come to know death, they tend to understand life. It is wise, in working with animals you are close to when garlic is utilized such as for deworming or cholesterol problems, that you recognize the life force may increase in the animal. Train the animal or help it to channel enhanced life force energy by playing with it or showing it constructive things to do with this energy. It is not a long lived energy; it will last from a few minutes up to one or two hours after the ingestion of garlic. But beware of this, so that the new life force energy or appreciation of life is cemented within the animal.

Garlic is, of course, an important herb to use in companion planting and as a spray. But these things help primarily on the physical level. At a certain level, the devic spirit may be available as an extremely intelligent organism to assist individuals who are studying and working with garlic in agriculture for use as a spray, for purification, or for companion planting with new and unusual plants that are now being bred. That is its primary use at this time, as one vehicle to combine spirituality and agricultural. The test point is the medulla oblongata.

Golden Seal

This North American native flowers in the spring. Golden seal has long been used as an antiseptic that is applied internally and externally.

This herb assists individuals in clearsightedness and in a deeper understanding of the spiritual purpose of groups and individuals. Golden seal is an herb that should not to be taken unless really necessary, because of its occasionally difficult antibiotic effects within the physical body. Indeed, it is better to use this herb in aromatherapy or as a flower essence for its spiritual properties. The spiritual properties exist in the herb form, but the antibiotic effect, which is often too strong, will be considerably weakened when golden seal is taken as a flower essence or an essential oil.

Antibiotics, including golden seal, will be used less in the future because they affect the entire system of the body. This has, of course, the negative aspect that the various things you are focusing on gather some strength. They are not so specifically affected, and so toxins may reform in the body in a more robust state. This is obvious with many of the various infections that are now present in the world. Many toxins are becoming resistant to antibiotics.

An antibiotic short circuits the natural defense processes of the body. It is harder for the physical and subtle bodies to recognize the signature, the vibration, and the lesson associated with the disease and toxin. The antibiotic affects, on a microbial level, the energetic processes that allow the replication of the invading organism. The individual may appear to be healed as a result of the antibiotic. Instead of working with the inner lesson or inner message of the disease, people simply rely upon the drug. Because of the general application and widespread use of antibiotics, the immune system has been negatively affected. The immune systems of individuals are less able to seek out and fight specific infections, while at the same time, the overuse of antibiotics has allowed many diseases and thought forms associated with them, as well as viruses and microbes, to become stronger and more resistant. It is a well-established principle in modern medicine that antibiotics do not work as well today as they did even a few years ago.

Syphilis is the obvious example of how the immune system response is repressed by repeated use of antibiotics. Syphilis now often takes much deeper hold in the cellular level of the body, even below the level of detectability with current medical tests. Thus, for antibiotics to have their true intended purpose, the physical body will naturally after a time reject them. Even with the powerful effects of golden seal as a natural antibiotic, it will only be used in dire cases. Antibiotics do not tend to focus or specialize within a person. This is their primary downfall. As one becomes more finely attuned to different spiritual vibrations, an antibiotic can affect one's spirituality as well as the physical body. Since the spiritual well-being of a person is also of great importance for an individual's health, it would be very unwise to reduce this by the use of any physical substance. This principle applies to all drugs that are antibiotics, while golden seal has slightly less potential negative effects. Golden seal is more mutable by thought than any other antibiotic because it works in a similar fashion to the physical body's natural antibiotic or immune system.

The pungent smell of golden seal is an important signature. The signature is a very pungent and penetrating smell, though not very strong; yet it is penetrating for any who are sensitive to it. Indeed, people can change their attitudes just by smelling it. The inner attitudes may be more revealed and clear.

Golden seal activates the ability to have clear insight into past lives and to understand not just the purpose of life but, more importantly, its direction. This yields more trust, so that intuition and clearsighted perceptions can be followed more easily. This also stimulates visions. What can happen is that a reverie state may be entered into in which visions of one's purpose are presented as symbols. The symbols are much more easily understood. What is suggested in such reveries is that a metaphor be created of something yielding clear sight. You could imagine in your visualization a magnifying glass, a great lens, or a powerful light that is put upon the symbols. As this happens, you may reach deeper states of oneness with and clearsightedness of these principles. This also assists in other areas when clearsightedness is necessary, such as in a relationship when there is confusion, a scientific problem, or some aspect to be overturned and looked at deeply.

This clearsightedness can focus on any part of life. There may be a particular attribute uncovered. When golden seal is used, there is likely to be less fear in confronting these issues, and an individual may develop courage to speak about various concerns. For those involved in counseling, especially on a psychic level or in helping individuals deal with fear of certain psychic abilities, golden seal may increase understanding of these concerns. Golden seal is useful for both the counselor and the person being counseled.

Golden seal developed in Lemuria but was not fully formed until the Atlantean phase. The great concentration of energy in golden seal took place in Atlantean times. It was then seen that it would be necessary at times for a medicinal to be used for what would today be called broad spectrum antibiotic therapy. At that time, it was used to flush many microorganisms out of the physical body. This was necessary because the small intestines then played a more important role in the physical body, because the large intestine had not yet developed to the extent that it now has in mankind. Its karmic purpose is to be available to mankind for a powerful medicinal effect, but gradually to show people that the exact spiritual counterpart of this, the clearsightedness into what the problem is in the physical body, is also available. The herb provides this in a gentle manner without the need to be taken into the physical body.

The second chakra is significantly energized, and the bladder, liver, and stomach meridians are also energized and better balanced. The etheric-physical body connection is enhanced. All the miasms are eased, especially the cancer miasm at the current time. The cancer miasm is today undergoing certain changes. In the deepening effect of the cancer miasm, there may be a more direct understanding of the way emotions and cancer powerfully interact. As a result of this, it is possible that golden seal may not continue to weaken the cancer miasm. The fourth, fifth, and sixth rays are brought into more clarity, and negative aspects associated with Neptune are eased slightly. There is, in the heliocentric chart, something called the Sun return which occurs around your birthday. Those individuals who use aromatherapy with golden seal may find it much easier to understand the information and symbols provided by this configuration. The test point is the hara center.

Grapefruit

A tall fruit tree, grapefruit produces large white flowers and a round yellow fruit.

People using grapefruit have a clearer attunement to their spiritual goals. There is also a greater sense of global community; the perfectly round shape of the fruit reflects the idea of resonance to the Earth. However, the juice of this fruit engenders an unusual response in most individuals. This response is one of released acidity from the physical body. Because of this response, the current body state may be more utilized and understood spiritually. This unconscious evaluation of the physical body is a way to tune into the shared morphogenetic field called humanity, the way people are interrelated worldwide. This impact enables an individual to attain spiritual goals more easily, particularly when such goals relate to humanity. Individuals sometimes use grapefruit to lose weight. Such individuals may find greater success in losing weight if they also bring their spiritual focus and attention to various global activities and projects.

There is an enhanced perception of direction for groups. There can be assistance with group energy as it focuses on a given goal. Individuals become better leaders as a result. The self-image of a person gradually shifts, bringing more energy to this task.

The plant has come into its own only recently, with a larger fruit developing because of the great necessity today of global community and the alignment of individuals spiritual goals. The fruit has been available for a long time on the planet, but only recently has the energy been available for it to expand by the various techniques of hybridization and crossbreeding, and the devic spirit associated with this fruit is now stronger. As grapefruit gets larger and larger, more people will understand the importance of the Earth being significant to all people. This is personified in the fruit. It was not seen by the Lemurians as to when this capacity would be necessary. However, it seems that this is the time for this to occur.

The plant was much smaller in Lemuria. But through the constant use of love, especially through communication with the grapefruit devic order, it gradually grew in size. In Lemuria, the plant was not utilized for food until the end of the Lemurian phase, but the various concentrations of the specific types of sugar found in it were developed towards the end of Lemuria.

The stomach meridian is energized, which is profound in the way this affects the second, third, and fourth chakras. The energy in the third chakra in particular may be stimulated and brought into a much deeper state of balance. There is also a slight cleansing of the liver meridian. The etheric body is cleansed, the emotional body is strengthened, and the causal body comes into a sense of greater harmony. There is an easing of the syphilitic and psora miasms, and the seventh ray is brought into clarity.

There is some assistance for animals seeking to purge various substances from their bodies when they are in the presence of individuals on a strong spiritual path. This inner cleansing may be something the animal seeks if grapefruit juice is provided occasionally. Once a year is enough. The animal may drink a small amount of it which is usually sufficient. The test point is the navel.

Hawthorne

This tree produces white flowers and berries. Hawthorne is traditionally used for a wide range of heart and circulatory disorders.

Its ability to create greater attunement to the choices in life is one of its important spiritual characteristics. And it has the ability to assist individuals in understanding how they manifest God in their lives. The way a person manifests their own particular vision of God is unique to each individual. The way some of these properties are transferred naturally leads to a great focus of energy on the heart center. What occurs as a result of this is that an energy is formed in the heart that can be quite warming and remains long after the herb has been used or has fulfilled its function of aiding the blood or the heart. These energies surround mankind. The etheric signature of the plant appears to have a pulsation that is close to the tempo of a heartbeat. Before taking hawthorne, it is wise to tune into your heartbeat for a few minutes to activate its spiritual properties.

The ability to let go is greatly enhanced with hawthorne. This is not just on the medicinal level with the release of stress, but in the heart, as individuals learn to let go so they may trust. What happens in the psychic journey of letting go is that an individual reaches a point of psychic and spiritual merging in which they realize that the body will function by itself. They do not need to put any attention on it; they could just as soon die. What happens as a result of such an attitude of release is that great psychic energy is liberated, primarily in the heart center. As a result of this, the ability to love someone that you may have perhaps hated in the past comes more easily. Negative thought forms lodged in a person's own aura may be dislodged or even utterly destroyed. Therefore, there is some benefit in using this herb, along with loving meditations for oneself, and especially for loving others that you may have hated in the past. This implies forgiveness, but it is not quite so; it is more forgiving yourself than anyone else. Simply the awareness of this energy of love beamed at someone may be sufficient.

In Lemuria, the plant was often used as a symbol; the fruit or berry was used as a decoration or gift and a way of sharing. This is because the energy of the heart was always seen as a pulsation that could be felt by the individuals involved. There is a certain kinship with quartz crystals in the current time because of this. In Atlantis, one gave hawthorne to a friend just as one might today give someone a quartz crystal. Love was imbued deeply by the Lemurians into this plant. The devic order was gradually affected by this. This was not the more conscious direction of energy, but one that developed alongside the Lemurian civilization. This is why the energy of hawthorne even today is relatively subtle, yet it may have a powerful effect with certain individuals very attuned to Lemuria. The karmic lesson here is to again allow this energy into the Earth, if people wish to choose it.

The heart chakra is energized, which naturally balances and aligns through love the other main chakras with the heart chakra. The chakras and nadis in the hands may be quite stimulated. Spiritual healing may develop, but hawthorne does not so much stimulate the transfer of energy as it stimulates the energy of love. The pericardium meridian is energized, and the etheric and emotional bodies are cleansed. The first, second, and third rays are much more focused within an individual.

It is sometimes wise to give hawthorne to an animal you have a loving relationship with when the animal has done something wrong. You as well as the animal should take a small quantity of the herb, perhaps in the tea form after meditating on it and pouring love into it for a moment or two. Allow your heartbeat to touch that of the animal, and notice its beat too. This may cause a temporary realignment with one's pet. The test point is the heart center.

Hemlock Spruce

This tall evergreen tree produces a bark that is gray-brown on the outside and red on the inside. This herb is used as a mouthwash and eases bladder and kidney problems.

The inner bark and sap from the tree are of benefit as an herb. There is sometimes what is termed 'psychic debris' that accumulates in working with third eye vision. In the accumulation of unwanted psychic vision, blockages can develop. This is natural. This tendency is very similar to the blockages to past life information. Filters are interposed. If the filter begins to affect you, if by opening the third eye you become aware of difficulties in your life, experiencing greater blockages of many different kinds, the inner bark particularly, is indicated. Or apply some of the resinous substance directly to the third eye. A gradual releasing of these blocks will take place; it will not be a sudden energy. It will let one come into contact, gently at first, with the purpose of this psychic debris.

If you are open and sensitive to what another being is saying, if you begin to acknowledge various capacities of empathy and sympathy, and at the same time work upon opening your third eye, you will begin to observe that accumulating in your aura are many parts of what you have received from others. These energies may not be exactly that which you feel is good, that which you want in your aura. For instance, some of these things may relate to negative experiences, negative thought forms, or difficult feelings that you have experienced with other people. This energy may have accumulated gradually over the years. Most of this is unconscious but, as the third eye opens and you become more aware, you may see that it is hard to cleanse this away. Sometimes, this can negatively impact the third eye opening process. That is an especially good time to use this herb. Hemlock spruce can also be used to remove negative thought forms.

For an individual seeking to fine tune third eye energy, it is wise to experiment with many of the evergreen trees to see their different effects. Trees of the needle and evergreen variety often assist in opening the third eye.

The pungent bark, the inner bark in particular and its aroma, can deeply affect the emotional state of an individual. There is a certain resiliency of this woody substance to difficulty interposed from outside. This is well known to insects. This is due to the cleansing effect that its etheric nature has on the vibrations around it. This may be perceived and observed as characteristics of the plant itself, but for a person, this may be something that they would learn from. The nature of vibrational matching at the third eye level receives some of this. It is almost like making the signature of the plant your own for a time.

The use of this tree in Lemuria was primarily for beauty. Trouble with insects or working out psychic difficulties associated with insects was not of great importance in Lemuria. But it was seen that in Atlantean times, soon to come, it would be of far greater importance, because the Atlanteans would probably alter and change the Earth's natural environment. Therefore, deep resiliency, resistance, and inner strength were magnified in this tree. Its karmic purpose, of course, is to make these available to mankind.

There can be a strengthening in the throat and the third chakras. It will depend on the nature of the blockages. As the third eye opens, deeper understanding not only of religious or scientific states but of your internal point of view may result. This enables one to understand how a blockage may exist in various areas, such as the ability to assimilate power or difficulty in expression. Thus, the energy of the third eye chakra becomes intertwined with the energies of the other chakras.

The chakras are strengthened as one moves from the third eye outward. If an individual, in opening the third eye, sees that some chakras are blocked, perhaps noticing a band of energy at the third chakra, they may find it much easier to dispel this energy when working with this herb. The stomach, bladder, and gall bladder meridians are strengthened. This is not always beneficial for a person. If headache results, discontinue using this tea for at least a week. Such headaches can be a result of intensified energy through the gall bladder meridian. The nadis in the forehead are all stimulated, the psora miasm is eased, and the eighth ray becomes more clearly seen and focused. The etheric and mental bodies are cleansed, and the mental body is slightly stimulated. The test point is the third eye.

Hemp Agrimony

Hemp agrimony is a European plant that flowers during the summer. It is an emetic that also eases liver problems.

The plant's reddish color and profuse nature of subdivision and blossom signify an attunement with the Earth. This energy is too subtle for most people to understand. However, the plant is unique in that it provides the individual with more choices which are in harmony with all that they uphold and believe as beautiful and important about the Earth. People who grapple with the more difficult issues of spiritual ecology, of understanding how the entire Earth works together and that they are part of it, will benefit on the mental level by using this herb.

There can be, as mental clarity opens regarding alignment with the Earth, a deep sense of frustration or anger, as if the difficulty the Earth is now experiencing is something they would like to remove but cannot. The emetic nature of hemp agrimony may influence an individual, and they may find it a little difficult after drinking the tea to keep anything down. Thus, the individual should use it only in small quantities, perhaps as little as a quarter of a cup of a weak tea. This might be quite sufficient for the spiritual properties to be awakened.

There is also a strengthening of desire to remain in incarnation. Use this plant for those who are suicidal, especially with individuals who do not understand exactly why they need to leave the Earth. Such people are tired of it all but do not understand exactly why they are thinking of suicide.

There is greater coherence and integration to bring together many different ideas. There is a deeper understanding of universal laws, as one contemplates and reflects on the world. This is indeed a psychic gift, because there is a stimulation of the heart, an awakening there. The true birth place and home of universal laws in mankind is in the heart, not the mind. This awakening may be strengthened with greater understanding in the presence of this herb.

The plant in Lemuria was understood for its gentle nature and awareness of the Earth, as if the nature spirits associated with it participated in many of the ritualistic experiences in ancient Lemuria. It was seen that mankind might forget some of the wholeness of creation, so the nature spirits working with this plant have worked to preserve this attunement. In the mid-Atlantean phase, hemp agrimony was required to preserve this teaching. Then there were some difficulties, as if the Atlantean civilization was not able to appreciate fully an awareness of the Earth. This led to various difficulties, including some problems associated with nuclear weapons. In that time period, the plant mutated slightly into its current form. At the same time, the devic order associated with it became a bit stronger. This had a powerful and beneficial effect for the balance of the Atlantean civilization. Their understanding of the biosphere, how the interdependence of all things was so important, continued for most of the Atlantean civilization.

There is a stimulation of the heart chakra, and an awakening there, as if the eyes of the heart see more clearly. And there is a strengthening of the minor chakras in the hands and feet. The bladder meridian is slightly enhanced, and there is added movement through the pericardium meridian. The etheric and mental bodies often merge more clearly, while the emotional body is cleansed. The psora miasm is eased, and the eighth and tenth rays are made stronger and clearer. In sidereal astrology, there are some negative aspects that may be observed between Mars and Earth. Such indications in the natal chart show an added susceptibility to the positive influence of this herb. The test point is the center of the chest.

Henna

Red flowers are produced by this shrub that is native to North Africa and the East Indies. Henna is used as a gargle and for treating headaches and skin problems.

There is a tendency to change the understanding of karma, as if to change the possibilities by simply revealing more information about your own karmic purpose. This herb spiritually awakens one to past lives, to the possibilities for changing future lives, and more importantly, to certain gifts relating to the balancing of karma that an individual has not paid attention to in their lives. Sometimes the use of henna, even externally on the body, can stimulate this effect. The self-image of a person may be shifted regarding past life negative karma, as well as possible future positive karma that an individual may create for themselves. This change of view is what is emphasized with henna.

Henna has the unique ability to change the color of human hair. This property has existed since even the earliest Lemurian time. It was used as a playful herb, and this playfulness is again re-emerging. Its karmic lesson is to provide these attitudes of change in a playful and relaxed manner, so that individuals may come to them willingly and with knowledge. Henna was often used in ancient Egyptian rituals for coloration, especially as a part of the death rituals. There were many ways henna was used in Egypt. Mankind went through several periods of rediscovery of henna. One is currently opening at this time; Egypt was another one of these periods. Then there was a deep attunement to the future lifetime that was to be seen as enjoying the company of the gods. Henna was also used for past life therapy.

The ability to stimulate the crown and third eye chakras, to have a new point of view, to reveal future and past lifetimes as reality so that one may work with them directly are all attributes of henna. When one is working with another individual, it may be much easier to deal with the past life regression process. Past life therapists often experience an unconscious bond or tie to the person they are working with, which naturally surfaces as past life memories for the therapist. These bonds are sometimes unconscious and difficult to deal with. This herb, taken as a tea or just rubbed externally over the skin or hair, can ease this problem. The therapist may be more able to accept their own past life connection to the client and become more aware of their own past lives that have surfaced in the therapy.

The third chakra is slightly energized, and the syphilitic miasm is eased. The astral body is stimulated, and it may expand. The fourth ray is focalized, and the test point is the back of the neck at the third cervical vertebrae.

Horehound

Found in waste regions in the United States and Europe, this plant grows white flowers during the summer. Horehound is a prominent expectorant especially useful during coughing.

With horehound there is an alignment with pure physical energy so that individuals may accept such an energy as useful on the Earth. People involved in manual labor, or who need to work with difficult physical tasks, may find their spirituality assisted. They may acknowledge God in all that they do, even that which is the most physical. This spiritual property also assists the muscles to rest during meditation. There is less distraction and difficulty during meditative states. The awareness of God in all that is physical matter is enhanced. For instance, this can assist engineers or scientists seeking to understand microscopic matter.

One better learns to accept what one sees. This is not always an easy matter. Ancient tales show this more clearly, such as the ways new techniques from the space brothers and others were rejected for some time. This is currently in vogue as a tale of Magellan in discovering the New World, as it was then called. Those who lived in America were not even able to see his ships. With horehound the physicalness of existence is seen more clearly, and individuals' fears relating to what they see are eased. Psychically, this means that one can see very clearly what is actually transpiring. This is of some assistance with deep hypnosis. Individuals who fall into trancelike states quickly or easily, perhaps falling into a trancelike state while driving, will benefit from using horehound. Doctors would find this a good remedy to ease narcolepsy.

The past association with the animal kingdom is quite strong. This herb is indeed attractive to animals of the canine species. There is a tendency for individuals to have a deep remembrance of this from Lemurian times. The signature relates to its ability to assist dogs to come closer to mankind. This has been a general tendency throughout the evolution of the entire canine species. Over and over again, these animals respond to this plant in an emotional way. It is as if they are intermingled at the soul level. One of the dog's important lessons is to know this physical existence more deeply, to provide it as an explanation or understanding of one facet of Earth to mankind. This is a gradual unfoldment of this life stream. But this is a two-way street, and that is why dogs are man's best friend, as the expression goes.

The root and second chakras are coordinated, and the gall bladder and bladder meridians are strengthened. The nadis in the legs are energized, and the second ray is clearer for people. There is a clear relationship to the planet Mars, for Mars and its ability to focus on the physical is very important for mankind. The planet and the herb often work together. When one is having difficulty with Mars, there will be enhancement of the herb's spiritual properties in taking horehound. This may also be true when Mars is in positive aspects to other planets. The test point is the navel.

Hyssop

This short herb produces bluish-purple flowers. Hyssop is used as an expectorant, stimulant, and to relieve inflammations.

This herb stimulates a deeper connection to people. This leads to a release of guilt, as with the flower essence. But this is an example of the more concentrated energy in the flower essence versus the more spread out or less dense energy in the herb. There is a deeper sense of relationship, a greater connection on the physical, emotional, and mental levels with all individuals. Spiritually, this creates a greater sense of harmony and oneness. It is an excellent herb to share in a group. There is a relaxation of an individual's judgmental side as they see themselves judged by others. This is important, because most individuals contend and work with the right to judge themselves and are seeking to ease the way they judge others. However, they do not always understand or accept the way they feel others are judging them. This presupposed self-judgment can be quite difficult and largely unconscious, and sometimes leads to states of guilt. That is the relationship to the flower essence. However, on a deeper level, this uniting into group energy clearly enhances states of group meditation in which the energy focus is placed outside the group. For instance, a group may assist in a political endeavor, a meditation on peace, or certain areas of the world where people are suffering.

The reddish color of hyssop tends to last through all the seasons. This represents the fact that etherically there is a vibration of uniting individuals at the root chakra level. This is a vibratory feeling, and some may have a sense of calmness in sitting near the plant.

In Lemuria, this energy was better understood. Hyssop was seen as a vehicle to connect what individuals wished to combine with the very best parts of themselves as relating to the will and the physicalness of being. The higher spiritual aspects, later created in the plant in Atlantis, were not much a part of the plant's initial development. This development has largely remained in place, so this is something that humans can again tie into without moving into levels of rarefied spirit that can lead to some of the Atlantean difficulties with technology and abuse of the will. The karmic purpose of the plant is to provide an overall energy again for humans to draw into themselves if they wish.

In this combining of energies, many psychic abilities are unleashed. These include the ability for energy to be focused on one person for healing or on worldwide events to affect many individuals. There is a self-regulating effect, however. If individuals, in coordinating these energies, seek to focus them towards negative ends, there will be a debilitating energy associated with the group. And so it is self-governing and generating on that level. The highest and most beautiful aspects of interpersonal relationships are brought out by the herb. What occurs is a natural self-focusing of the group. These energies, when various people work together, can indeed make some difference on the planet.

The second and third chakras are brought into a better state of balance, so there is a uniting of the first, second, and third chakras especially towards the heart chakra. The conception vessel is energized, the spleen meridian flow is better balanced, and the nadis in the hands and feet are stimulated. There is also a temporary balancing of the mental, emotional, and etheric bodies. As a result of this process, some energy may be focused in the astral body, which becomes more calm and peaceful. Thus, hyssop can be useful in certain difficult sleep conditions when an individual is waking up quite tired due to extensive astral travel.

There are several connections here to the sign Aquarius. This sign tends to rule and work with hyssop. Individuals especially attuned to Aquarius, as it may assist them in any group endeavor, may find direct correlation. When the Sun or Moon is in Aquarius, this is a second indication that a group will be particularly enhanced by this herb.

There is some assistance for those who seek to develop new properties of massive growth techniques for food crops. This herb, when applied to the soil in diluted quantities, enhances the crossbreeding of plants, pest infestation prevention, growth, and growing conditions. Less water and sunlight will be needed. The proper proportion here would be one drop of the hyssop tincture to about four gallons of water. The test point is in the center of the chest.

Iceland Moss

This lichen is commonly found in northern climates. It is used as a tonic, nutritive, and demulcent.

The signature of this plant is very obvious. The idea is that it can achieve the highest height, and it will remain there in very difficult environmental conditions. Spiritually, there a direct correspondence. Individuals struggling in difficult areas of their personal evolvement to attain higher development, and who are also in difficult environments, will be nourished by this herb. There is an inner strengthening that takes place to remain fixed in one's goals; it is a little like mountain climbing. Indeed, mountain climbers are aware of this herb and see it frequently.

Many times, however, when an individual comes close to achieving this higher spiritual peak of a deep awareness of God or of how their work towards attaining spiritual goals has brought fruit, there is a deep fear. There is an unwillingness to continue. Sometimes this is due to the fear of facing oneself or of facing God. But sometimes it is also the simple idea that, after this is accomplished, there will be nothing left to do. This is important. It is in a direct correlation to how the mountain climber feels when reaching the top of the mountain. There is a great joy but, sooner or later, it is time to climb down. In actuality, what is happening is that the trust level of the highest vibration one is attaining is not being permitted. And this inner trust of what occurs when the spiritual evolvement is complete is not understood. The herb helps greatly in accepting this, allowing this to be deeply felt. It cannot be understood or explained, but it is useful for individuals who are attempting these difficult feats.

Thus, this herb is useful for individuals who are working towards spiritual goals that are not part of society. For instance, if you have been taught western ways and are now studying eastern mystical traditions, this herb would be of assistance. In the martial arts there are specific applications when individuals are seeking to let go of the mind and yet be in a position of full physical response. This involves the ability to work with energy coming at you from all sides, as if the mind itself is let go and the body becomes one with the action that is happening around you. These things can be difficult because the individual is unable to trust fully. Iceland moss helps with this trust.

There is an enhancement of the courage principle, which is very important when psychic abilities blossom suddenly. Sometimes individuals will not be able to face the level or power of their own spiritual awakening. Some individuals experience spiritual emergence that is difficult. It causes fear or misunderstanding, yet it is in alignment with their spiritual purpose. You may ask yourself, in such a situation if your spiritual purpose is a deeper love, an understanding of God, or working with other individuals. And these psychic gifts could perhaps be seen to help. Then if they are not in alignment, why do you need them? If you see that they are in alignment, and yet are frightening, it is because you have not experienced inner trust at these higher vibrational levels. In working with these abilities and using iceland moss, the person gradually learns to trust them more. This is especially true with clairvoyance, intuition, psychometry and mental healing.

The plant existed in various forms, a little more rudimentary perhaps, long before mankind came upon the Earth. As the ancient Lemurians began to understand and admire it, it was seen that the spiritual properties of its ability to exist in the higher regions in a harsh environment and to exist on very little sustenance would be useful as a symbol for mankind. However, it was seen that many around this plant would not even recognize these higher principles. And so a long process was put in place. When an individual was on a mountain, or working near the plant, they were in a state of deep meditation and love, as if observing mankind seeking the highest heights of understanding of God, not knowing it had an ally. So this secret friend and ally was awakened. Its own choice is to make this energy more available to mankind. However, its spiritual purpose in some ways is not directly intertwined with mankind's. Even after man might pass from this planet, this plant would continue, for it simply loves the way of the rocks and of the Earth itself.

There is some opening of the heart, crown, ninth, and tenth chakras. The gall bladder meridian is slightly stimulated, the nadis in the soles of the feet are opened, and there is an activation of the mental, soul, and causal bodies. The radiation miasm is eased, and the ninth and twelfth rays are made clearer and stronger for an individual. There is some correlation here to the planetoid Chiron and to Pluto. When these are in square or opposition use this herb. The test point is the crown chakra.

Indian Pipe

Indian pipe is unusual in that it has pipe-bowl-shaped flowers which turn black when bruised. It is used to ease nerve conditions, spasms, and fevers.

There is an enhanced ability to receive love. The love however will pass through if the individual does not understand its vibration. This is not necessarily love from a person, or even from a group, but universal love in the highest sense. This is very specific in an individual, because this receiving may be only one part of the process. Sometimes awareness of this love and the ability to put yourself in a position to receive it are needed. However, the plant increases the ability to know the correct time to open, to be mentally quiet, and to fully receive this energy. Sometimes this loving energy may be all around a person, yet they do not know it. Those who feel starved for love would certainly be advised to work with this herb.

It could be taken in a tea form, though it would be wise to brew it in low strength so that its vibrational capacities are primarily transferred. When you brew it in high potency, a higher concentration of the more physical effects are usually noted because various chemical agents are more concentrated. At a weaker strength, the spiritual effects have more impact. As one becomes more familiar with the spiritual properties of this herb, a stronger concentration can usually be taken. It is for one to discern. The flower in particular is useful. You will see an increased sensitivity to this love. It would be wise to use the flower essence of this plant.

Taking this herb gives an individual a chance to understand more carefully the difference between what might be termed 'personality love' and 'universal love.' The goal is to raise the vibration to work with these higher love energies. Now you might say, "But what is the source of this energy? From where does it come? Where should I direct this ability to receive?" On the highest level, universal love floods the planet and floods your being. You need not figure it out, but merely open to it. However, if you need to focus on it, be aware of the Sun and its energy pouring into you. Imagine the heart opening and being strengthened by this love. It is useful as the love is with you that you then let it go. Find some way to receive it and let your body be nurtured by it, and then send it elsewhere. Perhaps allow it to pour into the Earth, or send it across the world to another being.

This plant may learn a great deal at the devic order level from the manifestation of Christ consciousness. It will come to understand loneliness and community. And through the action of Christ love, it may come to be one of the first plants that will assimilate and work with human love. As a result of this, the energy associated with the plant will spread. This may allow it to grow under varied conditions, to be utilized by many people, and to grow in new areas of the world.

The signature of this bowl-shaped plant indicates the receptacle. But, you will also see that, if the love that is brought into the plant is of a physical nature, if it is touched, in other words, it may be bruised and turn black, as if the energy itself is changed. The symbol here is clear and obvious. The individual receives only the highest love, and whatever else there may be is released. It is useful for individuals struggling with the principles of universal love to investigate and utilize this herb.

The plant also brings peace among people. This is a natural adjunct. You may wonder what is the purpose of universal love in the cosmic or even human sense. Only through that can a deep and lasting peace be created. There is a direct correlation to the symbology of the peace pipe, but there is more than this. There is, among individuals who are awakening to this kind of energy, an awareness of their unitedness. Many times, the reason for war is difference. As differences are eased, there is recognition of love among people.

There is an increase of the heart's ability to receive energy. In certain types of healing, such as reiki, this energy is specifically utilized. In many people, reiki may be assisted by this plant . The ability to utilize heart energy can be useful for many different purposes. But because this energy is of the highest level, it is useful when doing such healing not to figure it out. The mind is quiet. Do not direct energy specifically to a particular part of a person's body, rather, make it as available as possible, with as many possibilities to move through you and the person as you can imagine.

The plant stood as a symbol of peace on the planet in the transfer of energy between Lemuria and Atlantis. It stood as a reminder for individuals to know that they could have differences yet remain in love on the planet together. The Lemurians, in bringing this as a symbolic energy deeper and deeper into the plant, made it part of its life purpose. The plant received this willingly, and the devic order associated with it has been aware of a constantly growing awareness in humanity of universal love. The karmic purpose of the plant will change from generation to generation as mankind's ability to manifest, learn about, and work with universal love also changes. It is keeping pace with mankind in this way.

The heart and throat chakras are opened, the heart, small intestine, and circulation sex meridians are energized, and the nadis in the chest and back are opened slightly. The emotional body is cleansed, while extra energy is imparted to the mental and causal bodies. The syphilitic miasm is slightly eased, and the fourth, fifth, and twelfth rays are strengthened. The positive aspects of Jupiter and Venus are indications for using this plant.

Many who seek a greater friendship with animals that must be kept in captivity will find a deeper sense of forgiveness in the animals by offering this herb. This is one of the properties of universal love. However, it is wise, if you are the zoo keeper or someone taking care of animals that wish to be free, you must find a way to balance the karma of the lack of freedom. Then take this herb and give some to the animal and there will be a greater sense of forgiveness. Eventually, however, you will have a greater sense of love and you will wish to do something for animals, perhaps for a similar species roaming free somewhere else in the world. The keepers of animals as well as the caged animals should take this herb at times. The test point is the center of the chest.

Unfortunately, this herb is not readily available in stores. I have only located it as a liquid tincture under its Latin name *monotropa uniflora* from Boericke and Tafel in Philadelphia. This product is sold in some health food stores. I recently met an American Indian who was selling herbs. His tribe has long used this herb, calling it Indian pipe. However, he was unwilling to collect the plant for me or others because his tribe considers it sacred.

Indian Turnip

Found in the Midwest, Indian turnip has traditionally been used by the American Indians to alleviate asthma, headaches, and rheumatism.

The plant has powerful medicinal properties, especially when one is working with the flowers, but it should be used cautiously. This herb has the interesting property of helping an individual awaken to their spiritual purpose. This can even be beyond life purpose, as if understanding more of what God has intended for them or what they elected for their lives before coming here. However, in a more practical way, this means an opening or release of energy. When an individual works on a spiritual project, it will be greatly enhanced by this plant.

Spiritual work or life purpose goes through an individual in cycles. The appreciation of the way these cycles take place is enhanced. This is not easy. You might think your spiritual purpose is a constant and continuous thing. Of course this is true to some extent, but it must also coordinate with mankind's spiritual purpose, with an awareness of your life, and how you integrate what you do. The way energy of a spiritual nature manifests in your life must follow patterns that cooperate and harmonize with the physical, mental, and emotional levels. It would be wise to use a flower essence of this plant. The signature relates to the flowers, their unique shape and way it seems to hold back energy, as if waiting to be welcomed.

There is enhanced ebb and flow of energies, particularly those associated with lunar cycles. Part of this is because the natural spiritual energy associated with the plant works well with the energy of water as it is utilized in the leaves, and especially in the flowers. Water retained there is often, on a spiritual level, associated with the Moon. Thus, there is a release of energy of a spiritual purpose in coordination with lunar cycles. For individuals who are also seeking to understand the interrelationship between the Moon and Earth, this is one form of geomancy. Understanding the flow between humanity and the Moon is of great benefit. It is that which is the inner reminder of cycles for a person. People come to understand the way psychic abilities work within them. This is especially true with abilities that relate to other people—the reaching out for healing, the way of counseling, and the gathering of intuitive information in working with a person to assist them in their life.

The plant was much more primitive in Lemurian times, but the Lemurians saw that it had great capacity for developing into a symbol of great spiritual purpose that could be held within humans. The Lemurians saw that this embodiment of purpose, God's purpose through mankind, was necessary in this plant. And so they spoke of this and brought it into the awareness of the devic order associated with the plant, and this spiritual purpose was directly placed in the plant. This was accomplished in a hundred year period when energy was focused into the plant by many Lemurians and understanding of God, Earth, and the Moon was brought deeply into the form of light. The light was poured into this plant, and the plant's devic order, knowing how to use it, began to change the plant. Physically, it became larger, stronger, and clearer and began to take on its current shape. Some native Americans understood these properties and how spiritual purpose moves in cycles. Thus, some of its inner message was released. However, by and large, the inner message, or karmic purpose, of this plant has not been accepted or fulfilled.

There is some stimulation of the root chakra and added energy in the eighth, ninth, tenth, and eleventh chakras. There is a strengthening of the conception vessel meridian, and the nadis near the crown chakra are stimulated, as are the mental and causal bodies. In some individuals, the causal, soul, and integrated spiritual bodies are brought into a temporary state of alignment. There is some release of the stellar miasm, and the eleventh and twelfth rays are strengthened. Press the medulla oblongata and top of head at the same time to activate the test point.

Indigo

This wild plant is found in the east-central United States. It is an antiseptic and purgative. Large doses can cause poisoning.

There is one prime use for this herb. Its indigo color may be of benefit for some individuals. The coloration is used in clothing, pieces of paper, and may be placed upon the third eye center to accentuate energy associated with the third eye. Thus, there is a deepening of psychic abilities associated with the third eye. Clairvoyance is significantly enhanced as is clairaudience and the ability to see auras. The result of this is that spiritual understanding associated with some of these properties may be more easily available. The signature is the color associated with the plant.

Indigo has been used in ritual for most of mankind's history for it colors. Its patterns will bring this to mankind as the color associated with the sixth chakra is focused upon. The sixth chakra is activated. There is a strengthening of the mental body as well as some enhancement of the fifth ray. The test point is the third eye center.

Irish Moss

A sea weed that grows along the Irish coast, Irish moss eases various respiratory conditions.

There is a strengthening of environmental spirituality, so that people can firmly and clearly work with the environment. This is reflected in the way Irish moss intermingles with the sea and Earth. It is also a way for people to understanding their environment in a more direct fashion. This is sometimes necessary before true environmental work can be done. In seeking to help areas affected by acid rain or to assist animals in jeopardy as a species, it is often necessary to have a deeper love, forgiveness, and understanding, as if spiritual ecology is just as important as actual physical ecology. This greater awareness is directly stimulated by this herb. There is a consequent release of anger, of a particularly negative thought form, perhaps of hatred that may be stored in the emotional body, as one contemplates these things. There is a direct correlation between the herb's ability to assist in purging radiation from the physical body and the way emotional release takes place. Many times, on the higher levels, emotional entrapment causes increased susceptibility to radiation poisoning as well as other difficulties relating to the environment.

There is a direct enhancement of the ability to see all things happening at all times. Some gain proficiency in psychometry by using this herb. When the herb is utilized for such a purpose, do not think about various places, just hold an object to understanding it better. People seeking to understand harmony with the Earth on an environmental level will find a deeper understanding and creative energy. There will also be a consequent release of blockages, creating a deeper understanding of the Earth, especially when making physical contact with a rock.

In the more primitive forms of creeping moss and those plants associated more with the Earth and sea, the Lemurians saw an interesting possibility for merging. They saw the possibility that mankind would misuse the inner energies associated with the atom, that these energies of radiation might be exposed and misused. Thus, the plant was also developed for some of these physical cleansing properties. The plant was given the opportunity of helping humanity to harmonize with the environment, particularly the environment of the sea. This task was taken willingly by the plant. However, that secondary purpose, the harmonizing with the sea, has not yet been fully revealed to mankind. This higher purpose of the plant may be revealed in the coming ages.

There is a strengthening of the third eye, and of the minor chakras in the feet, hip region, and throughout the legs. The bladder meridian is directly stimulated. There is enhanced energy in the etheric, emotional, and mental bodies, which temporarily aligns them. The radiation miasm is eased, the fourth and tenth rays are brought into clearer focus, and the test point is the third eye.

Ironweed

Found in the Midwest, red or purple flowers grow in the summer. Used as a bitter tonic, ironweed promotes digestion and stimulates the appetite.

The plant takes its name and signature from the way it appears as a solid form with its reddish color. There is also available on the etheric level the added strength that the plant establishes between the Earth and the environment around it. A strengthening of this deeper connection to the Earth may be felt by people. There is also an inner constitutional strengthening that is related to the action of the etheric and emotional bodies. This is directly affected by ironweed. This may yield greater ability to manifest on the physical level various attributes one wishes to create. This gives a greater sense of groundedness, solidity, inner knowingness, and willingness to remain on the Earth. This plant can be useful on the emotional level for individuals contemplating suicide, for people who are struggling with a vision of the Earth they have lost or a vision of their incarnation. This can be made clearer and stronger for the person.

There is clearer insight into the purpose of immediate affairs and practical attributes, such as a job. Sometimes this is very difficult for an individual to recognize, because they are so enmeshed in their work, it is so much a part of their experience.

The idea of this plant has long been to personify some of the attributes of the mineral kingdom, particularly the strength found in iron. The idea was for individuals to retain this understanding as if they have that iron, or that inner strength of will. The Lemurians understood this quite deeply, so they attempted to leave this as a legacy for mankind. Thus, the idea of the will as revealed emotionally to people was placed in this plant. The devic order associated with ironweed took this on willingly; it understood that this would be of great importance in mankind's future. During the Atlantean epoch, this plant was hardly recognized or used at all. Understanding the will was not then seen to be of great importance.

There is added energy in the root and second chakras, and there is a definite strengthening of the gall bladder and liver meridians. The etheric and emotional bodies are strengthened; they often come into a state of temporary resonance which also affects the mental body. There is an easing of the petrochemical miasm, and the third and fourth rays are made clearer. Those working with the planet Vulcan may find some benefit in observing and working with this plant. It can be taken at times when Vulcan, as described in esoteric literature, is in a position of negative aspect to natal Mars. The test point is the coccyx.

Jasmine

A tree growing thirty feet tall, jasmine is found in India and other Asian countries. Jasmine calms the nerves and has often been used as a carminative and astringent.

Jasmine enhances the tantric function. This property has existed for a long time, and indeed the more aphrodisiacal properties associated with jasmine are now undergoing change. The ability to see God in sexuality is more strongly available to individuals by the use of jasmine through aromatherapy. This has increasingly been the case for the last fifty years. The reason for this is that mankind's attitudes towards sexuality is changing. This is partly a result of the consciousness of the specialness of sex associated with the changing thought forms coming from a fear of AIDS. Jasmine affects this by easing people's fears of the God nature of sexuality. Many who have strict views regarding sexuality and the way pure pleasure is experienced, are now confronting fear around sexually transmitted diseases, especially AIDS, in relation to previous attitudes. Using the essential oil or small quantities of the herb eases these fears and attunes people more to the Godlike properties of sexuality. This involves tantra in its purest sense; the way inner sensuality is nurtured in an individual. This has nothing to do with physical contact, but is simply a deeper awareness. The purpose of sexuality is also to experience pleasure deep within an individual. The guilt and fear associated with sexuality eases, and gradually the God nature emerges. Individuals who are not part of a couple can take jasmine alone to better understand the essence of tantra. Jasmine could also be used with persimmon flower essence because they both have a similar function.

The aroma of jasmine runs very deep within an individual. However, there is no direct correlation to such a sweet aroma in sexual functioning in most individuals. The sexual glands give off an extremely small quantity of an oily substance that has a similar odor to jasmine. This is largely masked by the function of the other lubricants and chemicals in sexuality that the body gives off, so it is largely received unconsciously. As the individual attunes more and more with God, the sweeter smelling body odors emerge, and one begins to smell more like jasmine. Indeed, this is the way the physical body tended to smell in Lemurian times. This is the signature of jasmine that runs deep in the unconscious of people.

The ability to perceive sexuality and accept it is enhanced, as is the acceptance of God energy in the moment of orgasm. This means that in the sexual union, energy that is transferred from male to female and female to male is more easily absorbed and consciously brought through the physical body to the heart center or even to the higher centers.

The origin of jasmine in Lemuria led to the refinement of the plant to develop a smell similar to that of human beings in sweetest sexuality. However, sexuality in Lemuria was very different than it is now. Jasmine continues now as a reminder to individuals that sexuality and the use of the physical body for pleasure can be done in a relaxed and calm manner.

The root, second, and third chakras are united to function closer together. The heart, small intestine, and pericardium meridians are all stimulated. The nadis in the genital region are given extra energy. The connection between the physical and etheric body is energized, and the syphilitic miasm is eased. Also, the third and fourth rays are brought into greater prominence.

There is an association with the higher aspects of Venus. Use this herb, in any form, whenever Venus and the Moon are in conjunction, opposition, square, or trine. In each of these cases, the individual will be more sensitive to the effects of jasmine. In the past, jasmine was used to relieve some relationship difficulties with the animal kingdom. But this is largely related to past lives and does not occur much now. Today, most people who work with animals do so according to accepted methods of society, which are often dictated by various considerations such as economics and rearing standards. However, a few individuals are learning to appreciate the animal kingdom in new ways. This will eventually create changes and, hopefully, a greater recognition of this herb's properties. The test point is the pubic bone, pressing on the top.

Kidney Bean

This annual, probably from South America, is used to lower blood sugar levels.

The balance between fear and love can be quite strong. For individuals who are learning to understand this balance, this is a very important herb. This is not too different from the flower essence properties in easing fear. The relationship between love and fear is understood better, and greater love is manifested in life because you come to understand and therefore release fear. This leads to interesting states of greater oneness with the very thing you are afraid to love, the very thing that you fear in your life.

Many times, when receiving love, the individual stops the process at a certain level. The body can handle only so much love, or perhaps you feel that you deserve only so much love. This often results from training received during childhood. All these things are fears, a fear of deserving, a fear of full receptivity, or perhaps a fear of not being approved of by your parents. These thought forms will often act to resist love. At a certain depth of love received, with the assistance of kidney bean, there is a strengthening of the essence of universal love. The individual may at last come to recognize some of these resistances and fears that develop in conjunction with love and may release them once and for all.

The ability to speak your mind in a true and penetrating manner is also enhanced. To know the exact thing to say, when and how to say it, and how to share this in such a way that the other person knows the lovingness behind it is not couched in fear is an important attribute.

The shape of the bean obviously symbolizes the kidney. In the human being there is an unconscious but long standing connection between the kidney and attitudes of love and fear. Part of this is because these emotions are engendered to some extent by the adrenal glands, which sit above the kidneys.

The plant originated in Lemuria but was not developed into its full form until the early Atlantean phase. This was so that all the herb's properties would be available to mankind with this balance of love and fear. The plant did not fully accept this, because there was very little to illustrate to it that fear was necessary. This was shown gradually as the Atlantean civilization developed, and the plant and associated devas have since willingly taken this vibration on.

The second chakra is given greater energy and ability to release stored energy, while the minor chakra in the kidneys and the kidney and spleen meridians are also strengthened. The astral and emotional bodies are changed slightly to be in better communication with each other, and the heavy metal miasm is eased. The influence of the planets Mars and Venus can, in some instances, represent fear and love when they are in opposition or square. In such times, there is added benefit in taking this herb. If you are working to domesticate a wild animal that is particularly fearful of humans, which is often the case, there is benefit to giving this herb to the animal. The test point is the navel.

Knotweed

This annual usually grows to two feet tall. In Chinese medicine, knotweed relives toothache and stops bleeding gums.

The juice has a powerful dissolving effect, which is the signature of the plant. It is a way of intensifying solvent action. This is why the plant is so effective in dissolving stones in the physical body. This powerful property extends to the spiritual level. It has the ability to dissolve a number of blockages in your path. This can often be simple things such as little annoyances or difficulties. A strengthening of positive affirmations may also develop. Those who work with affirmations and yet struggle to truly feel or know them, are greatly aided by this herb. This dissolving effect may also remove negative thought forms, though here it is not so much in the etheric or emotional body as in the mental body.

On the physical level, this dissolving property has beneficial effects, but must be used with some caution. This is not so much from the tea as from the juice of the plant. This is similar on the spiritual level, in that if one dissolves and empties there can be a filling effect, a way one is strengthened with the positive nature that one receives, as negative thought forms dissipate and positive ones replace them. For most individuals, this leads to a place of imbalance in which practicality is ignored. What one wishes to happen is what happens. It is like wishful thinking. This is a way in which intuition is displaced with these positive thought forms. The action of this herb in the tea form, or in a very dilute concentration of the juice, even prepared homeopathically at 2x or 3x potency, has a balancing and self-governing effect in which these affirmations are taken in balance. Relinquishing of practicality is less likely to take place. This is useful, because when using affirmations it is wise not to swing too far into wishful thinking.

There is, with this cleansing of negative thought forms, a definite enhancement of energetic process in the physical body. Thus, all forms of meditation are enhanced, the ability to receive information from guides is stimulated, and an ability to understand the nature of negative thought forms is strengthened. Some people develop a deeper ability to see auras, including their own. This is not directly related to information as it pours into the third eye, so this type of aura reading takes place with the eyes closed. One imagines a form, perhaps a rose or a plant, and the person becomes this form. Then what is observed around it are colors, shapes, and energy patterns. This is an internal way of seeing, which is enhanced by using knotweed. Also, with this dissolving property, individuals come into greater harmony with the entire water element. This is not done as if attuning to marsh plants, but rather is done as if one consciously becomes the water. Meditation at the seaside, or working with water in many different ways is slightly enhanced using knotweed.

In Lemuria, the plant was first developed for its medicinal properties. Being a powerful solvent, it was seen as useful later to many people who might accidently eat foods or substances that could harm the body. Dissolving stones was important also, because the accumulation of particular debris often found in foodstuffs was common enough that the creation of urinary stones was a strong possibility. However, the spiritual properties were understood by a gentler process, a way of anticipating how humanity might be plagued with negative thought forms and would need to dissolve them and understand their process. The devic order associated with the plant studied for a long time with the Lemurians. This is not the kind of learning that you do in a school, but was a way of love and joyful exchange. This energy was utilized in Atlantis, but did not fully come into its own until about 3,000 years ago when the problem of particulate matter harming the urinary tract became rather common. Then the plant was rediscovered.

There is added energy throughout the second, third, and fourth chakras. At the third eye chakra there may be a strong sense of opening and greater clarity, though there is no added energy to this region. The bladder meridian is slightly energized, but its primary effect is with the liver and kidney meridians. The etheric and emotional bodies are significantly cleansed, and there is added clarity in the mental body. The petrochemical and heavy metal miasms are eased, and the fourth and tenth rays are made stronger for individuals. There is some correlation to the water signs in general, but this is a more esoteric link. Medically, it is extremely important for animals struggling with the problem of stones. The test point is two inches below the navel.

Lady's Slipper

Native to the United States, golden yellow and purplish flowers appear on this plant in the summer. It has long been used as a sedative.

It is wise to use this herb when fully dried to avoid any toxic effects. This also enhances some of its spiritual properties. Lady's slipper affects people on two essential levels. One of these is the level by which the feet come in contact with the Earth—the way the Earth speaks to you by motion. This enhances the ability to achieve a trance state while dancing, called trance dance. It also makes it easier to achieve ecstatic states brought on by Sufi dancing and other similar techniques. Individuals who seek greater energy through the feet will find this accelerated and assisted by the energy of the plant. The technique of walking on the dew in the morning, may be supplemented afterwards by drinking some lady's slipper tea.

When the dew is still fresh on the ground, walk on it with your bare feet. Visualize the sun and its light coming into your body, passing through to the center of the Earth. Then bring energy from the center of the Earth through you to the heavens, releasing all negativity and imbalance. This gradually establishes a much deeper spiritual connection with the Earth, certain physical imbalances are alleviated, and emotional calm is easier to attain. Do this several times a week for up to a few minutes each time.

The other spiritual effect is what happens to this energy. It is not only achieving a deeper trance state and a willingness to experience God's energy in such a state, but to utilize it in a way of fluid grace—a way the Earth is connected through your being to God, and together God and the Earth dance through you. A gentleness and grace may be achieved. Sometimes this energy has a tranquilizing or headache relieving effect because it is a potent and powerful tension reliever. Many times the tension is between society and an inner grace that you may experience. As inner grace becomes stronger and as your connection to the Earth and to God deepens, then inside your being a deeper calm and sense of inner knowingness develops. Being alive in itself is often a state of stress. And so for many it is important that this process be resolved, so that the life they live is graceful on an internal basis.

There is greater ability to understand the value of dance. Then the correct way to utilize this on a mental and emotional level combines with the physical body. This leads to greatly inspired states for some individuals. But, more importantly, the way they visualize dance and motion of all kinds, is significantly enhanced. In creative visualization, when one is aware of movement, there is definite assistance in taking lady's slipper.

The signature is quite obvious, from the pod like shape. And one may notice on the etheric level that from the sole of the pseudo foot or shoe there is an energy that proceeds straight down to the Earth. A connection is set up, and a resonance takes place between the Earth and the plant that is external to its leaves, stem, and roots.

In Lemuria, naturally, this plant was quite amusing. It was loved and used as an important decorative item in many places. It reminded individuals of the inner capacity for dance and joy. However, a great sadness came upon the Lemurians at the point when they recognized that at some future era, this joyousness might leave the dance. The idea was to put it back in some way, to bring it into the plant so that it might evolve with mankind as was appropriate. The joyousness in dance may yet be rediscovered more deeply in individuals, but at this time it is more important to amplify and strengthen internal grace in a person. That is the mode in which the plant now operates.

There is a strengthening in the minor chakras in the feet, the back of the knees, and the hip region. The root and second chakras are also nourished. The meridians in the liver, spleen, bladder, and kidneys are all strengthened. The nadis in the region around the eyes, fingertips, and toes are slightly stimulated. The emotional body is cleansed, and the mental body is stimulated. The cancer and heavy metal miasms are eased, and the eighth and ninth rays are made stronger and clearer for individuals. Positive aspects between the Moon and Venus are excellent indicators for using this herb. Dancers who keep pets may notice that some energy they bring through their bodies are not energies the animals fully understand. This occurs particularly when an animal suffers a minor injury to any part of its body, especially those that affect its ability to walk or run. It is wise then that both of you take some of this herb. The test point is the soles of the feet.

Larkspur

Blue or purple flowers appear on this herb during the summer. This plant is occasionally used as a purgative and insecticide.

There is increased understanding of the animal kingdom and an awareness of the coordinated purposes of various life streams with that of mankind. To some extent, this is specialized in the larkspur flower essence with certain sea creatures. It is sometimes wise to take the herb and flower essence together. The plant grows in the wild near certain animals who are quite comfortable around this plant. Indeed, it is often wise to have larkspur growing in your house if you have pets. It can assist them in becoming more acclimated to the human frame of mind. Its spiritual purpose is to attune mankind to the purposes of the other kingdoms that work with mankind, particularly the animal life streams.

There is greater ability to diagnose or understand what an animal is working with. Sensitive veterinarians will develop more psychic attunement and telepathy when using this herb. However, be aware that animals do not think in the verbal fashion, and telepathy these days tends to imply such. What is transmitted is a picture of the difficulty the animal is struggling with, from its point of view. And this can assist the veterinarian or those who might help heal an animal by providing an accurate diagnosis. It does not assist very much in direct healing, but aids in a deeper understanding while working with animals.

The karmic lesson here is profound for humanity in learning to accept animal life streams. Originally, larkspur was seen as a bridge that the nature spirits associated with this plant created between mankind and all animals. This was an important aspect set up by the Lemurians and an energy that continued into Atlantis. It was quite honored and understood for such a simple purpose. Only near the end of the Atlantean phase was this understanding lost.

The fifth and sixth chakras are activated, particularly when attuning and working with animals. The nadis in the arms and hands are stimulated, and the etheric body is slightly stimulated. Some individuals may find increased attunement to the sixth and seventh rays, especially when they work with animals. Although there are some interesting attributes connecting larkspur to certain planets and fixed stars, this is still a relatively subtle pattern. The test point is the soles of the feet.

Lavender

This shrub produces lilac-colored aromatic flowers. A very prominent essential oil, lavender is often used for stomach and head problems.

The signature coordinates its powerful aroma and the violet ray to yield a spiritual property of greater relaxation in higher states of spiritual ecstasy, oneness with God, and deeper states of meditation. The tensions that may be associated with such states as one returns to normal waking consciousness are eased. This is because the spiritual states of oneness and an inner understanding of God are brought more into the everyday patterns of life. Gradually, daily patterns will be infused with this spirituality. This allows the patterns themselves to be altered and shifted to be more in alignment with God. The ultimate spiritual benefit of this plant is to bring everyday actions into more association with God.

A certain gentleness takes place in men. In women there may be a tendency towards greater strength. This is also because of a greater acceptance and understanding of old age and the way action in the physical world wears out the physical body. Gradually, with such an acceptance, there is actually less fear of old age, particularly in women. As a result of this, there is greater physical stamina, health, and strength.

Sometimes lavender enables an individual to reach much deeper trance states. This can, of course, relate to deep trance channeling and states of hypnosis in which it is desired to change particular habits. The relaxation that takes place as higher consciousness is achieved is often the last and most important step in truly working with these higher energies.

The Lemurians used this herb to achieve ecstatic states. There was an actual release from the physical body of important energies. These energies attracted certain devic forces, and as the Lemurian civilization grew and matured, it was understood that eventually the ability to reach such states would be lost to mankind. The devic spirits volunteered to work with this property, so that mankind could achieve higher ecstatic states at a later time. It was seen then that the relaxation experienced in such states would be critical for mankind to continue to reach these higher states in any form later on. Therefore, activating lavender to preserve higher states of relaxation and ecstasy for the future benefit of humanity was a task willingly taken on by the devic order associated with lavender.

The root, heart, seventh, eighth, ninth, and tenth chakras are all energized and brought into a greater sense of harmony. This creates the possibility for energy to flow in more ecstatic states and for more relaxation to take place. The small intestine meridian is stimulated, all the nadis are enhanced, the emotional body is cleansed, and the gonorrhea miasm is eased. The rays from the seventh upward are brought more clearly into focus. In coordination with joy, it is often necessary to know one's purpose better, and that is where the rays assist. Moreover, there are some connections to the planetoid Chiron. This will be sensed mainly when Chiron is in conjunction or opposition with the Moon. The test point is the top of the head.

Leek

Leek is a popular food that is often cultivated. Leek stimulates the appetite and is a good diuretic.

Spiritually, there is a parallel to garlic in that there is assistance in the birthing process; there is greater awareness of the child to be. Cooked leeks are full of excellent nutrients for the growing child and are often recommended for expectant mothers. Leek, in appearing as a cluster, can bring energy from the Earth more strongly into action, almost as if a birth is taking place. This energy is symbolized in the signature of the plant. What occurs in spiritualizing the birthing process is an easing of the fears of expectant parents, a greater sense of calmness, and the sense that the life that has been before the birth will be continued into the birth. This is the parallel with garlic, that it is one continuum. These energies can be more easily expressed in the child, so it is wise at least once a year for any child to eat some of the actual plant. If cooked, it still transfers some of these spiritual properties.

Those who emphasize variety in a child's food provide the child with a more conscious choice with leek. In early childhood years, there is some benefit in this plant being taken. We are not referring to large quantities, but just the vibration of the substance. After the birth, there is a tendency in some women to have what is termed 'postpartum depression' or difficulty after the birth relating to the loss of the connection, bonding, and deep sense of oneness with the child. Leek eases this by enabling the mother to better see the continuum and understand that the child's life was very strong on a consciousness level even before conception. The mother will better understand that the bond with the child will continue into the child's later years.

The ability to bond with the child in the uterus in enhanced. Of course, this can have a negative aspect. If one is seeking a child but the unconscious is saying, "No I do not wish a child," there can be a conflict. The bonding may bring this more clearly into focus. This can lead to a miscarriage, because the bonding is deep enough so that both child and mother cooperate at the unconscious level. Leek makes this attitude more conscious; as bonding takes place, the unconscious energy that is released becomes conscious. The psychic ability to bond with the child in the uterus can actually take place before conception, but generally, is recommended to start from the period of about three weeks after conception. In that time period, others such as the father may also bond with the child.

In Lemuria, there was an understanding of the sacredness of how leek related to the birth process and the way creation took place. Lifetimes then were far longer, and the lines and divisions between life, birth, and death were not nearly as clear and distinct as they are now. Therefore, the substance was taken by those who were suffering and seeing the possibility of death and knowing that birth would eventually be theirs again. These were the people who brought into this plant the devic energies that continue with it even today to ease the birthing process.

The root, second, and abdominal chakras are given added energy. The conception vessel meridian is stimulated, and the etheric body is strengthened. There is some assistance for animals that traditionally seem to have difficulty in the birthing process, especially horses. The test point is the base of the spine.

Licorice

Licorice is found in northern China and Mongolia. In Chinese medicine, licorice is often used for the throat and a wide range of chest problems.

There is a tendency here to allow deeper states of emotional release in a person. There may be problems due to blocked understanding of one's purpose or difficulty in understanding a relationship, such as the way people are struggling to understand each other. When these energies are held deep within, there may be some difficulties relating to the emotions that come to the surface. Excessive states of anger or fear may result. The use of licorice may affect these blockages, so that an individual is able to release them more easily. In emotional release work, there is often some benefit in using the herb.

A cleansing of the blood also occurs as a result of this release process. This can be of some assistance on the physical level along with other blood cleansers. This herb is generally for those who are more aligned with their spiritual purpose, because a full understanding and use of the emotions is not easily available to those who are not aligned with higher spiritual purpose. Emotions are energy, and that energy is understood and realized as a greater manifestation of God in one's own being when licorice is used. This pure energy is quite useful, and with licorice, one may be able to release it more easily.

Emotions, which might otherwise prevent the development of psychic abilities, are allowed to come to the surface to be worked with and released. This may prevent the development of most psychic abilities. For instance, one who is becoming a conscious channel may develop blockages because of self-doubt. This doubt may be brought more fully into focus by licorice so that you can realize its roots and allow it to be released. This is true for any psychic abilities when emotional blockage prevents their full flowering.

As for the signature, there is the stimulating ability of the taste. It activates enthusiasm, urgency, and many other emotions. It also increases the production of saliva in the mouth. This is symbolic of its etheric ability to stimulate wanting or desiring. It stimulates the formation of emotions on the etheric level. Its karmic purpose is to allow this for mankind, and for mankind to choose it. It is no accident that licorice is a popular flavor for candies and other condiments. It is the emotional level that many individuals need today. Eventually, licorice should be seen by those involved in spirituality and other levels of understanding God as a taste that is too strong, one they do not desire anymore. Then they will know that licorice has served its purpose.

The second and third chakras and the liver meridian are stimulated. There is a tendency for the emotional body to be compacted for a short period of time and then to expand. This affects other subtle bodies as the images and understanding of the emotions takes place. There is some assistance when Jupiter and Mars are in square or opposition; negative aspects associated with this expansiveness and this difficulty with emotions may be eased. The cancer miasm is eased, and the test point is the navel.

Lion's Foot

Found in the eastern United States, lilac-colored flowers appear on these plants in the late summer. It is used to relieve diarrhea and dysentery. The shape of this plant looks like the foot of the lion. The plant stimulates the development of deeper courage. On a higher level, praise develops. This praise strengthens the desire for life. Indeed, in the essential form of beingness, the first thing considered is life, whether one is to be, to experience the properties of life and beingness. This is what the kingdom of air contends with. This property is again nourished when an individual takes this herb. This also provides some of its tonic abilities.

The herb's reputation for treating snakebites is not accurate on a medicinal level. However, on the etheric level, there is some truth here. This is because the plant's juice has the ability to strengthen, deep within the body, the willingness to be. And so the great fear of death that is the first reaction to a snake bite, especially in the adrenal glands, is released. Death is accepted a little more easily. Less attention is placed upon death, which allows greater life force to manifest within the person. This type of courage, this strength of being that is more an appreciation of life, is gathered more strongly within the person as a result of using this herb. This is very useful in spiritual states when patience or trust of what is to happen takes place.

There is an enhanced ability to commune with the nature kingdom. This includes greater telepathy with plants and animals, if this is what the person desires. This develops from a strengthening of a deep sense of praise within a person. Visualize this energy as a powerful sense of love for someone you love dearly, and project that feeling outward to the nature kingdom around you. The herb allows the response to form into a deeper sense of praise. As a result of this, in whatever pathway is most available, you become more aware of the nature kingdom.Welcome the nature kingdom and be aware of the energies of love that you transmit because this is the key to making that contact stronger.

This was one of the early plants used most often in the beginning of time on this planet. The original use for lion's foot in Lemuria was to ease the thought form of fear. However, other plants and techniques were developed to deal with this issue, as it was seen that fear would become more prevalent. After a while, it was seen that understanding fear could lead to a deep sense of praise, towards the original beingness principle. The devic order readily and lovingly took on these characteristics to remind humanity of this, which is its purpose.

The heart chakra is opened, and significant energy is added to the chakra immediately above the head, the eighth chakra. Increased energy flows in the governing vessel meridian, while the nadis throughout the chest are stimulated. The etheric body is cleansed, the emotional body is stimulated, and the causal body is temporarily brought into greater alignment and harmony with the soul body, particularly in relation to the beingness principle. This creates an energy that gradually permeates into the person.

There is a easing of the stellar miasm, and all the rays are slightly enhanced. This herb should sometimes be given to young animals. The ability to assimilate mother's milk is enhanced, and bones and teeth are strengthened. In a similar fashion, the early growth phase for plants is stimulated. It also helps plants assimilate nutrients better. The test point is the bottom of the sternum.

Loosestrife

This perennial grows in swamps, marshes, and other moist places. Dysentery, diarrhea, and fevers are some of the imbalances loosestrife alleviates.

There is an association here on the spiritual level with the element of water. This is obvious because of the plant's habitat. How an individual comes to understand the spiritual lessons of water is an important consideration. Water has the ability to cut through stone, given enough time, but it is also able to fill a container. There are individuals who struggle with such lessons. People are often required to be flexible but also to have great power. This often occurs in management type positions.

Greater understanding is imparted concerning the ability to be fully flexible yet remain strong and focused as to what one can and cannot do. An individual develops extra confidence to get involved in new spiritual activities. One learns to trust the way they work and, at the appropriate time, to share with others in a way that blends personal experiences with that which one has newly learned.

In healing, the energy of pure softness develops. This is very important for many healers who are working with people who have hard muscles, a rigid disposition, or who are struggling with concepts that are binding or chafing. Therefore, despite what healing techniques are used, there is an added softness. What occurs as a result of this is greater flexibility and, ultimately, the inner strength the individual is actually seeking.

In Lemuria, the plant was understood for its ability to transform water. It actually raised its frequency so that individuals near the plant understand the water more directly—where it had been and the things it had worked with. As a result of this, a deep cleansing of the aura took place. However, the physical body was not affected. This was not a medicinal purpose, although it was as close to that as one came in Lemuria, especially in early Lemuria when there was little disease. A sense of joy developed between the plant and the Lemurians, and this became part of the plant's purpose that has continued long after Lemuria. Through attuning to loosestrife, aspects of water can be transferred to humanity. Today, a massage application can be made with loosestrife for athletes, especially runners, to ease tired muscles.

The chakras in the knees, calves, thighs, and the root, second, and third chakras are energized. The kidney meridian is less stressed. This allows the energy from it to transfer into the other meridians, which is often necessary. The emotional body becomes more relaxed, and the radiation miasm is eased. There is a clear connection here to the sign Cancer, which epitomizes many aspects of this watery plant.

There is some benefit in using this plant when there is difficulty with plants being watered too much. Root rot or certain fungal difficulties at the root stem and bottom stem of the plant can result. The use of this herb in small quantities mixed with water can be of some benefit. A tincture at a ratio of one or two drops to ten gallons of water may be sufficient to impart the vibration into the water. The test point is the bottom of the feet.

Loquat

This evergreen fruit tree produces white flowers in the fall. In Chinese medicine, loquat is used to treat the lungs and stomach. The leaves or flowers can be utilized as a tea; however, stronger effects will be noticed from the fruit. Its signature is the unique taste. This engenders an emotional response, so there is a deeper sense of understanding nature and civilization and praise for how civilization can function with nature. Today, this is a temporary sensation. However, it is hoped that occasional exposure to loquat will generate an inner appreciation of the sweetness and bitterness of civilization and co-shared creative reality as a part of daily life. Individuals, as they work with this spiritual energy, may unite in a sense of deeper love. This inner sweetness opens the heart in a way that is a little more grounded, firm, and clear than many other heart opening techniques. It is a way of absorbing and realizing spirituality as it exists, not as you wish it to be. Some images that are incorrect are dispersed, so individuals cut to the truth of the matter, or they see things in a clearer and more loving light.

There is an enhancement of heart energy that may be used for healing and clearheadedness. Counseling may be particularly assisted. Others may be shown a clearer heart's direction when you bring some of this into yourself. As the inner sweetness of loquat is appreciated, there may result an inner heart strength that can withstand very difficult outside circumstances. Individuals who perceive that they are under psychic attack may find this inner heart strengthening to be of great value. What they perceive as an outside attack may simply be released by greater love. Even as they discover what has happened, they may then change their level of vibration so the forces that they perceive as attacking them simply pass through them.

The taste for loquat developed gradually in Lemuria as a loving reward for little children. It was a way the existence of heart opening energy might be that which the children played with. However, gradually, it was perceived that this heart opening that allowed perception of immediate truth might be something necessary for mankind at a later date. Thus, this fruit was given to children in Lemuria so they would work with the devic order of loquat. Some of the childlike attitudes associated with loquat have given it some of its present day capacities. Attributes of youthfulness, childlike attitudes, and ways of remaining youthful and rejuvenated are associated with the fruit. Loquat is sometimes understood to have such properties in Chinese and other oriental medical systems. The devic order associated with loquat brings the heart opening to greater clarity with the clear eyes of the child.

The heart chakra is strengthened, and the eighth chakra is slightly opened. There is a strengthening of the lung, pericardium, heart, and small intestine meridians. The emotional body is cleansed, and the cancer and gonorrhea miasms are eased. The fourth and ninth rays are made clearer for most individuals, and the test point is the center of the chest.

Lungwort

This herb has flowers that turn from rose-colored to blue. As the name suggests, this plant is used to treat various lung and throat problems.

Here we are dealing with the air element. As is evident from the signature of this funnel-shaped flower, some people can etherically almost see the breathing of the plant, the drawing in of pranic force, and its conversion and assimilation through the plant's body. Spiritually, this is extremely helpful because today there are many difficulties in fully utilizing prana. All who work with breath can benefit occasionally by using this herb. Various yoga techniques such as pranayama, kriya yoga, and techniques in which breath is focalized as part of meditation are all enhanced. If taking this herb as a tea, take it anytime up to one hour after such exercises to aid the transfer of energy. Prana, which is everywhere and pours through individuals, is a circuit. It moves through individuals out again into the world and is reabsorbed again and again. This energy is made more available with lungwort.

Prana becomes available in the lungs, moves through the physical body, focuses in the brain, and then transfers as light into the mind. This is a reversal of the usual process by which light moves into thought, then into the brain. What happens is that the mind is stimulated. At a certain point in this process, there are corresponding interchanges of energy into the physical body. As this transfer of energy takes place, prana changes color. This is signified by the fact that the flowers of lungwort change from rose to blue. People doing yoga or who are specifically working with prana should often visualize the air as blue, or electric blue, or a mixture of rose and blue. It is wise to visualize a mixture of these colors, so that those who cannot often attune to blue can absorb the reddish hues that affect the lower chakras. This herb enhances understanding of how breath and pranic force, affect the physical body. This energy is made more assimilable because of increased understanding. There is a transfer of light. Some will simply feel a deeper breathing, while others will be aware of the light.

There is an easing of blockages relating to anger, and the ability to utilize pranic force is enhanced. However, most individuals do not understood this today. Energy can be focused from the breath, by deep inhalation, holding of the breath, and by focusing as if to pour energy from the entire body to the third eye. There is danger in doing this, because blood pressure can go up dramatically. But individuals who clearly have no problem with blood pressure can do this exercise. In holding the breath and focusing energy into the third eye center, one can have a momentary increase in the ability to see auras.

In Lemuria, the plant was observed for its potential to assist the development of the lungs. However, this use did not develop until Atlantean times. Then it was necessary to focus primarily on the flower, because the Atlanteans did not fully understand the plant's capacities. However, in tapping into certain storehouses of old knowledge, such as certain crystals relating to the Lemurian experience, the ability to change this plant took place. The devic kingdom readily accepted the karmic purpose of increasing mankind's lungs to work with pranic force.

The karmic lesson is for this plant to remain intertwined with humanity and to grow with it. There will be a change for humanity in a few hundred years towards even greater lung capacity. It is hoped that this will occur within about two hundred years. Lungwort may be of some benefit on the spiritual level, as the devic spirit incorporates itself as part of this evolutionary change.

The third eye and eighth chakras are enhanced. Of course, the lung meridian is energized, and there is a positive effect on the stomach meridian. The nadis all through the chest and back are stimulated, the mental and emotional bodies are cleansed, and the tuberculosis miasm is eased. The eighth and ninth rays are made clearer. Certain individuals may experience lung difficulty when Mars is negatively aspected to certain planets such as Saturn, or when Mars moves through the first house. These are good times for this herb to be utilized. The test point is the center of the chest.

Magnolia

This tree is found in central China. In Chinese medicine, magnolia is used to treat the spleen, stomach, and lungs.

Through using this plant, one may absorb lessons from past lives in a relaxed state. The odor of the plant is a guiding signature here. It relaxes an individual. Those aligned to spiritual paths and able to work with higher energies may find it beneficial to rest with the aroma of magnolia or with a quantity of the bark as a tea after reflecting on past lives. It is also useful to apply an oil from the bark to the third eye center. This assists in achieving a relaxed attunement with past lives. When past life information is revealed to an individual, there is a natural tendency to build walls around it, to try very hard to understand it, and to struggle with it. This is because there are innate fears associated with such lives. You can send loving energy to the beings you have been, but sometimes even this is not enough.

If you are delving into past life areas in which the information is not clear, this herb may help. Sometimes, when you are doing past life hypnosis or various conscious channeling techniques, blockages develop in which the full information cannot be assimilated because there are no longer languages or cultural expressions of the techniques as used in ancient times. With magnolia, the lesson or message can be absorbed in a more relaxed fashion. The ability develops to go beyond one past life to connect it to other lives. Sometimes, one life is seen as a core lifetime, and through that core life, other past lives are perceived. The full absorption of the messages from a core life becomes easier to understand. Past life therapists also develop a deeper understanding of themselves which they can apply to their clients.

In Lemuria, the plant was understood to assist with astral travel. Individuals slept beneath this tree, inviting the devic kingdom to be with them. They relaxed deeply, almost becoming part of the tree, and then imagined another time or place and journeyed to it. Later in the Lemurian phase, past lives and their significance became much clearer. It was seen that the devic spirit could be invited to assist in a better understanding of past lives. It took this on a bit reluctantly because it saw the difficulties that mankind was creating for itself around this issue.

In the future, it is hoped that the karmic purpose of this plant will again be revealed to humanity and that safe, deeply relaxed astral travel will again be permitted. But it will take a much safer Earth for this to happen. Right now, certain dangers are present for astral travelers. For example, when an individual brings their astral form into a highly emotional area such as a war zone, the fighting and hatred can strongly affect the astral body, bringing a great deal of fear and difficulty back into an individual as they sleep. The main difficulty is in astral work with emotional levels of the world. The current purpose of the plant is to assist in a deeper understanding of past life information. Ultimately, it is also to assist in deeper levels of astral travel.

The heart and fifth chakras are brought into greater harmony. This creates a sense of relaxation as one looks into the past. The astral body is very relaxed as is the mental body. The triple warmer, heart, and gall bladder meridians are strengthened. The effects of the third and fourth rays are strengthened, and the test point is the navel.

Ma Huang (Ephedra)

Popular in Chinese medicine, this plant is found in northern China. Ma huang eases asthma, fever, and coughs.

There is a definite enhancement of the physical body's ability to utilize prana that is drawn in by the breath. Yogic processes are enhanced. This is different from other herbs that assist in pranayama and prana absorption in that it allows the spiritual energy drawn in with the pranic force to be concentrated into a well-entrained vibration. Instead of it just being forms of prana which nourish the body in many ways, it becomes a coherent force. The way this energy is absorbed at the moment of breathing can be easily influenced by the mind. That this was understood by the ancient Chinese is shown the way ma huang was often given. As a being was seeking to rid themselves of a cold or cough, or when they saw the effects of the imbalance on their body, they visualize clearly the dry, clearing, and opening effect that they wished. This definitely enhances the use of ma huang.

When ma huang is utilized with pranayama, deep breathing techniques, and other various ways people work with the breath, there is a definite enhancement of the ability to utilize pranic force instantly. This can be extremely useful for people who need a quick boost of their energy level. There are no debilitating side effects, such as can develop when taking stimulants. Instead, it is the pranic force that is the stimulant, and ma huang simply allows it to be more easily drawn into the physical body. There is also a strengthening of visualization states as a natural result of the way this entrainment, or standing wave pattern of the thought form, becomes more energized. Concentration also improves.

There are certain keynotes and times when not to use ma huang. It is often stated that it should not be used in pregnancy. Its powerful energy may cause a miscarriage, because this concentrated focus actually pulls energy out of the fetus and into the lungs, the mind, or other places where it is being directed. It is not wise to use ma huang if there is a great dryness because it will naturally tend, by this focusing of energy and concentration, to release pranic force in water form from the body.

There is an enhanced ability to concentrate at a much deeper state of meditation that is also energetic in nature. Individuals who utilize rapid physical motion and yet use this for a meditative state should often use this herb. This could include jogging, a powerful yogic dance, or what is called 'trance dance.' A greater focusing of energy in the person can result. With breathing and yogic work, generally take a very small quantity, perhaps less than a quarter of a teaspoon in a cup of water in a tea form. The reason for the small quantity is to impart to the individual working in this area only a general sense of this concentration and movement of pranic force. Then it will assist in their own visualization as they do this work.

Anyone working in movement, particularly when it relates to spiritual functioning, will benefit from ma huang when they are seeking to increase lung capacity, to draw in greater pranic force. It may also be utilized in times of sickness. However, when it is utilized simply to gain greater stamina, there will not generally be much improvement.

The plant appears in some ways to look similar to the branches and stems of the alveoli as they branch throughout the lungs. There will also be tasted with ma huang a sensation, almost emotional in nature, that relates directly to the element of air; the wind itself appears to be captured within ma huang.

In ancient times in Lemuria, it was observed how the wind changed as it passed through the branches and leaves of this plant. This was particularly true with the stem branching points, sometimes called the crotch of the stem. It was as if the wind was changed and nourished by the plant. In understanding this, a subtle connection became established between the devic order associated with ma huang and the Lemurians, in which they saw that the wind and the plant seemed to work in harmony. The question was asked, "Can these energies of working with the air element, with wind, be coordinated with mankind?" The question was posed to the plant which it took about fifty years to answer. It took so long partly because it was not entirely certain that it could coordinate with mankind and the devic order had quite a bit of difficulty in discerning this. The eventual answer was yes, but the negative effects of the drying process on the body, such as during pregnancy, made it clear that ma huang would only gradually come into use with humanity. This is a very slow process. The karmic purpose of the plant is not just to work and coordinate with humanity. It is also to understand the wind element, to work with it deeply. Therefore, you will see that there are many applications of ma huang and many ways it will be utilized in the future, because it has as its essence the purest, most essential form of the air element.

There is a release of energy from the third and fourth chakras, and a connection between the fifth chakra and the lungs. Presently, this is more specific to the lungs. In the future, some of ma huang's energy may be released more to the fifth chakra. There is a definite strengthening of the lung meridian that is transferred to a number of the other meridians. Sometimes this can be felt, after taking ma huang, as a slight sensation of warmth at the top of the head where all of the meridians join together. The nadis in the chest area and the etheric and mental bodies are stimulated, and there is a release of the radiation miasm. A greater clarity of focus in the third, fourth, and eighth rays will be noted in some people. The most positive aspects of Mars are brought into much greater clarity by ma huang. When Mars is in trine or in the sign of Scorpio or Aries, it is wise to use this herb. The test point is the center of the chest.

Mango

This popular fruit tree produces pink, red, or yellow flowers in the spring.

There is a significant enhancement of a person's idea of what spirit is. The shape of the fruit signifies this, as its signature. When fully ripe, there is a sweetness on the outside, and a strong inner center. It is also well attached to the rest, as if the inner idea, that which you know as your inner being, is firmly attached to your outer belief structure.

Mango is useful to individuals seeking to change their belief structures. Though they have been trained in a certain way and told of many things, when it comes to spirituality and spiritual investigation there is often a tendency to resist new belief structures. This will be eased significantly for many people. This is more applicable to westerners who do not regularly eat mango. When it is a regular part of the diet, as in Hawaii or southeast Asia, where it is more common, people may find that this spiritual property has led them to a sense of deeper grace as they accept with an open mind many possibilities of different spiritual paths. This belief restructuring is a tendency that will be incorporated in their makeup after a time.

For most westerners it would usually take two and a half to three months or so of eating mango on a regular basis for this inner spiritual reserve to build up. As part of this process, there will be a natural questioning of inner beliefs. This is good. When it is completed, one will have a long-lasting, deeper ability to work with outside belief structures. This new trait may last for the rest of your life.

One important core concept of the universe is that you are a part of it, are firmly enmeshed with it, and are aware of its beauty, sweetness, and uniqueness. The fruit of mango gives this spiritual property most strongly to individuals. There can be an added gracefulness in accepting new ideas. One has a willingness not to criticize others for their belief structures, but to hear them out completely before revealing your own views. There are, of course, some properties of the flower essence transferred into the entire plant, but this particular property is more concentrated in the fruit, and that is the recommended part to eat.

There is increased ability to be in a state of telepathic empathy. This is a little different from the usual telepathy or empathic skills. It is a way you truly see through another's eyes. Because of the warming and loving effects of mango energy, there is a strengthening of the heart. When you are in someone else's skin, you are not using so much the physical eyes or even the third eye to view the world, but the heart's eyes. Seeing through another's heart, allows you to truly receive the inner message of their belief structures. You understand not just what they say, but who they are and how they feel. This is a powerful empathic skill that can be useful in counseling, assisting children, and working with people in whom psychic abilities are emerging in uncomfortable or difficult ways. Naturally, other levels of clairvoyance are enhanced.

It is a plant of great beauty and inner strength, but in the beginning its fruit was much smaller. It was seen that symbolism would be necessary to increase the ability to receive thought impressions and ideas from many points of view, so that people's universal belief system could be larger and larger. The pit of the fruit was allowed to grow. Those Lemurians who influenced this process were aware of many of mango's characteristics. They saw that these properties would be transferred naturally, as people who were attracted to it for its pleasant taste and nourishing benefits to the intestine used it at regular times in the future.

There is a strengthening of the heart and third chakras and of the etheric and emotional bodies. There is an increase of energy in the kidney meridian, which cleanses the physical body. The large intestine meridian is enhanced, the nadis in the chest area are stimulated, and there is a release of the psora miasm. The fourth and tenth rays are enhanced and made clearer, and the test point is the sternum.

Marshmallow

This hardy perennial produces pink or white flowers. It has long been used to ease inflammations of the mouth and throat and as a poultice.

Using this herb allows individuals a place in which they may soften the way they speak and the way they understand life and relate to others. This is particularly useful in extreme or difficult states of anger or irritation—especially when there is a spiritual purpose involved, and the individual is struggling towards greater love and understanding of another but the anger or hatred gets in the way. This energy can be converted into enthusiasm. There are many techniques for doing this. However, when the individual has these capacities for nurturing, softness, and love, and sees that these are being withdrawn or pushed aside by stronger negative emotional states, marshmallow is indicated. The individual should chew some of the root, if possible, and then meditate for a while. Allow the heart opening to become warm and radiant and the energies of love to become focused on someone you care deeply about, instead of focusing on the person you feel anger at. You do not have to give up the anger, but simply experience loving that individual for that time period. It is a mere transference, by will, of emotions from one being to another. We are not expecting this to have a profound effect. However, when done repeatedly, inner softness may return. Marshmallow assists deeply in this. This is evident in the signature of a sweetened taste and the way an individual may indeed feel softened simply tasting this herb.

There is a great strengthening of the bond from the heart to a little child. When you are teaching psychic abilities to children who are manifesting such talents, there is some benefit to using marshmallow. Part of this is that, as you speak about these things to a child, your own unconscious blocks—fears, angers, and difficulties with psychic abilities—will surface. A child will know and feel them unconsciously along with the transference of the techniques, abilities, and ideas that flow between you.

In Lemuria, a great deal of love was associated with all of the plant kingdom. Many plants were able to respond to this, and marshmallow was one. However, it was not until the end of the Lemurian phase that it was seen that this softening would become very important for humanity. Indeed, it was extremely difficult for most Lemurians to even imagine that states of hatred, anger, or fear could stand in the way of deep love and deep spiritual attraction. However, the devic order was able to provide a sense of stability, which was almost like an insurance policy. The energy associated with marshmallow was periodically focused on by the Lemurians and then made available throughout the planet for all species in all lands. This energy lay dormant until it was needed again by mankind, which took place near the end of the Atlantean phase and continues to the present day.

The third chakra is relaxed, while the heart and throat chakras are energized. What occurs as a result is a flow of energy into these two areas, and usually a resonance takes place in which the energy then moves back into the heart chakra. The liver meridian is eased, and when energy accumulates there, it disperses more easily. The emotional body is cleansed, and the fourth and seventh rays are more focused. There is a clear connection with Mars, particularly when Mars and Venus are in square or opposition. Difficulties are eased then by taking marshmallow. In any trine between Mars and Venus, the deeper lessons associated with the emotions one is struggling with in a relationship may be much more easily assimilated. The test point is the center of the chest.

Matico

Eight feet tall, this shrub is native to South America. It is used to alleviate diarrhea, dysentery, and ulcers.

Matico has the property of drawing in powerful energy. This is how it appears to one with etheric sight. The height of the plant is a direct consequence of this. When you look at the ratio of its height to its roots, it is surprising that it grows as well as it does. This symbol is the signature. It can be used as an aphrodisiac when the sexual energy is drawn up through the body. It is like the kundalini energy moving up the spine. This is a more holistic sexual energy than might be conceptualized in the usual way an aphrodisiac is used or understood.

A compacted, cylindrical energy is created in the etheric body of the plant. There is a similar pattern in man's etheric body. To some who are sensitive to this, it can be felt when putting the hands within a few inches of the plant. A swirling vortex of cylindrical-shaped energy is created that extends upwards, sometimes twenty feet over the plant, and down through its root system. A swirling energy is drawn into and out of the plant. When the herb is taken internally and one becomes more aware of this energy, it increases the way the ray pouring into them supplements the physical body, giving greater energy. It also activates greater coordination in all the chakras.

There is a similarity here to the flow of energy through the governing vessel channel or sushumna of the spine and the way this energy pours through the body. When this energy is focused, particularly with the higher chakras, upon spiritual understanding and a deeper sense of oneness with God, it can be transmuted from what is essentially a sexual energy into an energy that is very spiritual, awakening, and enlightening. There may be a sense of warmth as a result of this. It is very important that people have an awareness of how good it is to experience this energy in body, mind, and spirit.

The ability to energize is enhanced, so techniques involving ritualistic energy of a sexual nature, such as in tantra, are definitely aided. However, it is recommended that an individual utilize this energy in other ways, such as in clearing energy. Imagine an energy like an arc, perhaps ten feet in radius, coming from the top of your head. The energy arches gradually and lands on the Earth near you, nourishing a person, healing a plant, or working with an animal. It could also be spread, as it pours out of the crown chakra, to accompany or work with a group of people. Since the higher chakras are stimulated, after such a creative visualization, the energy should be drawn in through that arc, and into the body by a deep inhalation. Then the circuit of energy is more easily completed. When awakening the higher centers, especially the third eye and crown chakra, there is benefit in using this herb. It does not matter exactly how these centers are awakened. If striving for clairvoyance or a greater sense of oneness with others, creative visualization is specifically enhanced by applying this herb.

The karmic pattern of the plant was established independently, as if almost on its own. The Lemurians created a powerful example of the way will was able to pour through their bodies and merge with the loving energy of the Earth, moving with it and assisting in others' healing. This energy occasionally formed into a rodlike pattern moving into and out of the spine. Since this plant was beginning to form somewhat similar to this, it began to imitate this process. The Lemurians recognized that this could become a reminder to others of this energy that could be utilized in the most basic functions, for reproduction and use of enhanced sexual functioning to bring greater states of enlightenment. This was requested of the plant. The devic order of the plant gladly took this on, and that is its karmic purpose.

There is a temporary alignment of all twelve chakras. This is quite temporary, and will generally take place about ten minutes after ingestion of the herb and usually last for half a minute or so. In this temporary alignment, it is wise for an individual to visualize the energy pulled from the feet through the physical body, through the root chakra, and all the way up through the top of the head. This is similar to the arc of energy we mentioned before. This exercise stimulates all the chakras, especially the root chakra.

There is a strengthening of the bladder, gall bladder, and governing vessel meridians. The nadis at the very top of the head, back of the knees, and soles of the feet are energized. The causal, soul, and integrated spiritual bodies are augmented. The connection between the mental and causal bodies is strengthened, the gonorrhea miasm is alleviated, and the eleventh ray is activated.

There is a connection between Mars and Chiron, particularly when they are positively aspected. An individual who has them in trine in the natal chart should work with this herb. A person stimulated slightly by this herb could project healing energy into an animal, especially if the animal is sick. This is also true for plants. It is wise, however, when using it that your subtle bodies not be in contact with the subtle bodies of the plant or animal; stand at least seven feet away from the plant or animal. In most cases, ten feet away is better. This corresponds to the ten foot radius or arc of energy referred to earlier. The test point is the top of the head.

Meadowsweet

This plant is often called queen of the meadow. Salicylic acid, from which aspirin is derived, was first isolated from this plant's flower buds in 1839. It is an astringent, antiseptic, and antirheumatic.

Energy that flows through the body is enhanced by this plant. This is particularly important on spiritual levels, when energy towards a project is dwindling. This plant has a certain degree of inner or innate intelligence, so it should often be recommended for various herbal blends. At the same time, its angular stems impart the signature of the ability to change direction, to utilize various possibilities in different ways, and yet maintain an alignment with the original purpose.

The herb is useful for individuals involved with groups, especially when there is a common energy towards a given project. This is particularly true when it is of a spiritual nature. The flexibility to continue with a project is given. If you are working on a project, especially one with a spiritual end, and encounter obstacles in which the usual patterns of intuition, understanding other points of view, or working with other individuals have been unsuccessful, this herb can be useful. It may give you a new direction, an entirely new place to start, or stimulate your finding this inside yourself.

There is increased ability to be flexible and change direction. This greatly enhances the intuitive process. Many individuals need only to be exposed to other points of view to know that taking new directions is possible. Intuition is not only enhanced but cemented within a person, as if they acknowledge that it is possible for the intuitive process to be strengthened. Willingness to see a problem right to the very root of it may be improved by the use this herb.

The necessity to be flexible and, at the same time, to have a strong or powerful energy was an important attribute of the leaders of the Lemurian civilization. It was what made them the leaders. They were united telepathically, and it was not always necessary for leadership in the usual sense. A strengthening was seen in the way energy was made stronger as an

example for others. The leaders were asked to bring some of those qualities to bear upon the devic order. This plant was chosen because it also
has the capacities of leadership and coordination. Today, it is useful in
various combinations, particularly when dealing with arthritis. For individuals aware of the necessity for flexible leadership, some of these ancient
Lemurian qualities may still be present. This is not an easy thing; it is not
the usual way of leading. It is more what is currently termed management,
when the group does the essential effort. However, the thought form for
this flexibility was the most important attribute of Lemurian leaders, and
this is the energy that the plant primarily took on and thus is its karmic
purpose.

Because of the presence of salicylic acid and other important medicinal
substances, it is wise not to abuse this plant. Do not take it for the spiritual
properties in large quantities, concentrated doses, or for regular periods of
time.

There is a stimulation of the throat chakra, and energy flow through
this chakra can be useful. It pours down to the hands and nourishes the
neck in many different ways. The meridians that run through the throat,
the triple warmer meridian, and the nadis in the throat are energized, as are
the etheric and mental bodies. For some individuals, the effect on the mental body will not be discernable, but others may be able to work with that
mental energy in a more concrete fashion. The gonorrhea miasm is eased,
and the fifth, seventh, and eighth rays are made clearer. There is some
strengthening of the impact of Uranus, particularly as it progresses through
the natal chart. When it is negatively aspected, and one is involved in a
project of some importance, this herb should be used. The test point is the
base of the throat.

Milk Thistle

Native to Europe, this herb produces large purple flowers in the summer. Recently, it has become increasingly popular in the United States for
its impact on the liver.

A juice exudes from milk thistle, which helps explain its name. This is
its signature, and this milk has a rather stimulating effect. On the spiritual
level, this herb stimulates greater forgiveness within a person. This has a
powerful effect, as if the energy of another being is pouring through you, a
being who is greater and more forgiving than you could imagine yourself
to be. This also has a powerful cleansing effect on the emotional body.
There may be a strengthening of many organ systems in the body. And indeed, this is why it has the holistic effect of working on so many organ
levels at once.

With this greater release, a sense of loneliness is eased. This is more
than emotional loneliness. The plant originated early in the Lemurian
phase. The complete understanding of soul division was then not yet a part

of the collective unconscious. The oneness of all things was more known and felt. This is the essential core of forgiveness, that "if it were not for my circumstances or my environment, I might be you and do the same thing that you did. Therefore, it is easy for me to forgive you." That is the conceptualization or affirmation associated with the thought form of forgiveness.

This oneness is also personified in the way this plant now appears. It seems as if you would not want to touch it. It looks prickly and keeps you away like a cactus. Yet deep within it, the juice has a stimulating and forgiving effect. This is a paradox for people, and this is its karmic purpose. It is as if providing this allows individuals to decide for themselves whether they choose to be separate or to find a deep forgiveness and thus join humanity.

The psychic abilities stimulated by this plant include merging, greater telepathy, and a feeling of oneness with others. This forgiveness principle can also be applied to the misuse of any psychic power. Individuals seeking to change matter, to alter its form or shape, can more easily forgive themselves if they have misused this energy in the past. For example, alchemists who have abused their power would benefit from this herb.

Strengthening the emotional body takes place in a holistic manner, enabling it to come into greater resonance with the etheric and mental bodies. This has a powerful effect on the heart, which is stimulated secondarily by the action of the subtle bodies. This effect may come and go. It may change with the diurnal and nocturnal cycles a person experiences.

The minor chakras on the soles of the feet and palms of the hands as well as the gall bladder, kidney, and liver meridians are directly stimulated. There is also some release of energy throughout the back region, particularly throughout the bladder meridian. The cancer miasm is eased, and the fourth ray is particularly energized. Some aspects of Venus are made more easily available to individuals. Times in which Venus and Saturn are in square or opposition are excellent times to utilize this plant.

Animals often need this plant, partly as a self-medication and often just to experience forgiveness in themselves. It might be wise, from time to time, to add a small amount of it in juice form to an animal's food, or give it the seeds to chew on if it wishes. The whole plant should not be provided, as the animal might injure itself trying to get at the seeds or fibrous juicy part of the plant. The test point is the center of the chest.

Milkweed

Growing to six feet, this herb produces purple flowers in the summer. Milkweed is used to treat the kidneys and is an emetic and purgative. It can be poisonous in large quantities. It is called milkweed because it produces a milky substance.

This plant imparts a deep sense of nurturing in some individuals. It can be difficult at times for men to understand the nurturing or loving side of themselves. And women may sometimes struggle against this, as if in taking care of others they neglect to take care of themselves. This involves not only the nurturing of children but the nurturing of the child within an individual. It is also seeing the child in others. Nurturing and caring for others, as God cares for humanity, is one aspect of the way a person can be. In accepting this, your innate nature toward such nurturing is manifested.

The ability to release problems and truly love another individual and oneself is enhanced. This involves a deep set of psychic abilities that is very helpful for the development of many other capacities. The ability to send energy of a feeling and nurturing nature to an individual that one normally does not care for also develops.

The Lemurians discovered a technique by which the watery substance of milkweed could be vibrationally changed. The sound vibrations applied allowed milkweed to become easily assimilable by a person. This allowed an energy of the Earth to permeate into a person's body, yet it had a certain nourishing capability as well. Only small quantities of it were necessary, but the vibration was changed in a similar way that cooking is now used to change various herbs, plants, and food substances so they are assimilable by humans. What took place then, when the vibrational change occurred with milkweed, was that its life stream was affected. The devic spirits associated with it reflected on what was happening to the plant and what was working then for humanity. The question asked was, "What can be contributed?" It was seen that this nurturing ability would be useful in the future, so the plant and associated nature spirits willingly took on the task of developing this nurturing ability in mankind. This is the karmic purpose of milkweed.

The second, third, and fourth chakras are coordinated better, causing more energy transfer and deeper states of relaxation concerning issues of nurturing. The stomach meridian and nadis in the hands are energized. There is a slight benefit for mothers giving massages to children with milkweed. The emotional body is slightly cleansed, and the syphilitic miasm is eased. There is some enhancement of nurturing abilities when planets one has negative aspects to pass through the sign of Cancer. The test point is the base of the throat.

Mouse Ear

This plant is found in the eastern United States. Yellow flowers appear during the summer. It is used for liver, throat, and spleen problems.

This herb softens the etheric body as well as the physical and mental bodies. This creates a deep seated healing that comes to the surface. This is why mouse ear has so many different applications. It also symbolizes the mouse—its small size yet its great power because of the way mice influence the environment. There are many areas in the forest, for instance, in which they play an intrinsic ecological role. Individuals begin to recognize their own role in life, a greater sense of humility is created, and an inner sense of the self manifests.

This inner sense is not always understood. It is not just a matter of recognizing what you cannot do; it is the way your whole being exhibits humility in what you do that is received by others. This way of humbleness is well respected in the natural kingdom. It makes no statement about itself except by what it does. Therefore, the ability to trust oneself more deeply is made very powerful.

There is an enhanced ability to make a temporarily telepathic link with another individual. With humility, relaxation, and absorption, the inner message of another person may emerge. Besides the slight enhancement of the usual forms of telepathy in which an idea or an image is transferred, you recognize the inner being of the person more easily. There can be a great joy as a result of this, and this joyousness can become deeply ingrained. It is also useful in easing fears about telepathy. For instance, when individuals develop psychically a little faster than they had thought they should, or when they make mind-to-mind links more often than they thought they were capable of and fear results, mouse ear is indicated.

Its particular shape and form reminds one of the many characteristics of the mouse. In its softness, there is also the sense of multiplicity, that is, fecundity. Mouse ear is able to replicate itself and grow fairly easily in a number of different environments. This is again the essence of humility. As Christ said, "the meek shall inherit the Earth."

In Lemuria, this plant had many different uses, but it appeared to be quite helpful as individuals began to recognize the transition through adolescence into adulthood. Then the ego state was extremely stressed, even as in the current time period. We do not specifically recommend mouse ear today except for highly evolved individuals making the transition from adolescence to adulthood because many of these ancient properties have been lost in the plant. In Lemuria, it was played with and was amusing to those who enjoyed it, and it was used in certain rituals. The devic order associated with this plant gradually came into confluence with the Lemurians around this plant, and ego issues where humility became more important were then considered by the Lemurians as a whole. The assignment was made for this humility to be more firmly ingrained with the devic order, and that is its current purpose today.

There is an opening of the root and third chakras. The liver meridian is significantly balanced, the nadis in the fingertips are energized, and there is a strengthening of the emotional, mental, and etheric bodies. There is an easing of the syphilitic miasm, and a strengthening of fifth, sixth, and seventh rays. There is some connection to negative aspects of various planets to Venus. In particular, aspects of square and opposition between Neptune and Venus are eased. In mankind's past, this plant was used to work with the mouse kingdom, but these patterns will not work very well today. The test point is the wrist.

Myrrh

This tree is found in east Africa. Myrrh has long been used as an ingredient in tooth powder and as a stimulant.

This herb has been well known in legends for the last few thousand years for its ability to align Christ consciousness with aspects of a person seeking to love others more and to understand oneself better. However, these aspects on a spiritual level also extend into areas of which most individuals have no conscious understanding or recollection. It is the energy by which, before being born, they created various life tasks and purposes to accomplish in the coming life. This is the symbolism of the gifts to Christ of frankincense and myrrh. The way this operates with people is to illustrate for them more clearly their unique gifts. This has a great psychic effect, but spiritually what occurs is an alignment with the God nature of an individual. Most people do not appreciate themselves on such a level. With myrrh, people learn to view these gifts and to understand these higher abilities.

Myrrh is most easily taken in the aromatherapy version and should usually be applied to the forehead. However, it has a greater impact if taken in the herb form as a tea or chewed once or twice a week, because then myrrh can penetrate into an individual unconsciously, and people will not be so clearly aware of it. That which you know as your spiritual gifts are usually called your talents. As you come to know and become acquainted with them, your attitude about them changes. This changing attitude is what is enhanced by myrrh.

The willingness for an individual to put their energy into new psychic abilities without fear and to make rapid progress with them is enhanced. This is notably true regarding the ability to understand where things are located and to find lost objects or people. One learns to better use psychic gifts in which one needs to see clearly into the past or future or to see objects which are far away.

If someone is exploring an area of psychic development, and they begin to have second thoughts about the process, it would often be best to take frank. Those more interested in developing psychic abilities from a more spiritual perspective should often use myrrh.

The smell of myrrh is part of its signature, but also those opening clairvoyantly may see pure spiritual energy pour into this herb. It is similar to the way the rays work as potential energy fields pouring into humans. This pattern is a little clearer with myrrh because the vibration of the plant draws in such high energy.

In Lemuria, these energies were perceived, especially at night. The way energy poured into the plant was praised and loved; it was seen that in mankind's future this higher energy attunement would be needed. However, the devic order associated with myrrh was simply shown this light to know itself better. It took a long time before the herb was really used. Only in the later Atlantean phase was part of this higher alignment recognized. However, in entering the age of Pisces and the focus upon Christ energy, more and more individuals became attracted to myrrh. Increasingly, its full energy is being permitted to be used, partly because its vibration is striking certain resonances so that higher energies may be felt more easily within the plant.

The seventh chakra and soul body are energized, and the connection between the causal and mental bodies is enhanced. The stellar miasm is slightly eased, and the seventh, eighth, ninth, and tenth rays work more easily with myrrh. There is a positive connection to the planetoid Chiron, which is associated with Christ consciousness. When Chiron is positively affecting an individual, use myrrh in any of its forms. The test point is the medulla oblongata.

Nasturtium

Native to South America, this annual produces flowers with many colors. Nasturtium stimulates the appetite and is good for the blood cells.

The spiritual properties activated include the enhancement of joy within an individual. Part of this is because blood cell development is enhanced, and emotions that stimulate joy in the body tend to enhance the production of red blood cells. This has been shown by those who study mood states and the ability of the body to heal itself. The state of joy is also imparted by the taste of nasturtium. Nasturtium can be eaten newly picked from the ground and is sometimes mixed in salads. The taste stimulates in the saliva the production of various chemicals that impart this sense of joy, or an uplifting and lightening quality. When an individual takes nasturtium, the Earth's energy and the vibrations of the wide variety of minerals in the plant are brought into greater coordination. This resonates with the joyousness of the plant in its willingness to now work with humans. This is a relatively new development. More and more focus on nasturtium as a food may result over the next ten or fifteen years. As a result, this joyousness and karmic purpose of the plant will be enhanced and will move to another stage.

The joy associated with nasturtium extends deep into an individual, especially affecting dance and movement. There can be new ways to understand the awakening to God's joy in loving a human, to see the silly things that humans do, and the perspective people may take in looking at the world and understanding themselves. These properties may give rise to a humorous frame of mind. It is not only that humor is encouraged, but the joy of existence is made more clearly available. Sometimes, people desperately cling to deep states of meditation, following a guru intensively, or experience deep spiritual attunement. They become frustrated because they do not understand why they are doing this but feel drawn to do it almost unconsciously. This plant gives greater perspective on this process, and a tendency may develop for these people to laugh at themselves, to 'lighten up.'

A much clearer perception of the light energy or life force in other people develops. This is useful when you are healing or counseling another person, because the light energy is easier to evaluate and work with. This evaluation must take place at the heart center and not with the mind. You will know that you can say provocative things to those with a strong life energy. With those whose light is not so strong, you can use nasturtium to see and know them. You would be gentler with these people. This is an important intuitive ability for those who counsel and heal.

The plant's use for enhancing joy made this one of the staple foods in Lemuria. The energies associated with the plant could be drawn directly into a person without harming the plant. It was the plant's contribution. It posed the essential question through its devic order to the Lemurians, "Would this be of use later? Will humans always assimilate our energy in such a fashion?" The clear answer was that yes, people probably would need to eat the food substance to activate the plant's properties. The plant willingly allowed the devic spirit to make the minerals of the Earth more available on a physical level in the plant so that indeed this could take place in the future.

Its karmic purpose is to bring this joyousness to mankind, but over the next twenty years or so to allow this to change. Individuals will make this sense of joy more conscious in themselves and thus gain a greater perspective of the world. In one sense, nasturtium is the plant of peaceful action, a way in which individuals, by the use of this joyousness provide a greater perspective for each other and enhance the possibilities for peace on the planet. When you take the bigger view of things in love and joy, many individuals are affected and work together to help each other. This greater perspective is often all that is needed for simple and logical choices to be made. That is why it is hoped that this substance will be ingested as a food more often in the future.

The third, fourth, and fifth chakras, the gall bladder meridian, and the nadis in the hands and feet are energized. The astral and emotional bodies are able to communicate more easily, and the etheric body is strengthened. The third, fifth, and eighth rays are made clearer for an individual, and the test point is the base of the throat.

This is one plant that animals are drawn to and will take when necessary. It is wise, once a year or so, to make nasturtium available for domesticated animals. If they consume it rapidly or eat all that you provide, continue providing the plant. This is not only for its mineral content, but also because these creatures are connected to each other on a spiritual level worldwide and sometimes need this perspective. This is not the same as the mental understanding of joy that can sometimes happen with nasturtium for a human, but it is there nevertheless in the forms that animals work with. When animals leave the physical body, they do so more easily than people, and they rejoin the overall thought form or soul stream of animals more easily than do people. The soul of animals is not so differentiated as with people. Nasturtium can also be provided to animals when they are dying, but it is more important to offer it to them at various times over the years.

Olive

This Mediterranean tree produces fragrant, white flowers. It is a popular Bach flower with an oil that is commonly used in food.

A great condensation of energy takes place here. This means that individuals who seek to work with energy condensed in any of its forms can be aided by this plant. This is obvious in the continuing need for greater energy in the physical body, as olive oil is now used more and more extensively and appreciated for its interesting culinary properties. What happens in this condensation of energy is that a greater strength for one's purpose is allowed. One can concentrate greater energy to accomplish a task.

However, there will generally be some difficulty. An acceleration of blockages towards achieving a task can take place. The power unleashed by this process is directed in a correct manner; it is coordinated with the heart, in a way in which loving energy allows this concentration of energy and strength to take place with a person so that others are not harmed. On the level of sensation, the taste of the olive, olive oil, or even the roots and flower of this tree can impart these vibrations. As for the signature of olive, there is a full concentration of an extremely strong oily substance and the condensation into a particularly dense fruit. The fruit or berry is the signature.

There is also an association with science. What occurs relates to the particular shade of green that is sometimes seen in this fruit; those seeking scientific discovery experience greater understanding of God through science. There are individuals who have completely forgotten about this, such as those involved in nuclear weapons development. These individuals will be affected slightly by the use of olive in any of its forms towards a deeper understanding of just what they do. For science itself is compacted energy, a true concentration on a given problem to yield certain results. That compaction and concentration of energy is very important, and in mankind's current state of development is depended upon greatly by society for results. It is said over and over that you must specialize in order to work, you must focus your energy in order to produce results. This is not always true, of course, for many great results take place by integrating many levels of information. But this concentration can drain an individual's higher energies, and that is when olive is of some benefit.

Olive can even be considered a tranquilizer, but the tranquilizing effects are relatively temporary. They take place when it is consumed. However, the spiritual effects take place gradually and in a much more subtle manner. They are not compacted energy, but the ability to concentrate energy is enhanced.

There is an enhanced ability to focus energy into a specific meditation, into a ball of light, or into pinpoint areas. There is enhanced use of acupuncture, when an individual seeks to focus energy in the acupuncture process. Olive oil, of course, is utilized in massage, and when acupressure is combined with massage, olive oil is of some benefit. This is partly because energy is being focused by one individual into another.

Olive has long been a plant of many uses. However, in Lemuria the plant was not used as a food substance. It was used for its decorative capacities because the berry or fruit was not seen as particularly beneficial for the Lemurian people. It was also seen that, at some point in the future, it would be necessary for mankind. However, even through Atlantis, the full use of this plant was not developed. Ultimately, as energy and civilization developed in the Mideast, brought on by the concentration of intelligent energy by the pyramids, this plant came into its own. The plant's devic order, which had by then learned much of the movement of energy by the various civilizations on Earth, was able to more easily bring this energy to mankind. The plant was recognized almost magnetically. People were drawn to it and found many important uses for it.

In Egypt, olive was often used in ritual, because of its gentle odor and because of its ability to smooth digestive functioning. Olive symbolized some of the merging of energy that is often necessary in a ritual, bring together many different people with their different beliefs and values. There is a sense of deep unconscious peace. Olive was seen as a symbol of peace and for uniting. The idea of the olive branch as a symbol of peace goes back to even before Egypt.

In Lemuria, the olive branch was used in games the children played together in nature. When the children played, swam together, or focused their minds on a certain area, sometimes competition came between them. An adult then presented the children with an olive branch, giving the children a chance to choose. Over and over again, the children moved away from competition and used the olive branch to choose a closer connection with nature and the Earth. This is where the symbol of the olive branch actually got started. In ancient Greece and Egypt, the Lemurian use of the olive branch as a symbol of peace and unity was again resurrected.

In time, medicine will discover in olive oil complex organic substances which have a strong cleansing effect on the liver and gallstones. These substances also aid in liver regrowth, bile production in the gall bladder, and a cleansing of the bloodstream. Chemicals or heat used to extract olive oil damages some of these organic substances. Animals will especially benefit from these substances, although in time medical research will also focus on treating people with the extracts of olive oil.

The third and fourth chakras are brought into a better state of balance. The gall bladder meridian and the nadis throughout the chest and abdomen are strengthened. The etheric and mental bodies are cleansed, the syphilitic miasm eases, and the fourth and fifth rays are strengthened slightly. The test point is the bridge of the nose.

Onion

This common vegetable produces greenish-white flowers. Onion has long been used to treat a variety of digestive and heart ailments.

The tendency is to open the heart to release sadness. This is a common blockage for individuals working in almost any area of spiritual wisdom or understanding, especially when greater love is manifested in their lives. The signature here is, of course, its pungent smell and vapor which cause tears. As the eyes of the heart open, sadness is seen in the world, and this is more easily released and understood. There is also a tendency to broaden love energies. Thus, there is a greater strengthening of the entire attitude of lovingness regarding spirituality. This strengthening is very important.

Another part of the signature is the relatively dense and compact structure of the onion. It has layers. Each can be peeled to yield another inside. And so it is also with the heart. As one comes to know and understand oneself better, layer upon layer is peeled away. The understanding of this loving energy is different than with most other foods or herbs that relate to the heart, because the element of sadness is intimately intertwined. The full understanding of what one creates allows this sadness to be released. More energy is available for that which is created, the way one works with people, and the energy available for spiritual understanding of God as it runs deep in the heart. This property is retained even when onion is cooked or taken in a juice.

There is a much clearer ability to know the difference between what is another's point of view and what is yours, an ability to understand the difference between sympathy and empathy, and a clearer emotional frame of mind in which it is easier to release feelings rapidly. Sometimes, feelings of sadness are felt as one awakens to levels of telepathy with other beings. This is because you see through their eyes for a moment, and they also see the world and the difficulties within it. There is also usually greater energy available for all forms of psychic healing.

In Lemuria, the plant was much smaller. The bulb shape was even seen on the etheric level. It was seen that the essential oils within it could have this triggering effect to bring tears into the eyes. This was an interesting ritual, because the tears were generally tears of joy. There was then no need to be sad for the world. In the later Lemurian phases, the possibilities for mankind's suffering became apparent. With that understanding, energy was brought into the plant to strengthen it and to enlarge it to let the effect on the physical eyes be there to release sadness that would block joy. Gradually, mankind's own energy has changed this thought form until today the plant's karmic purpose is simply to remind individuals that this release of sadness can yield greater clarity.

The second chakra and all the nadis in the eyes, face, and upper part of the neck are energized. The emotional body is cleared, the tubercular miasm is eased slightly, and the third and eighth rays are clarified. Some individuals develop a greater sense of life purpose and are able to see where sadness has blocked them in understanding this purpose when these two rays are coordinated together better. In the heliocentric system of astrology, there is an association with planet Earth. This causes some intensification of any Earth energies as projected in the heliocentric chart. The test point is the shoulder.

Pagoda Tree

Native to China its flowers have long been used to treat a variety of blood disorders in Chinese medicine.

When this plant is viewed etherically, in a state of deep meditation, the natural energy flow from one part of the plant to another looks like the human circulatory system. This occurs not only within the plant, but external to it as well. Pagoda tree has a great affinity for the human circulatory energy and for the way blood is created.

On the higher spiritual level this relates to the circulation of energy throughout the physical body as received in states of deeper insight, meditation, and understanding. But on levels beyond this, it relates to the interconnectivity and replenishment of all aspects of society and people. This is a good herb to take for aiding the circulatory system, but it also helps people work together and understand each other in groups. Group meditation is enhanced, as are ways people can work together to co-create an endeavor of any kind.

Many emotions that stand in the way of group interaction are released. The cleansing of the emotional body is fairly deep. People feel greater space and energy. The relaxation associated with this also allows some physical changes to take place. The emotional body, with its direct connection to the blood, allows a richer, more nutritious blood. At the same time, it stimulates dilation of the capillaries so that plaque and cholesterol-forming substances are released. This takes place at the highest spiritual level as a beautiful merging of levels of time and ways people understand their past, present, and future. This embraces mankind's purpose, and there is a direct alignment between the spiritual purpose of the devic order, the plant, and mankind.

There is an enhanced ability to understand an entirely different point of view, to see things from another person's perspective. Even stronger for some people will be a willingness to totally understand another person's choices, thus giving people a deep sense of forgiveness, helping them to discover that they would have done the same thing in the other person's shoes. There is also a gentle enhancement of telepathy and a willingness to receive impressions through the eyes.

In Lemuria, the plant was often found for no particularly understandable reason in areas where religious ceremonies took place. Even to the present day, it relates to religion in Japan and other places. The Lemurians, in noting this, asked the devic order why this occurred. What was shared was that the plant needed to circulate energy, and the Lemurians quite obviously could see the way the tree moved energy throughout its body. But there was some difficulty with this circulation, as if without sufficient spiritual influence, without sufficient love of the Earth felt by the Lemurians and the understanding of God brought by them, the plant would die. It was by a process of natural selection that those plants nearest areas of religious activity prospered and grew while those further away did not.

Thus, in a willingness to cooperate with this plant the Lemurians enmeshed into its devic order the ability to assist the human circulatory system. It was a natural adjunct to the way the plant grew. However, this meant that in mankind's future it would be intertwined; it would be utilized over and over again for its herbal effects. It would never be allowed to die out, even when mankind turned its back upon various ways of religion, and of understanding Earth, God, and higher spiritual principles. This assured the plant's existence into the future. Its karmic purpose is to assist mankind in understanding this inner uniting, this way people, plants, and animals have a common bond in understanding God. In this way, the circulation of energy becomes similar for all species.

There is a stimulation of the heart chakra which increases energy throughout the third and fifth chakras. There is also added energy, as if in a concentrated form, at the crown chakra. There is a strengthening of the pericardium and heart meridians. Energy related to the circulatory system is strengthened, and a transfer can take place to any of the other meridians, particularly at the transfer points in the hands and feet.

There is a strengthening and sometimes a cleansing of the emotional body. As this takes place, there is a transfer of energy to the mental body for clearer understanding. The cancer and heavy metal miasms are slightly eased, and the fourth and sixth rays are made clearer for most people. The plant has similar effects with the blood and circulatory system in animals. When an individual is training or working with an animal, it is often wise to use this herb, particularly if the animal is showing any signs of difficulty with cold temperature. This also assists in the spiritual bond and connection between the animal and the person. The test point is the back opposite the heart.

Papaya

This fruit tree produces male and female flowers. Papain, one of the constituents of papaya, is often used as a digestive aid.

The spiritual properties can be profound on the level of complete assimilation. Assimilation implies that any blockage that may reduce assimilation is also brought to the surface and completely released. This can be seen not only in the way eating papaya aids digestion, but also in the way papaya greatly speeds up colon transit time, even causing diarrhea in some individuals. The idea here is that what is held on to is released making more room for what is needed. This means that new ideas of spirituality and new techniques are much more quickly absorbed and utilized. There is a tendency to attune to specific vibrations more easily. In working with a teacher, one is better able to apply the teachings. Such assimilation takes place primarily on the level of resonance. Papaya enhances the resonant properties; it focuses energy into specific bands or frequencies associated with the resonances of new teachings. That allows information to be transmitted easily and quickly by the resonant capacities between you and another person.

The plant has been used as a food substance for quite some time. In Lemuria, it was utilized towards the end of the Lemurian phase, as it provided a great deal of nourishing substance. What was different then, of course, was that the full utilization and assimilation of the tree's properties were more concentrated in the flower which was of a purely spiritual nature. This changed gradually until, at the end of the Lemurian period, direct contact with the newly budding Atlantean civilization was necessary. Then papaya was often eaten. Papaya was eventually shared with people in tropical regions the world over to remind people of these ancient times. Its primary karmic purpose is to remind individuals of this innate ability to absorb and work directly with information.

The root chakra yields greater energy directly into the heart. This energy then pours directly into the third eye. This is what allows assimilation to be enhanced. A circuit is established between these three chakras. The mental body is brought into a higher state of vibration. Greater resonance between the mental body and that of another being takes place as a result. The gonorrhea miasm is eased, and the ninth, tenth, and eleventh rays are made stronger in an individual. The test point is the third eye.

Passion Flower

This vine produces blue, pink, or purple flowers during the summer. Passion flower is traditionally used to alleviate neuralgia and insomnia.

There is some transfer of the Christ properties and vibration of Christ consciousness that the flower essence activates into the herb. However, the flower essence of passion flower is much more effective to activate these principles in people, so this is one herb that is best taken with the flower essence associated with it. The energies associated with channeling, clairvoyance, heightened spiritual states, greater awareness, and even peak experiences of a religious nature take place much more easily with passion flower. The channel is opened, so that energies are not held within but are released. Any negativity, such as fear, resulting from these higher states is released into the Earth. In addition, there is a tendency for the individual to be better protected from negative or difficult vibrations that emanate from electronic devices such as computers, televisions, and microwave ovens. Many such devices produce what are called ELF frequencies (extremely low frequencies), which create biological stress on every cell in the body. The herb will assist in the release of these negative energies into the Earth.

The psychic abilities activated are somewhat similar to the flower essence, but when there is difficulty in the greater awakening to levels of higher consciousness this is eased because the energy itself is released. As a result of this, what usually comes to the individual is greater understanding of how to use these abilities. Greater application of psychic gifts becomes much clearer. The plant reminds one of Christ energy. It is not only in a reaching out manner, but etherically there is a direct relation to the great passion that Christ felt for the achievement of God on Earth.

The plant was used in purely sacred or sacramental rituals in Lemuria. It was allowed to grow wherever there were ritualistic places where worship, understanding of God and Earth, and working with energy of a more spiritual nature was taking place. The Lemurians, as they saw these energies in their rituals become permeated into the various plants, felt the loving and joyous energies from passion flower and from its vines and roots. This created a resonance, so passion flower was often used to close ceremonies. The resonance was experienced and an energy was created almost like a shield, ball of light, or intense area of energy that was then allowed to sink gently into the Earth. This sometimes gave people who used this herb a greater reverence for Earth as it related to God. This is the plant's karmic purpose today, to allow this more deeply into people's lives.

The crown chakra is stimulated, with the energy likely to move in both directions, vibrating and creating resonance with the sixth and eighth chakras. There is a strengthening of the nadis in the neck, wrist, and arm areas. There is also a strengthening of the kidney meridian, especially where it runs through the interstitial spaces in the chest. The soul body is cleansed, and there is more attunement between the etheric, emotional, and mental bodies. For many people, this causes a deeper reverence, and it is easier to release energy that may accumulate in the etheric body. The eleventh and twelfth rays are also strengthened. There is some connection here to the planetoid Chiron, which is associated with Christ consciousness. But the primary connection here is that when Chiron is positively aspected with Jupiter or Uranus, there is an added effect in using this herb.

Paw Paw

Native to the Midwest, this fruit tree produces dull red flowers. The American Indians use it as an emetic.

There is an enhancement of the ability to receive what one has already learned. This is an important contribution to spiritual growth. Most individuals partly acknowledge who they are and what they have done, but they do not recognize the intrinsic uniqueness of their own being, what they have already accomplished and learned. In many cases, this is not of any importance on the level of knowledge. Rather, it is the way this reveals your willingness to be here, your strength of understanding. The strength within you to continue growing and understanding is seen as a continuum extending into the past with your appreciation of what you know. This then extends into the future with what you can know.

This property is seen in the signature of the plant, its unique taste. An individual is reminded of this uniqueness. Also it has the unusual property of tasting somewhat different to most people. One will say it tastes like this, and the other will say it tastes differently. This signifies uniqueness, a recognition of that which they know is real in themselves.

The paw paw flower essences, and to a lesser extent the fruit, are quite beneficial in treating anorexia nervosa, because many times that illness relates to poor self-image. A person is not able to receive love and to know that they deserve love.

There is an enhancement of the ability to sense uniqueness and to project healing energy to the psychic level in other people. This can be very beneficial for individuals who are developing psychic gifts. But this is not of any help if they are in a state of spiritual emergency, where they are seeking other areas of deeper cleansing. This will be especially enhanced in states of fasting. A fruit fast that includes paw paw enhances third eye sight, clairvoyance, channeling, and the ability to see auras. There can be a strengthening of many of these effects if a good teacher, in appreciating his or her own uniqueness, speaks of this in a way that you also receive it. It is like a modeling process. In appreciating your inner strengths you become willing to develop new abilities that are rooted in the old ones.

The unique character of this plant was recognized in Lemurian times, although it was similar to mango, quite a bit smaller than it is today. The concentration upon the fruit to provide this uniqueness to all individuals as they may wish to explore it was understood to be an important property. In Lemuria, it was seen that this division of the soul into finer and finer parts, until at last a continuous soul stream of a single individual could be maintained from one lifetime to the next, would give individuals some degree of identity difficulty. They would not know exactly who they were. There were many things that could be useful here to alert people to their inner identity, but paw paw was chosen, particularly the fruit.

There is a strengthening of the fifth and ninth chakras. The ninth chakra sometimes affects this characteristic of unique spirituality in an individual. There is slightly speeded up energy in the liver meridian, and the nadis in the fingers are slightly stimulated. There is a significant cleansing of the mental body, and there is a slight release of the syphilitic miasm. The fifth, sixth, and seventh rays are made clearer for an individual, and the test point is the base of the throat.

Pear

Producing white flowers, pear is a popular fruit tree originating in Asia Minor and eastern Europe. It is rich in nutrients and is used to treat various kidney problems.

There is a significant strengthening of a person's willingness to remain grounded and strengthened, while at the same time reaching for other areas in life. This is an important attribute when exploring new pathways. We have focused on this quality when describing a number of herbs, when new pathways are provided to people, because this is appropriate for these times. Today, with enhanced communication, much new energy, and many people appearing on the planet, there is a great deal of choice. It is wise to remain well grounded when exploring these choices and working in different spiritual areas.

Pear has a unique shape; it is larger at the bottom. You can see that if it is tossed into the air, it is likely to fall with the larger part down first. You land upon your feet and find a center or balance. The spiritual properties of centering are enhanced by pear. This is different from grounding or centering by using specific techniques such as various herbs. Rather, this is a way in which a person can return from spiritual exploration, with an inner strengthening and a feeling of groundedness. One can explore new pathways without feeling lost or confused.

This exploration can extend to ecstatic states or peak experiences. Sometimes, individuals approach a peak experience with great fear, feeling, perhaps unconsciously, that they will change too much as a result of the peak experience. Of course this is true, but it is the fear that is more important. With pear, in particular, there can be an inner strengthening of the person's will to make such a change, knowing that not only is it for the better, but those parts of one that remain will be the most important. Then the deeper states of ecstasy and peak experiences may be enjoyed. The use of pear in a fruit fast is sometimes recommended. It can have a cleansing property on the body. Part of this is because of the deeper grounding combined with an ability to experience higher states.

The psychic properties that let one know their center has been enhanced should be explored by all individuals sometime in their lives. We must be careful to distinguish this from grounding per se. For when you know you are centered, you may then choose to move off it to learn other things. But you do this consciously. It is this conscious exploration that pear enhances.

Some individuals have a negative physical reaction to pear. An accumulation of gas in the large intestine may result. Individuals may experience this in particular with pear juice. For such people, similar herbal properties that we have described may be attained by occasionally using pear leaf. This may also relieve gas pains.

In Lemuria, the plant was utilized as food. It has a particular unique character of a certain grittiness as the fruit is chewed. This has a stimulating property to the mouth. This can be quite useful for individuals to know more of the physical side of things, as well as to allow them an awareness without heaviness.

In ancient Lemuria, it was realized that later individuals would probably take fruits away from the trees where they naturally grew. Pear was the first fruit to be imbued with a spiritual presence to return the life force essence from the fruit after it was consumed back to the tree from which it was taken. After pear is eaten, its life force always returns to the tree from which it was picked. Thus, it was able to develop this ability to find its center more quickly and easily ahead of many other fruits. It was experimented with for quite some time before it was perfected. As a result of these experiments, other fruits were given these properties.

The return of the life force of pear to the tree from which it was picked occurs on many levels, although it primarily occurs at the etheric body level. At the level of the physical body, this energy is generally not seen or noted, but can be felt by some individuals when they eat the fruit directly underneath the tree. The reason for this is that the Lemurians trained with the devic order associated with each different fruit-bearing tree, so the ability to return the subtle vibrational energy back to the tree was developed. If you eat the fruit right under the tree, the devic order doesn't need to return the subtle energy to the tree. Under such circumstances, many individuals will feel the difference. It was necessary to set up this pattern with fruit trees because they would wither and die unless some energy was returned to them.

It appears that this pattern of energy returning to the original tree from which the fruit was picked is more important and necessary when the plant's way of propagation is to drop its berries or fruit to the ground. The pulpy material around the seeds creates the growth for the plant and sustains it in the early period of its initial growth. This process is not critical for other plants or trees.

When its initial characteristics were completed, it was seen that the fruit might choose how these properties of finding the center would be transferred to humanity. Pear was allowed to decide this for itself. Gradually, in working with the Atlantean civilization, a settling in of this thought form became apparent, until in this civilization it has taken on its role more clearly and firmly.

To a certain degree, the ability of the flower essence to amplify the creative process for musicians when combined with quartz crystals, harmonics, and sound structures carries over to the fruit. It is very important in musical expression that the center be known. This property was particularly brought into resonance and perfection with quartz crystals during experiments in Atlantis. In amplification of this property, the musical tone center was made clearer and more apparent. In current musical vernacular, this may be called the tonic.

In various forms of musical expression, the central or pivotal tone is one that is begun with or returned to during the musical piece. In some types of musical expression however, this tonal center is deliberately not utilized or is only discovered as the music gradually evolves. An example of this would be the percussion instruments. They will create many different tones and the exact central tone or tonic will not be clearly felt or seen by many individuals. The use of pear may assist individuals who attune to this to find this inner tonal center even in percussive type music. The tonal center is utilized in many different areas in music, so it is important that an understanding and clear, conscious conception of it be allowed for those using music involving this tonal center.

However, in musical explorations in Atlantis there were flights into all kinds of variations of harmony, sympathetic resonance, and various varieties of frequency both harmonious and dissonant. The finding of the correct center, or tonic, was critical because people's consciousness, as they were affected by this music, needed to be brought into some awareness by which they could utilize the new energies they received.

There is a strengthening of the third and fourth chakras, the flow in the triple warmer meridian is speeded up, and the large intestine and lung meridians are cleansed. The nadis in the palms are stimulated, the etheric body is strengthened, the mental body is cleansed, and there is a temporary coordination of all of the subtle bodies. There is some release of the cancer and heavy metal miasms, and the tenth ray is made clearer. There are some connections in sidereal astrology to the Earth. This is a symbolic center. In the sidereal chart, when Earth is in negative aspects to other planets and one is working to cleanse the body, pear is particularly recommended. The test point is the medulla oblongata.

Peppermint

This aromatic plant produces small reddish-violet flowers. Peppermint is often used as a stomach tonic and to aid digestion and ease nervousness.

If too much peppermint is taken, a reduction of its spiritual properties takes place. This is important because many feel attracted to the taste. It is actually an aromatic taste that is connected in the nervous system and the taste sensory organs. An addiction to this taste and smell may develop so that peppermint is overused. This also reduces the plants ability to cleanse.

What happens when mint is used appropriately in smaller quantities—a cup or two of peppermint tea once a week—is that there is a strong tendency for a cleansing of the entire physical vehicle so that the vibrations of each chakra and the various subtle bodies draw energy from the soul and the higher self, through the being, and release it to the Earth.

You might think this would make a greater contact with the Earth, but this is not what is usually sensed spiritually. Instead, what happens is the energies blocking soul lessons diminish, so that these lessons pour more easily through a person. This occurs because the person is more rooted or grounded, but also because of a great flow and attunement with the chakras, subtle bodies, and the soul. Symbolically, the deep and unique odor stimulates the etheric fluidium so that this flow takes place. The way it works is almost magnetic. Magnetism involves movement of the ethers. As the etheric fluidium is stimulated, an individual moves through blockages to achieve more purpose in life.

When too much peppermint is taken, this flow takes place at too great a pace. This causes the systems that have allowed energies to flow through an individual into the Earth to slow down or shut down. The pace is simply too high a vibrational level for one to work with. Some people have noticed that taking peppermint negatively affects taking homeopathic remedies. Peppermint in large quantities blocks the life force flow, so the individual is less sensitive to a homeopathic remedy. This issue is less of a problem with flower essences and gem elixirs because then the vibrations often work in harmony. But there is a threshold of tolerance. The threshold is much higher with flower essences and gem elixirs than with homeopathic remedies.

Through this increased movement and attunement with the soul, there is an ability to get far beyond oneself, to help in areas of counseling, to listen clearly to another person's problem, and to get instantaneous answers. Some of the lessons held deep within the soul are revealed rapidly. Fears are eased, especially those involving motion such as in skiing, driving a car, or flying. Some of these developments create greater energy in the individual. This greater energy can be applied in many areas, but this will usually be easiest when there is a connection made to another person. A polarity is struck. At the ending of this polarity, there is no debilitating or difficult effect with the person. This is why peppermint tea is often of some benefit after a polarity healing session.

In Lemuria, the plant was seen to impart motion to the ethers. This was praised. It was incorporated in many interesting dance rituals in which the smell of the herb went into an individual as if in meditation, and an inspired dance took place. It was realized that mankind would eventually lose the reason for doing such a meditation, so the energy of the plant was incorporated to include this motion whenever it was taken in an herb or tea form. Its karmic purpose is to remind individuals of this dance or motion ability, as if imparting it into the etheric body so that individuals will feel it. This is very unconscious in most individuals today, and it is the karmic purpose of the plant to eventually reveal this more consciously to humanity.

The third chakra is slightly stimulated, and movement up the front and down the back of all the meridians is enhanced. This includes all the meridians except for the triple warmer meridian. The etheric body is exceptionally cleansed, and the magnetic forces that affect the etheric body are activated. The thermal body connection between the etheric and mental and etheric and physical bodies are enhanced. This sometimes stimulates faster healing in an individual when visualization is used. This alignment can also assist when there is temperature difficulty in the body, especially when the temperature is too high. Peppermint could be used in emergency rescue when the body temperature is too high or too low. In addition, the magnetic force has a particular pattern associated with it through which information is transferred from the etheric body to the mental body. This transfer of information is enhanced.

There is a slight easing of the stellar miasm. An individual perceives all the rays slightly differently, especially the sixth and seventh, and can work with them more easily. When Mercury is in retrograde, individuals who suffer emotionally and have great difficulties in their lives will be aided by using peppermint. Mercury's swiftness and ability to impart rapid mental states and quick thinking are activated. The same spiritual properties are imparted to animals, which can sometimes cause slight behavioral changes. Animals often seek the mint plants. The test point is the top of the head. The other forms of mint have very similar properties to peppermint so they are not discussed in these books on the spiritual properties of herbs.

Pimpernel

This short perennial is usually found in Europe. Pimpernel eases diseases of the brain, stomach, and heart.

There is a tendency to allow the raising of energy. This applies to any chakra; therefore, this process creates knowledge of the Earth spiritualized for individuals, knowledge of working with the emotions, knowledge of power, knowledge of the heart, and knowledge of expression. The basic teaching of each chakra is brought closer.

Pimpernel has an upward motion through it. Its circulation and strength are derived from this motion, which can be observed by those who work with this signature on etheric levels. Because of this upward motion, energy associated with an area in which there is a blockage or a particularly strong expression in life is spiritualized. It changes your point of view. This is not the same as raising energy through kundalini yoga. It is a way to spiritually understand God's purpose. God's way of expression and an understanding of how these things are beneficial for you in your relationship with God are brought more clearly into focus.

There is some concentration of psychic energy as a result of this motion. Whichever chakra has blocked energy or a strong amount of energy associated with it, can have its energy released and raised to the next chakra. Individuals developing the abilities of self-expression may find psychic gifts such as clairvoyance, telepathy, and deeper understanding of the self associated with the third eye becoming stronger and more focused. Deeper states of healing may result as individuals who work with love use this herb.

In Lemuria, pimpernel was used extensively in dance. The devic spirits associated with this plant were quite clear and easy to work with, and indeed, they even helped to choreograph some of the dances. Joyousness, motion, and strength were imparted as a result of this dance. The devic spirits have continued to maintain this energy. Today, mankind is not able to dance in such a fashion; however, there is the karmic purpose to wait and allow this when mankind is ready.

The simple meridian flows up the front and down the back are made stronger and clearer. This includes all the meridians except for the triple warmer meridian. Some of the nadis in the legs and feet are given added energy. The emotional and etheric bodies are cleansed, and the tubercular and cancer miasms are eased. The second, third, and fourth rays are made stronger and clearer, and the test point is the knees.

Pine

This tall tree has many commercial uses. One of the Bach flowers, pine is used for kidney, bladder, and rheumatic disorders.

With pine there is an ability to activate energies associated with the third eye. This is distinct from many other herbs that work with this center. What happens is that the energies of your life become naturally coordinated with energies of the third eye. The way one uses psychic abilities becomes apparent, and there is a sense of relaxation associated with various psychic abilities. At the same time, the ability to work with the nature kingdom, especially nature spirits, is enhanced. There is a much greater awareness of nature and of the purpose of nature spirits. An ability to interchange love with these beings develops. One could send love to them and feel love when it is receive back. For this psychic ability to be firmly rooted in an individual, free will must be part of the process. The secret of properly using pine is that love is directed so that the heart and third eye centers work in coordination. One then sees that all ways of psychic powers, as rooted in free will and love, make sense. This is honoring God's principle of free choice for all mankind.

Clairvoyant sight is enhanced. This affects the perception of nature and the ability to sense the shape and color of auras, rays, and the energies of subtle bodies. These things can be perceived more easily by the physical eyes. After pine is taken, meditate with the eyes closed upon something alive that is known to have an auric field, allowing the imagination to stimulate the third eye. Visualize a clear and beautiful blue eye in the middle of the forehead opening up and looking around. A slight pressure might be imagined at the skin's surface. In welcoming this with the eyes closed, the energies associated with clairvoyant sight are stimulated.

As with frank and myrrh, pine resin can be rubbed over the third eye. Pine is especially balancing as it opens the third eye; it can be used in conjunction with frank and myrrh to develop these abilities, especially from a spiritual perspective. If headaches or lower energy develops from using frank or myrrh on the third eye, pine may be indicated.

Regarding the signature, the smell of pine seems to have a direct, almost neurologically measured effect, of stimulating the mid-forehead region. The needles appear to be pouring out from the tree, symbolizing penetrating insight. There is a tendency for these needles, when brushed by the hand, to make a rather piercing contact that does not usually reach a level of distinct pain, but is rather an interesting combination of an itch and a painful sensation that is really neither. This sensation is associated with opening the third eye.

Pine resin is rubbed on violin strings and in various waxes because of its strength and ability to create friction. This opens individuals to their gifts and to an understanding of God as the violin is played. The vibrational effects of pine are felt in the music produced by the violin. This is one area in which synthesized violin music cannot duplicate the acoustic instrument at the current time.

Pine, in its many forms, has been present on the Earth for a very long time. Its purpose at first was only to pave the way, because it can multiply and be in many interesting locations and is often able to survive in difficult climates and settings. The Lemurians recognized this property. They saw that within pine would be a receptacle to carry forth psychic gifts and an ability to understand the purpose of all humanity and the Earth long into the future. This is one tree that would likely survive even the remote but conceivable possibility of a nuclear holocaust, because of the tenacity and ability for its seeds to last long periods of time.

This tree is associated with tenacity and patience. The Lemurians specifically focused and concentrated this energy to work with the third eye, to make this energy more available to people to discover the nature kingdom. The Lemurians saw that eventually our association with nature would be forgotten, and this would become one of the key difficulties in mankind's civilization. Indeed, this was a correct prediction. In no longer understanding this kingdom, mankind has lost an interesting and important ability to make peace with nature. However, this tree was not chosen for that reason, but because it had the greatest chance of surviving no matter what would come between Lemurian times and times in which these abilities would be needed. The karmic purpose is to carry this energy forth, to allow it to be there until mankind is ready to work with it.

The third eye is directly stimulated. There is a slight easing of excessive or yang energy in the gall bladder, stomach, and lung meridian. And the astral, mental, and etheric bodies are stimulated and brought into a state of resonance. This assists individuals developing psychic abilities. There is a slight alleviation of the psora miasm, the eleventh and twelfth rays become much clearer and brighter, and the fifth ray is brought into greater harmony. Those already associated with such rays may feel increased energy in the physical body. There is some association with the planet Jupiter, but this alignment is temporary in the life of pine. It extends back in time 3,000 years and forward for about 3,000 more years. After 3,000 years the orbit of Jupiter will change slightly. The idea is that when Jupiter is positively aspected in the natal chart there is an added effect when using pine.

Animals in the feline family, when around people who are working with negative thought forms, tend to develop unusual ailments or strange difficulties that are hard to understand. In such circumstances, the animal can actually perceive negative thought forms, which can be quite frightening. Pine added to the diet enables the cat to know itself better and to relax about the conditions it is in. The test points are the third eye and medulla oblongata, when touched together.

Pipsissewa

This perennial herb is found throughout most of the United States. It is an astringent and diuretic.

This is a profound healer for deep release. It establishes an energy circuit in people that continues the function of the etheric or spiritual release beyond this use of the herb. The plant provides some of this effect as a medicinal release, but the spiritual effect of this circuit creates a spiral of energy in the persons' abdominal region that generally becomes an ongoing release system. This can have a potent effect regarding blockages to spiritual progress, such as fear or guilt. But more importantly, there is clarity in areas which one sees as blockages and is thus unable to receive God's love. There is a purging or cleansing from the heart downwards rather than upwards, as is more often the case, so that energy release can be profound and important.

At the same time, this vortex of energy cancels out some of the disharmonious effects of various negative thought forms that may have accumulated around the individual. In this way, the release function serves the individual on a high and important spiritual level, but it also makes use of many levels of unconscious energy. It is an herb that tends to bend the energy that one might emit unconsciously, particularly in the sleep state, into a path that is self-governing to release many levels of etheric toxicity and other difficulties.

Sometimes this energy transfers to other chakras, but it is primarily associated with the second and third chakras. For most individuals, it will tie in at a point about midway between them. These two chakras are usually influenced by each other. On the highest spiritual level, this energy release can be very liberating. Blockages, such as negative thought forms, may be temporarily released without the individual putting much attention on it. There is a slight danger of one becoming somewhat addicted to this process, to the point of repeatedly using this herb to release negative thought forms. It is far wiser, when they are released, to understand what their purpose was to allow a greater strengthening to take their place. But again, this is on the highest spiritual level. Most individuals involved in fasting, meditation, and creative visualization will reach these higher states and then be able to utilize the higher properties in a balanced fashion.

This release process aids in psychic development, especially when the intuitive process is blocked because of patterns from your current lifetime. This does not generally relate to past lives, because this herb does not have much effect on the astral level. Instead, on an unconscious level, the individual has attitudes and ideas that block psychic development in certain areas. For instance, if you are attempting to develop your intuition or clairvoyance, you may place a negative value judgment upon yourself because individuals in your past may have said only people who are crazy can do that, or there is something wrong with someone who does this. This area though, completely cleared out in many other ways in your life, may be more easily released when this herb is used. This is but one example of blockage removal.

Because this release is also taking place on the abdominal level, it is a release agent in relationships as well. If you are using this herb and are in an intimate relationship with someone, that person should also be fully aware of the herb's properties. They might take it with you. As you release negative energy, you will develop greater love. At the same time, the energy between you may increase. Agitation on an emotional level may temporarily increase in the relationship, but there will be a cleansing. This can be an interesting growth experience for two individuals who wish to purge some negative aspects of their relationship.

The whorl pattern on the leaf is significant. The energy that moves from it etherically generates a powerful spiral. This spiral of energy carries with it any psychic debris that you may bring into the living plant's field. For example, people beginning to open third eye sight, might be aware of some negative aspect of themselves, bring it more clearly into the aura by imagination, and then bring it near the leaf of this plant. They may see it carried away in the ethers that project from pipsissewa.

In Lemuria, the techniques of energy healing by which such vortices were established were relatively easy. When an individual had an accident or needed to have deeper states of learning, these energetic vortices were easily put in place. It was seen as a possibility that mankind's ability to heal in such a fashion might become more difficult or even be lost from the planet. Pipsissewa was chosen to preserve this capacity. It was not known when it would be needed again. It turned out to be needed more in today's civilization than in others when such energetic release techniques were more commonly used.

There is a strengthening of the kidney and bladder meridians, and the nadis throughout the abdomen are stimulated. Many of the energies that flow through the large and small intestine are stimulated, although not the meridians directly associated with these organs. The etheric body is usually first cleansed, and then a few hours after the tea is taken, the etheric body is strengthened. The cancer miasm is eased, and there is a strengthening and greater clarity with the third, fourth, and seventh rays. There is an easing of Mars negative effects when it is in square or opposition, and the test point is about two inches below the navel.

Pomegranate

A common fruit tree and popular flower essence, it is native to southern Asia. The fruit eases digestive problems including tape worm. The flower essence has been quite successful in treating a variety of woman's problems. Large doses of the rind can cause cramps and vomiting.

There is a tendency to understand and work with the emotions more easily. Most individuals compartmentalize emotions. The fruit has an interesting signature. When you break apart the fruit you will see that part which is edible, the seed structures are indeed quite separated and compartmentalized. This energy is brought together for an individual. The pomegranate devic order, as with most devic orders, attunes to the part of the plant that has the maximum concentration of energy. That point is the red-colored seeds.

Emotions are allowed to be understood—how they work together, and how they work with each other. Or one better understands how one feeling allows an individual greater peacefulness, while another feeling is difficult. These energies become more coordinated instead of seeming to fight each other. Ultimately, the emotions are seen as a source of energy, and indeed they are one. The strength in being on the Earth and learning the lessons of a difficult emotional world is to focus energy over and over in the heart center. Then these energies can be utilized appropriately. That is an individual's free choice. Pomegranate focuses and concentrates energy in the heart as the emotions are dealt with. Those involved in certain therapeutic practices, including techniques where screaming and anger are expressed and pain is released, may be aided by occasionally using this fruit.

As the emotions are brought together, there is a strengthening of the physical body. This enhances the individual's ability to manifest bodily changes much more easily. Most energy associated with changes on the physical level usually has its source in the emotional body. This is not because that is how it must be or how it was even designed for mankind, but because that is where people usually put most of their energy. As these energies are balanced, one may choose much more easily to focus such energies onto the etheric body. Then the mental body pictures truly make a deeper, longer lasting effect on the physical body.

As an example, take a man who is working with therapeutic practice to let go of being a child, to take charge of his life, to create mature adult relationships. He will deal with many emotions, primarily fear, pain, and sadness relating to the childhood experiences not fully acknowledged. As these emotions are released and their energies combined, there is assistance when using pomegranate. As a result of this, cleansing energy is released in the chest region. This can cause the individual to grow more hair upon his chest. Perhaps the pituitary will also be stimulated, and he may grow a few inches. This is documented in the way some individuals, working with powerful therapeutic practices, have noted such body changes, even though they might be well into adulthood. This entire process is made more conscious by pomegranate, so that an individual could choose where these energies should be focused.

In Lemuria, emotions were utilized in the way of ritual and were closely associated with sound. These were emotions that might be termed the higher or purer emotions. Feelings of awe, praise, and ecstasy were often experienced by the Lemurians. Pomegranate was seen to have the effect of assisting when an individual was enmeshed in some of the lower and more difficult emotions—those that humans now simply consider emotions. Then this fruit was allowed to take the role, aided by its devic spirits, of assisting Lemurians on this path. At such times, one, two, or perhaps three of the pomegranate seeds might be taken. It was also seen that later this would be quite useful for mankind. Thus, the devic spirit was allowed added strength to grow and continue on its own. It has observed mankind and seen the great importance of emotions. It has been able to gradually change the plant, making it a bit larger and focusing this compartmentalizing of emotions more deeply within it.

The second and third chakra are brought into much deeper states of harmony and balance, and the nadis throughout the front of the body are all stimulated. The energies that move from the chakras into the glandular systems are assisted, especially at the third, fourth, fifth, and sixth chakras. The emotional and etheric bodies are greatly strengthened, while the mental body is somewhat stimulated. The cancer, syphilitic, and gonorrhea miasms are eased, and the second, third, and fourth rays are activated. There is some easing of negative aspects of Mars and Venus to each other, particularly in the sign Pisces. These events can be quite difficult, and are good times to use pomegranate. The test point is about two inches above the navel.

Pumpkin

Yellow flowers appear on this vegetable during the summer. Pumpkin is sometimes used as an oil to ease skin conditions.

There is a clear association between the emotions and the Earth, which allows emotions to be better understood and balanced. As a result of this, there is a tendency to recognize Earth's properties, to be more at peace and at home upon the Earth. Pumpkin is an excellent food for those who have been associated with soldiering or warfare and who seek to change some of their points of view. This is especially true with the seeds. Because of a deeper connection between the emotions and the Earth, there is a release of energy. It is always hoped that there will be a shifting of such energy to more spiritual levels, and pumpkin assists in bringing more clearly into focus the possibilities for focusing energy on higher levels.

This is quite obvious when you see its physical appearance. Today, more than at any other time, pumpkin has become quite large. Individuals who have grown very large pumpkins exhibit a definite and clear bonding and emotional tie to pumpkins and often to many other plants. They talk to plants and give them special loving care. This is because, in this particular time period, human beings are able to wield and focus the emotions quite consciously. These energies of bonding between the Earth and the emotions are quite beneficial for most human beings today. It is a temporary easement and relaxation.

There is a tendency for emotional blocks to be released, and greater love, greater states of self-expression, and deeper healing abilities may result. Those who work with the plant kingdom and have emotional difficulties may especially notice these improvements. The 'green thumb' principle or greater attunement to plants while gardening increases when using pumpkin.

Pumpkin primarily works with the lower chakra centers, but there is some spillover into the fifth chakra. An increase in healing abilities will be the natural result. Because of the vibration of Earth energy, the opening of the root chakra is remarkably clear and powerful. The healing of glands connected to the lower chakras occurs. Eating pumpkin seeds also increases the energy available for individuals pursuing tantra or for raising the kundalini energy. Energy is concentrated, so it is more tangible.

In Lemuria, pumpkin was much smaller, but the orange color was extremely important. It was associated with the emotions. The symbolic nature of the later civilizations on the Earth was seen in the emotional difficulty housed within the plant. The devic order associated with pumpkin left the plant for long periods to commingle with Lemurian society. There was a wish to educate people as to the possible ways emotions could be used and understood. The devic order presented the idea of bonding with the Earth as an answer to the Lemurians' questions as to how emotional energies could be properly utilized in the future. The devas willingly took this teaching on as its own life force. Ultimately, pumpkin is likely to change again and revert to its smaller size. Part of this will be a result of the proper understanding of emotions for humanity, but also it is a way for the devic order to return deep within the Earth to again make contact there. Through a concentration of energy into pumpkin seeds, a deeper appreciation of Mother Earth will develop. This is the final spiritualization process that is the karmic purpose of this plant.

The kidney and spleen meridians as well as the nadis in the buttocks, base of the spine, and abdomen are energized. There is greater relaxation of the emotional and etheric bodies, and the cancer miasm is eased. The first, second, and third rays are made clearer. There is direct association with the sign Scorpio. This is obvious regarding the time period, which is relatively short, in which pumpkin is generally harvested. Scorpio emotional energy often runs deep into the unconscious. Individuals who are under the sign Scorpio, in reconnecting with the Earth, may indeed have greater energy released in which their deep-seated unconscious understandings are brought more clearly into light. This also means that using pumpkin seeds has a beneficial effect when various negative aspects with different planets occur in the sign Scorpio. The test point is the base of the spine.

Radish

Radish is a popular vegetable that produces white or lilac flowers. Conditions alleviated by radish include rheumatism, coughs, and headaches.

The primary property of radish is its ability to extend energy at certain levels of spiritual development in the seventh and twelfth chakras. The energy of a lifetime is opened and revealed to be God's energy in full splendor. As the crown chakra awakens, there is a gradual change in which one recognizes that this is only the beginning; the energy applied from God has much potential. In awakening and emphasizing the crown chakra, which is for many people an important focus at this time, more energy is available for people to work with their own potential. The white light of God is the energy of all the rays combined, of all of the energies of possibility for an individual.

This awakening is not something that is going to have a direct spiritual effect on most individuals. Most will be sensitive to its taste and this will be quite enough, because of the positive and cleansing effects that radish has on the blood and on the entire body. However, the seventh and twelfth chakras are important, because their potential gradually manifests. It is as if a manifestation of God within the person opens their particular talents. With this effect, there will be some spillover into the third eye chakra with a greater sense of purpose, but the eight through eleventh chakras are not activated. There is a relation between the difficult taste of radish to the difficulty on the physical plane of opening the higher chakras.

In awakening the crown chakra, certain states of ecstasy and a greater sense of purpose develop, and potential psychic abilities are activated. One better understands God's purpose for a group or race of humanity, and gradually there is a perception of Christ consciousness as it moves into unified energy fields that are then focused into certain individuals. There is some assistance in receiving high teachings from beings who are masters, teachers of wisdom, and great ones on the planet. Many times, these teachings as simply transmitted by words are not enough. They must be felt deep within the individual. This is not an ordinary merging, as in a healing. The merging takes place on a much higher level.

In Lemuria, radish was not primarily used as a food. It was grown to understand mankind's destiny of the heavens. And so the energies were seen through the ground. All plants appear glowing to those with etheric sight. This distinguishes live plants from those that are dying. This glowing in the radish is quite clear, even through the ground, and this is what the Lemurians worked with. They absorbed some of that energy directly in themselves to unite the highest spiritual aspects with that of pure Earth existence. This is different from what is currently understood, because the chakras in many Lemurians were better united and coordinated than is the case today.

The karmic purpose of radish is to provide all of these patterns as symbolic representations of what is possible for all humans. Many times, a plant is simply personifying, creating by something obvious in itself some symbol for mankind. With radish the symbol is not just the signature of the plant, but is a deep reminder for others to utilize it as a symbol—in the admiration of this beauty, as if somehow a universal knowledge appeared in front of you on your plate. You may recognize the way God's wisdom, the harmony of creation and nature, is all around you.

There is extra energy in the gall bladder meridian, and the nadis in the head are stimulated. The soul body is energized, the psora miasm is eased slightly, and the tenth, eleventh, and twelfth rays are activated. Sometimes, greater magnetism or a drawing up of energy can occur from this illumination. The test point is the top of the head or the crown chakra.

Raspberry

This small shrub produces white flowers. Raspberry is a prominent astringent and stimulant.

Some of the spiritual properties of the developing fetus are transferred into the mother, allowing greater communication between the child and mother-to-be. If there is a possibility of miscarriage, there is greater awareness of it and an ability to assist and possibly prevent it because of this increased attunement and bonding. The properties of raspberry are especially strong in the leaf. The mother of a newborn baby should often continue taking some raspberry leaf.

What also occurs for men, women, and children is the ability to have a childlike frame of mind for the incorporation of more joy. The awareness of the fun of life and a sense of relaxation develops, especially if one has been too intensely involved in spiritual practices. There is an ability to see with the eyes of a child. With the innocence of a child one may be open to many levels and understandings that as an adult one has learned to shut off. There is a certain danger and surprise in such seeing, because sometimes what an adult recognizes is more than they permit in their adult life. Eating raspberry may ease this. The plant's color and way children are particularly attracted to it indicate some of its energy. The signature includes such factors, but also allows a connecting energy between the tiniest of devic spirits. The spirits are then able to change vibratory reality and connect easily with the spirit in formation that is to become a child.

There is an enhancement of clairvoyance, especially in children. Children are in greater synchronization with each other. Raspberry's properties are often lost when combined with food high in sugar or other substances. This creates high blood sugar which weakens the deeper effects in the brain. If raspberry is taken in its less sweetened state, or not mixed with sugar or honey, higher states of consciousness develop among children. What occurs is similar to what happens in the prevention of a miscarriage. The energy of sibling rivalry is reduced, and greater harmony is found among children. What occurs when one takes any part of raspberry is a deeper sense of joyfulness and bonding between two individuals. Because this takes place in a childlike frame of mind, it is much clearer as a psychic ability if one or both of the individuals involved is a child.

In Lemuria, the way of the child and the available choices were not so clearly distinct from the levels of adulthood. Children were honored and seen as important contributors to society. Raspberry, with its associated devic order, was specifically selected to assist and help in the education of children. Education now is not what it was then. Education was an energy that created greater joy, relaxation, and openness to all levels of knowledge. Ultimately, the devic order associated with raspberry developed love for all children. As a result, it was seen that welcoming children into the world through the assistance of this devic order would be an important way to create greater joy and bonding in humans in the future. This energy was gradually infused into the devic spirit. But it was not until the advent of the Atlantean civilization that any of this childlike spirit was even necessary. Towards the end of the Atlantean era, the devic order was called upon to make communication with the childlike spirit in people clearer and stronger. That is its karmic purpose, to allow this childlike frame of mind in all human beings and for this communication to continue even into old age.

The root chakra and nadis in the feet, knees, and lower legs are energized. The liver and kidney meridians are strengthened, and the etheric and emotional bodies are cleansed. Raspberry has some association with licorice to release blockages in the emotional body. The syphilitic and gonorrhea miasms are eased, and the fourth and sixth rays are made a little easier for people to work with and understand. Children born with the planet Neptune in opposition or square to a natal Moon will often benefit from raspberry throughout their lives. This is because some of the unconscious abilities of the child may be quite difficult to contend with throughout life. There is some benefit in providing raspberry to animals that are pets of small children. The bonding creates in the child a deeper respect for the animal. Provide raspberry to a pet once a month or so. The test point is the soles of the feet.

Rhubarb

Originating in Tibet and China, this vegetable is an appetizer, laxative, and tonic. The oxalic acid content can cause poisoning. Pregnant women and those nursing babies should not use rhubarb.

There is a strong tendency for energy in the root chakra to rise through the spine. This liberates energy stored in the other chakras. Ultimately, this process focuses in the heart, the third eye, or the crown chakra. As a result of this pattern, the energy already dealt with in life is more available; there is a diffusion of energy that takes place in the root chakra center. This is why rhubarb can sometimes cause difficulty in pregnancy. A great deal of changing energy, which is largely under the control and direction of the being that is newly conceived, is taking place in the root and second chakras. Rhubarb also cleanses the root chakra. People may feel a closer attunement to the Earth, but this attunement will be different with each individual because of the association with accumulated root chakra energy.

There is an enhanced ability to accept sexuality, to share in the energy of creation, and to see the joyousness in being incarnated on the Earth. This energy is often with an individual for their entire lives but is not usually acknowledged. As a result of such an experience, a bonding or telepathic communication may take place between individuals. This is nonverbal and nonimaginative. It creates a sense of warmth in the heart center.

The reddish color of rhubarb suggests the relation to the root chakra, and there is a similarity in appearance to the human spine. Moreover, oxalic acid has an interesting odor that most individuals perceive as quite cleansing. The cleansing property of rhubarb releases energy associated with the root chakra.

In Lemuria, the energy of this plant was understood as a connecting force—one that aligned individuals with many aspects of themselves. It was also seen that this alignment, as part of the birthing process, would likely be lost in individuals who began to turn away from God, nature, and an inner connection with the soul. Therefore, the devic order associated with rhubarb focused more on helping mankind to relearn these things.

This was easier to do in Atlantis than in the current time period. Its primary focus now is to release root chakra energy. This karmic purpose will be fulfilled over the next few hundred years. Then it is likely that other purposes of this plant, including a greater acknowledgement of the joyousness of all aspects of existence, will be stronger. Rhubarb will then likely undergo a transformation in which some of the toxic effects will be lessened.

The root chakra is relaxed and its energy is dispersed, while the natural movement through the bladder meridian is slightly accelerated. The nadis in the abdominal region are energized, the etheric body is cleansed, the gonorrhea miasm is eased, and the first and third rays are energized. There is a gentle connection to the planet Mars. When Mars is retrograde for any individual, there will be some enhanced absorption in working with rhubarb. The test point is the base of the spine.

Sandalwood

This tropical tree, which is native to India, has a very prominent essential oil. It is an astringent, diuretic, and expectorant.

With sandalwood, deep states of relaxation take place on the spiritual level. It is not like a tranquilizer and is not just a physical effect. Rather, there is a deep calming effect when one is hard pressed towards spiritual aims or goals or does not understand spiritual teachings. This relaxation extends quite deeply in an individual. The idea of these states is to create an almost trancelike or meditative environment in which there is a focus on the information already garnered from past lives, the current life, and what is possible for the future. All these possibilities are relaxed and the energies associated with them are permitted to emerge. Such energies on a spiritual level are very useful, because one can attune more clearly to the spiritual teachings one is gravitating towards.

There is a tendency with sandalwood for this ability to relax, to occasionally go too far. This is natural because the current world creates the necessity for accomplishment, for doing many things, and for activities with outward goals. You must prove to someone else that you are worthy. In seeking relief from such constant pressure, it is easy to abuse sandalwood. The best way to use sandalwood is as incense, for its more spiritual properties. This should take place only occasionally, perhaps once or twice a month. Create at least a temporary environment in which society's constant requirement for accomplishment is absent. The release of such stress in an individual can be quite profound, but the need for such release must be balanced with the beneficial results of stress. Society pressures do lead to accomplishment and understanding.

Deeper trance, awareness of other realities, and deeper relaxation for increased healing all develop. Taking sandalwood internally and smelling burning sandalwood incense can benefit healing work, because sometimes the best approach is to be as relaxed as possible. We speak of the healer here. It is beneficial for the client too, but what happens as the healer relaxes completely is that increased spiritual energy of a more subtle nature permeates the individual. Sometimes the healer can get in the way of the healing process, and a deeper relaxed state will be of great benefit.

The smell of the plant can instantly have a powerful affect on an individual. In fact, those who are in areas where a great deal of sandalwood is growing may notice an immediate effect. This takes place because the olfactory mechanism can instantly make a link to the etheric body from its unique odor. This allows the deeper relaxed states associated with sandalwood to be felt and merged with a human. When joy is added to this process, the plant appears to be in a very happy or meditative state.

When such a joyousness and relaxation takes place between humans and sandalwood, there is greater power, greater strength of being, and greater acknowledgement of will. This occurred among the Lemurians. The Lemurians frequently depended upon and used sandalwood in many rituals, especially with dancing, prayer, and incense burning. Gradually, the ability to do this in a relaxed, openminded way was lost to mankind. In Atlantean times, it was seen that sandalwood would help bring deeper states of relaxation so it was again brought into popularity. The devic order associated with sandalwood saw that achieving a state of relaxation would be an on-going need for mankind and began to associate itself more directly with this relaxation thought form specifically for mankind. From that point to today and long into the future, the karmic purpose of this devic order is to provide a deeper sense of oneness and relaxation for all people.

The heart and fifth chakras are relaxed. The fifth chakra and energy stored in the throat region may then become quite available to move through the arms and into the face. And there is some relaxation in the gall bladder and pericardium meridians. There is a profound relaxing effect upon the etheric body. This can be useful in visualization therapy or techniques that influence the mental and etheric bodies to change the physical body. However, this is done in a state of deep relaxation and is an adjunct to more specific one-pointed visualization techniques.

The eighth and ninth rays become more easily assimilable. Sometimes the incense of sandalwood will be quite repulsive to an animal. Under such circumstances, do not expose the animal to it. Animals understand deeper states of relaxation and do not often need the extra energy offered by sandalwood. The test point is the base of the throat.

Sassafras

Ten to forty feet high, this tree produces small yellow-green flowers. It alleviates blood problems, rheumatism, and skin problems.

The roots of this plant activate higher spiritual energies of joy, praise of nature, and the full understanding of mankind's relationship to nature. Sassafras increases the ability to see praise. These are indeed high and important spiritual properties. They concentrate in the roots as the plant develops, and Earth energies commingle here. These things are now under the governing forces of the angelic realm, so individuals may find much greater attunement to angels. This is particularly true with people who seek to praise nature and the ways the Earth manifests beautiful and rather breathtaking forms of scenery, life energy, and new plant forms. These things cause a harmony between angels and mankind.

This is an energy that one can easily attune to or completely block. This is the nature of the attitude we call 'praise.' When you view these scenes in nature and come to know this sensation, these energies may be more available for the angelic realm to be closer to people. This is because of a commingling of a similar vibration—not because of a seeking from one race to the other. Both are praising together. This is greatly enhanced by sassafras and can run deep in an individual long after the experience of praising nature and mixing with the angelic realm takes place. It is today an important lesson for mankind to have these perceptions of nature. This is why there is such great attention now on pollution and other difficulties on the planet. How will mankind choose to work with nature? This is the question that is now being presented as the karmic lesson of sassafras is resolved.

There is an enhanced ability to see the angelic realm, to feel their vibrations, and know of their presence. This is a gentle perception. There is also greater clarification of the properties of free will. Exactly how will you apply the new found energies received while ingesting sassafras?

The plant has a continual concentration, particularly in the roots, of the energies from higher vibrational levels. On an etheric level the very tips of the plant may be seen to vibrate. These energies appear to travel downward into the roots of the plant. This provides some of the properties we have spoken of. However, the devic order associated with the plant often presents a miniaturized picture—actually a hologram—of itself as a being that looks very much like an angel.

In Lemuria, sassafras was observed to send radiations or signals from the Earth outward, as if to join with some other civilizations, loving and caring for humanity. However, the Lemurians did not understand the full importance of this. It was inconceivable to them, as well as to the Atlanteans, that mankind would not see the angelic kingdom at any time in the future. However, the angelic kingdom observed this, and saw that the essence of sassafras could be provided as an energy to enhance the ability to commingle with their kingdom and to view and know of the praise of nature. The plant then willingly chose this pattern of assistance, partly because it is very much attuned to human energy.

The fifth chakra is energized, the mental body becomes more relaxed, and the sixth ray is made clearer for an individual. There is an interesting change in the cancer miasm. Sometimes this brings on certain cancerous states in certain individuals, but it brings the cancer miasm into a place of clearer focus in which the use of various remedies and techniques for cancer may have greater applicability.

Use sassafras as a spray if you are growing entirely new or unusual species of plants. The greenhouse environment is particularly good for this. Combine a small amount of sassafras oil thoroughly with water and spray the room. The ratio would be five or ten drops of oil to around a gallon of water. This process provides greater energy to the plants. The test point is the medulla oblongata.

Schizandra

In Chinese medicine, the dried fruit of this tree is used to treat respiratory illnesses as well as insomnia and prolonged diarrhea. This is one of the few plants that contains the five flavors.

The interesting signature relates to the fact that the tree encompasses all five tastes. In Chinese medicine, this is of great importance. There are very few plants that have the sweet, pungent, bitter, sour and salty tastes. In encompassing all five tastes, it represents the five elements. In the Chinese system, this also relates to the five directions, with the center being the added direction. This is a fascinating relationship, yet we would also correspond this numerologically to the number five, which represents balance.

Beyond the balancing properties usually observed on the physical level, such as warming and accentuation of the female side, there is an internal balancing that takes place on a spiritual level. A person gains a much greater sense of purpose in life, how they may balance different emotions, and how they may balance a relationship. One better understands how one's path fits into the present and the immediate future. This facet of balancing is very important for many individuals. It can also correspond, as one is involved in spiritual practices, to the development of a greater sense of balance even on the physical level. Athletes, acrobats, gymnasts, and others working in areas where balance is necessary, would benefit if they were also exploring spiritual areas. However, we are not suggesting this herb for accounting. That is a different kind of balancing.

The way this balancing takes place on a deeper spiritual level sometimes causes a conflict within people that is eased. This conflict exists more deeply and more powerfully the more one explores spirituality. Sometimes, the resolution to this is called enlightenment. These conflicts can result from contemplation of destiny versus free will, or from the way one understands the teaching of someone else versus your internal teaching. Or conflict may develop when comparing the ideas of one teacher with those of another and not finding a satisfactory solution. These paradoxes can be balanced within a person—not so that they recognize them as the truth, but only as guideposts as they follow and understand their own truth. On the highest spiritual level, this balancing allows one to recognize that one is of equal importance in the universe with all other people, with God, and with the balance of all things in nature.

There are many examples of this balance promoting harmony. Schizandra is especially recommended for those forced into a mold of harmony, unity, or balance when they do not know of that balance within themselves. Schizandra can then be very useful on a spiritual level for people discovering that balance in themselves. Then they may change society to help reflect this inner harmony.

As energy is utilized in the physical body, it results temporarily in an out-of-balance condition. As the body rebalances itself to what is called homeostasis, the energy is utilized in the appropriate manner. For instance, in hands-on healing, or techniques such as reiki, there is a movement of energy and the body is temporarily out of balance. This herb usually speeds up stabilization and homeostasis. This also occurs in acupuncture, and this herb is often recommended for people who are strengthening and tonifying the physical body. However, when you are also working on a spiritual path, you will be more receptive to the healing energies around you. Then one comes to a state of greater balance more quickly.

One also recognizes left and right balance in the entire body. The left and right brains are balanced, so that understanding ideas and combining the intuitive with logic are both enhanced. The ideas that one may need for practical application may be speeded up and assisted, as in a creative idea leading to a sculpture or an engineering concept. These projects are made more real. This usually involves the blending of rational and intuitive faculties, which is enhanced as a state of greater balance is achieved with this herb.

In Lemuria, the fruit was considered quite useful. It brought many facets of nutrition to people. Yet, it was also seen that many fruits had the sweet taste. For variety this fruit, which was relatively bland at first, was utilized in ceremonies and gradually became enmeshed with the five different tastes. At various times in Earth's history, one of the five tastes has predominated in this fruit. Now it is the more sour taste, so that individuals may be reminded of a path in which they gather greater strength and bring a warming, particularly to the female side of themselves. But at various times in the past, the sweet, pungent, salty, or bitter taste has predominated. Each of these has been emphasized in different ways.

In Lemuria, it was seen that the ability to mirror civilization within the taste of this fruit would be an unconscious reminder of this balancing principle for some time to come. And indeed, for much of the Lemurian phase, the five tastes were quite well balanced within this fruit. At the end of the Lemurian phase however, there was an imbalance and some of the bitter taste became much stronger. This was partly due to the change in civilization, particularly the Atlantean influence. The Atlantean influence of culture and society created a mirror in which the Lemurians were able to experience this shift on the level of taste. The natural kingdom associated with this plant, particularly its devic order and the plant itself, understood that its purpose had been fulfilled and was able to continue in such a manner for the rest of mankind's existence. Its karmic purpose is to remain as this mirror at all times for mankind.

All the chakras are balanced and stimulated together. There can be some extra emphasis at the heart chakra level, because it has an intrinsic balancing capability. But there is no direct transfer of this to the usual functions associated with the heart, such as the thymus or the physical heart. Balance may begin at the heart chakra level, but it extends throughout all of the other chakras. The kidney meridian is cleansed, and there is a strengthening of the lung and triple warmer meridians. The nadis throughout the body are stimulated, as these relate to all the chakras. A temporary state of balance between the etheric, mental, emotional, and physical bodies usually takes place within a few hours after the herb is consumed. There is a lasting effect in this appreciation and understanding of balance in the mental body that extends for some weeks after using the herb. The psora miasm is eased, and the ninth and twelfth rays are made clearer for most people.

Some of the most positive aspects of balance associated with the sign Libra are emphasized for most people. People with a number of planets in this sign, or energy associated with the sign because of being born having the Moon and Sun in it can often benefit, particularly in times of crisis, with this herb. Because it does present the five tastes, it is wise to make it available to animals, particularly domesticated animals, so that they may choose it. From time to time, it is quite stimulating and useful to them. The test point is the bone at the base of the throat where it joins the rib cage.

Self Heal

This perennial plant produces purple flowers in dense terminal spikes. It is used as an antispasmodic, astringent, tonic, diuretic, and vermifuge.

There is a tendency here for some of the energy closely associated with the fifth chakra to connect with the third and seventh chakras. On the herbal level, this is of great assistance in working with the physical body's ability to transfer medicinal properties. Spiritually, there occurs a powerful energy that leads to deeper absorption and easier expression, and a greater sense of power and strength in the world results from this absorption and expression. Used properly, the energy accelerates all spiritual processes and lessens the need for all physical processes. There are correlations to its rather interesting effects in the proper assimilation and utilization of the finer energies associated with the flower essence. The herb and flower essence of self heal make a good combination for individuals who have trouble assimilating food substances. This herb is also useful for those making a transition to vegetarianism. The absorption and utilization of protein is enhanced.

What also occurs more deeply in an individual is that expressive abilities are made clearer, so that a person feels the willingness to express the truth, to understand what other people are saying to them, and to speak the truth to others in a way in which they come to know the truth more easily. The etheric esophagus is activated, but as a signature that is only the beginning. On a deeper level, you see the connection with the purple or violet color of the flower and the way crown chakra energy must be involved for full spiritual understanding and expression.

This expressive energy can be available for healing purposes. The healing, as applied on the highest level, is indeed in harmony with the name of the plant. It is self-healing. This healing is most effective from the crown chakra downward. The energy is applied first to the way you would heal any past hurts regarding how you expressed God in your life or how others expressed God to you. This can lead to forgiveness of some of the dogmatic positions taken by traditional religious institutions.

There is also greater understanding of the vibrations associated with food. This can be useful for those who are simply coming to know foods better, to know their vibration before eating them. For those who are fasting, there is additional physical benefit, not only from the herb but also from the flower essence. There is enhanced absorption on the psychic level of gifts that have been expressed in one's life but have not yet been accepted. And there is a tendency to release negative thought forms more easily in the fasting state. This pattern develops partly because individuals experience greater comfort and relaxation during states of telepathy.

In Lemuria, the plant was utilized for its ability to bring the capacities associated with fasting deeper into the individual. It was seen that the absorption of food substances for some individuals would inevitable be a primary point of health difficulty in the future. Thus, other properties were developed by the devic order associated with the plant. And the devic order was able to gradually increase its own assimilation of the Lemurian culture, which is a necessary part of the two-way action that takes place in the development of such beings. Therefore, with mankind's current focus on nutrition and new areas of assimilation and expression, mankind is giving a positive effect to the devic order associated with self heal.

For centuries, mankind's misunderstanding or, in most cases, total ignorance of the devic order has allowed a wall to be erected on the conscious level between the devic order and humans. This wall is gradually being torn down, as more people attune to these subtler levels through nutrition, meditation, and other conscious activities that open people to the natural orders. Indeed, individuals who are seeking to know the devic order visually may find it a little more apparent, especially in the higher spiritual states achieved in working with this order directly. This is done by being around the plant and then visualizing an energy field or a ball of light associated with self heal. Then you would call these devic beings into your mind, speaking with love in your heart.

Extra energy is released in the fifth chakra that can extend into the physical throat and the digestive system by means of the saliva and even stomach acid. The kidney, lung, stomach, and small intestine meridians are slightly stimulated. The ability of the etheric body to absorb and work with vibrational levels from all the other subtle bodies is enhanced. There is an easing of the heavy metal miasm, and the third and fourth rays are slightly strengthened. This plant can be applied with some effectiveness with many animals, especially when there is poor absorption of food or a significant change in the diet. The test point is the base of throat.

Shepherd's Purse

This annual produces small white flowers. It is used as a diuretic and to alleviate various blood conditions.

There is an acceleration of life force when taking shepherd's purse. This life force energy is usually unconscious in a person. There is an enhancement of the essential instincts for survival and a strengthening of the physical body. This enhances regeneration in the physical body, because energies that have not been used, which one has not paid much attention to, are again brought to mind.

The signature of the plant relates to its being found in waste regions; it is a weed that is found in many different areas, under many circumstances. The life force may run through the plant quite strongly. This will be especially noticed by those sensitive to the etheric when the sun is directly overhead. There is a powerful interchange at the sun's highest point. This does not always mean at 12:00 noon, but rather will be unique to each location on the Earth. At such times, an etheric flash of energy takes place. This plant absorbs that energy and holds it within for quite some time. This can be transferred medicinally to individuals in its ability to provide greater energy to the body's instinctual systems.

Individuals who are working with kundalini yoga, various slow-developing meditative techniques, or other religious experiences that gradually build to peak experiences, may bring such events into their lives more rapidly. Also, the energy associated with these encounters may be better assimilated. The life force energy, as strengthened within an individual, is a positive by-product of such peak experiences. This can be focused into spiritual areas in which meditations become clearer.

There is an enhancement of all healing abilities which make use of talents that the client does not fully recognize. For instance, if you heal a woman who is able to move in ways of great gracefulness, but you notice, that there is no particular application in this, that she is neither a dancer or a healer or engaged in areas where gracefulness is important, you may help her make use of these almost wasted talents. The life force in the individual becomes more clearly available. You, as the healer, are taking the herb, but she can also ingest it in a tea. Then the healing process between you is made easier; the deeper sensation of life force is shared between you temporarily in a common alignment or vibration.

The energy of the sun, as utilized by plants, was understood as a simple and beautiful natural phenomenon in Lemurian times. It was seen that mankind should be reminded of this. Thus, the devic order associated with shepherd's purse was given the simple task of allowing these energies to be strengthened within the plant. The purpose of shepherds purse is to act as a reminder of this for mankind.

The third chakra is energized, the crown chakra is opened, and the root chakra becomes more relaxed in the process of opening to the life force. Energy through the governing vessel is enhanced and the bladder and liver meridians are strengthened. There is also increased energy in the nadis in the feet. The soul body is energized, which activates life force throughout the body. All the subtle bodies are temporarily aligned during that period of energy transference from the sun. The stellar miasm is eased, and the tenth and eleventh rays are strengthened. When the Sun repeatedly causes difficulty in a certain sign, there is some benefit in taking this herb. The test point is either cheek.

Squaw Vine

This herb is found along the east coast and has funnel-shaped white flowers growing in pairs. It is an astringent, diuretic, and tonic. The American Indians have long used the herb during the last weeks of pregnancy to make childbirth faster and easier.

There is a tendency for an internal system of symbols relating to Mother Earth to be more easily generated in an individual. This is a little different than simply stating that there is greater communication with Mother Earth. Rather, what is understood is the nature of the relationship to the Earth, the specific ways the Earth has been your friend. Your individuality and the Earth as a being are more clearly brought out. This is seen in the signature of the plant, in that it supports and grows around pine and other trees, and in its flowers that grow in pairs. Its relationship to Earth is also expressed by its closeness to the ground. The American Indians understood this connection and used it not only for its herbal properties, but recognized this deeper bonding with Earth. Indeed, many of the herbs used by the American Indians have a special bond with Mother Earth.

Individuals who have certain unrecognized ties to the Earth will greatly benefit by occasionally using this herb, perhaps once a month or every other month. These individuals will often demonstrate spaciness and difficulty with the feet. They need to understand the purpose of this relationship. Understanding Earth on a mental level is not enough. It must be a love relationship that is created, for the Earth often loves you very dearly; it is a matter of recognizing this love.

There is an enhancement of the ability to dowse, to understand where objects are located, especially under the Earth. One can better understand the vibrations of the Earth. Those seeking ways to scientifically explore, for instance, the Schuman resonance, geomancy, or working with the Earth's grid system should consider using this herb. However, what is revealed is not just the psychic aspect. One asks what is the ultimate purpose of their work. It is not just to make money or to help another individual find water or minerals in the ground, but rather, it is a way they honor the Earth and come to know her better.

The Lemurians understood that this plant was sacred to the Earth. It was a plant that the Earth's energy was allowed to be within. It was also seen that gradually the application of individuals who would be born through a physical body would become very important. The chemical composition, the way squaw vine affects the body, was seen as having an interesting and beneficial effect. Therefore, the devic order associated with this plant was given the interesting task of alerting children to their relationship with Mother Earth. We have often recommended, especially in the last months of pregnancy, that the parents bond with the child by speaking to the child about how welcome it will be on the Earth, and how the Earth will receive the child. The devic order is doing this during the last months of pregnancy when this herb is present. When it is taken internally, this energy can become fairly strong, and that is why it is recommended at the end of childbirth. The nature spirits, in understanding this relationship between the budding child and the Earth found great joy in this task and asked the Lemurians that there be some utility to make this real for individuals. By the mid-Atlantean phase, there was the completion of the karmic lesson of this plant, to make Earth's relationship with mankind more available. This energy has been available within the plant ever since.

The chakras in the back of the knees, as well as the root and second chakras, are activated, and the chakras in the feet are particularly stimulated. The kidney and spleen meridians are stimulated, and the thermal body is slightly strengthened. The astral and etheric bodies communicate information more easily. There is some assistance in easing the gonorrhea and tubercular miasms, and the fourth ray is strengthened. With the heliocentric chart, there is some relationship to planet Earth.

There are certain animals who become quite depressed shortly after being removed from the natural environment into captivity. It is best to put them back, but barring this, squaw vine and skullcap can be of some benefit, in combination. Then the animal may receive more knowledge of why it has been captured and again attune to the Earth. It may also then choose more easily to be with a human. To allow this process to take place, it is best never to train or break the animal as is sometimes done with horses. Rather, gradually let the animal know of the love that you share with it. This is especially relevant with wild horses, bears, tigers, pigs, and boars, as well as with most of the wild and fairly ferocious animals.

Strawberry

A common garden fruit, strawberry produces white flowers in the spring. It is used as an astringent, diuretic, and tonic.

There is an enhanced ability to cleanse past life difficulties by means of joy. This is hard for some individuals. They move through levels of understanding their past lives from the point of view of karma, of forgiveness even, but they do not take joy from the lifetimes that they lived. Yet, look at your own life. You must have moments of joy, ecstasy, and pleasure just to remain here. A life full of depression would be one you would likely leave. This herb helps individuals return to the joyousness that they received in being on the Earth in the past. This is particularly true with the leaf, although the fruit also assists in this process. In those past lives, there may have been difficult periods, so there is forgiveness in looking at those lives. The way the plant tends to persist, its beautiful sweet fruit, its joy in taste, and the deep healing that sometimes occurs in eating it are symbols of the signature. What occurs as a result of this greater joy in looking at past lives is a release of karma. In fact, it speeds up the release of karma faster than regression or deeper understanding with the mind. This is because joy helps integrate all aspects of previous lives that one is seeking to understand.

There is some enhancement of the willingness to accept that one has been here on the planet before. And there is improved memory of past lives. However, there is also a slight tendency to accept many different psychic gifts for the joy that they bring.

In Lemuria, the fruit was much smaller and was often unnecessary. The joyousness was seen and worked with as a glowing and loving energy. There, past lives and the memory of them were, in some cases, entirely unnecessary and in others, not filtered or blocked. In Lemuria, the rare opportunity to incarnate naturally gave the person many opportunities to learn in numerous ways. No filters to block past lives were necessary. Towards the end of Lemuria, such filters became important as reincarnation itself became more and more prevalent.

It was seen that, in the budding Atlantean civilization, there might be some difficulty along this line. The Atlanteans were spoken to about this. They requested that, in seeing into the future and understanding what would come to mankind, some fruit be chosen that would assist regardless of whether mankind had or had not any spiritual understanding. Strawberry was chosen for this, and clearly it was a good choice, because it is still used as a flavoring agent for its pleasant and tasty properties. The plant took upon itself the karmic purpose of becoming a deepseated or unconscious reminder to mankind of the joy in remembering past lives. There were many in Atlantis who felt this joy, even into the mid-Atlantean phase.

Today, when you take on a physical body through birth, you generally have erected many filters to block remembrance of past lives. There are many good reasons for this. The filters block out behavior patterns and too much information, including past actions that bring guilt or difficulty into this life.

There is a strengthening of the third and fourth chakras, the nadis in the arms, as well as the pericardium and heart meridians. Difficulties in the small intestine meridian are released. The etheric and emotional bodies are cleansed. Sometimes, this cleansing is quite deep and extends into the mental body. The cancer miasm eases, and the fourth, eighth, and ninth rays are strengthened. When strawberry is eaten, the effects of Venus are more clearly felt in an individual's life. The test point is the center of the chest.

Sundew

This is an insect-eating perennial found in moist areas. It is used to treat a wide variety of respiratory problems. It should not be used continuously.

It is important to understand how viruses and thought forms interrelate. A negative thought form allows entry and growth of viruses in the human body. Medically, sundew relieves one of viruses as well as of negative thought forms. The way the process works is similar to the way sundew works with insects. When it captures an insect, there is a gradual absorption. It is not an instantaneous or rapid motion, as with venus fly trap. The individual absorbs the lesson behind the negative thought form. As a result, the thought form is gradually understood; it is not just released. The message behind it is absorbed by the individual.

This can create several difficulties. If a person has resistance to such energy, it can have a catalytic effect; there can be some great change. However, in many cases, there will be an easing of the problem. Often lung difficulties of any kind, including breathing difficulties, are symbolically related to deeper emotional states associated with powerful energy. The symbolism here is simply that insects, especially the smaller ones that can be particularly irritating or troublesome without being directly harmful, are those that the plant works with most easily. And these are the insects that often hold the most difficult negative thought forms for individuals. This is not so much because they are difficult in the sense of power or of changing your life, but because they are difficult to understand. These negative thought forms can affect levels of judgment, misunderstanding of others, misapplication of speech, and inability to forgive. Each of these is a lesson that can be revealed more easily by using this herb, but there are some constraints. If a lesson provided as energy is not understood and there is not some change in your life in taking the herb, the negative thought form will tend, over three days, to reconstruct itself. During that period, you have what you would call a second chance—another time to look at the negative thought form and understand it. Then it is activated more by your free will than by the additional vibrational or spiritual influence of the herb. If at that time you have not succeeded in understanding it or working with it, in other words, if there is any other external virus or other physical difficulty that is not relieved, it is usually not wise to take the herb again. Some other technique is then recommended.

There is a release of any negative thought forms blocking an individual from accepting their psychic gifts. The third eye is often opened, and some healing abilities in an individual may be increased. If you are working with a client and there are intense judgments or the client reminds you of yourself in some way, this is eased. A greater connection develops between you and the client, perhaps for counseling, psychic training, or healing.

The plant in its current state did not exist in Lemuria. It developed later and was seen as necessary as these insects and negative thought forms emerged. The plant existed in other forms long before Lemurian civilization, but its ability to create these spiritual effects in a person were added in the Atlantean phase. An independent source to ease negative thought forms was needed. The plant took this on in a gradual manner and is still holding this as its karmic purpose.

There is a balancing of the stomach meridian, which may release energy into the chakras, especially the third chakra. There may be a deep sense of emotional attachment or sadness. This is part of the process of dispelling negative thought forms as the energy of sundew is absorbed. The third eye chakra may also open. The etheric and astral bodies are energized, the psora and gonorrhea miasms are eased, and there is a strengthening of the third, fourth, fifth, and sixth rays. The negative aspects of Pluto are often released, and the test point is the navel.

Tamarind

A tall tropical evergreen tree, tamarind produces yellow flowers and a cinnamon-colored fruit. It is a mild laxative that is also used as a cooling beverage in the tropics.

This cooling effect can be felt by those who are sensitive to the plant, even to psychic levels. Some can intensify this effect by using crystals. Before taking it as a cooling beverage when the spiritual effects are to be amplified, place four or five quartz crystals around it for at least ten or fifteen minutes. Then when the plant is absorbed as an herb, fruit, or beverage there is a lessening of stress. The stress that may be felt on the spiritual path may be partly due to the inner goal, the necessity for inner growth in this lifetime. Many people experience great pressure in their spiritual work, because they sense what a special and important time this is. This energy is eased in an individual. As a result, they develop greater patience in their spiritual path and a greater willingness to absorb, assimilate, and work with other areas. There is also a tendency for individuals who, in ecstatic states, have too much energy in the physical body to release the energy so that it does not harm them.

There is a definite trance enhancement property here. This allows an individual to be more fully relaxed, even in states in which there may be greater agitation, as in group channeling when people are present who are opposed to the ideas being presented or the knowledge that is being sought. During the deeper states of trance, there is an enhanced ability to absorb the information afterwards. This is partly due to the more natural-ized or relaxed state. Such individuals, while working on psychic levels, experience a deep quietness. It may be quite possible then for the energy of channeling to emerge from the quietness. For some individuals, the bever-age may be of some benefit in learning channeling.

In Lemuria, the plant was greatly praised and understood for these re-laxing properties. Especially towards the end of the Lemurian phase, it be-came quite necessary for the devic thought form associated with the plant to carry this deep into the Lemurians. That devic order helped the Lemuri-ans to use the relaxing qualities of tamarind to release fear. There was then a great deal of agitation and fear about what was happening on the planet, regarding what was to come in Atlantis. It was also seen by this devic or-der that, eventually, mankind would learn all levels of being and ultimately would accept its own role. To help in such self acceptance by relaxation, this beverage is of great use. The herbal properties of tamarind combined nicely with its spiritual properties, and over a very short period of time, the devic order established this unifying force.

There is a release of energy that can be stored in the root, second, and third chakras that may cause detriment to certain individuals. The great change in physical body process that sometimes happens when two meridians are linked, such as when the spleen and stomach meridians get wildly out of balance, can be rapidly corrected with this plant. There is a temporary strengthening in the meridians all over the physical body as this balancing takes place. The nadis in the chest are slightly stimulated, the connection between the emotional and mental bodies becomes stronger, there is an easing of the heavy metal miasm, and all the rays are energized. The test point is the base of the spine.

Tarragon

This popular shrub is commonly used as a seasoning. A diuretic and digestive aid, tarragon also eases insomnia.

Its rather unique taste and especially its odor stimulate a deeper sense of the self. This refers to the true self, not to what one has been told in life. For some individuals this creates a conflict, as if what they are seeking to become or what they have been has nothing to do with who they really are. This is a generally positive effect, because such a deep question is often important with very little resulting harm. However, there is also a tendency for the individual not to understand fully the answers. And yet they may be felt within. A greater acceptance of purpose may come to the individual as an important thing to be explored. Tarragon makes the choices around life purpose much clearer.

There is, in deep hypnotic states, a greater realization of God's energy within a being. Thus, the period of time in which one is in a hypnotic state can be extended. There can be more conscious or lucid dreaming, and some individuals may learn to astral travel in the dream state.

In Lemuria, the plant was understood for its ability to help those who had forgotten why they were on the planet, who their deepest friends were, and what their purpose was. This was gradually seen as more necessary to understand, and so, towards the end of the Lemurian phase, this capacity was developed in the plant by the devic order associated with it. The karmic lesson of the plant, however, is a little stronger than this. It is to help mankind understand that it needs a purpose. This purposefulness and deeper understanding is not a part of all individuals. There are many who are here just to enjoy life, but even with these people taking tarragon will create more balance. The devic order of this plant is fairly active today. It can create questions about life purpose and God that may eventually be answered.

The fifth chakra is stimulated, which assists in the expression of what one receives. The third eye chakra is also stimulated. The astral body is balanced, the emotional body is activated, and the mental body becomes more relaxed. The stellar miasm eases and the fifth ray is affected, especially when an individual is just learning to understand this ray. Those who are negatively aspected by Jupiter will find some benefit by taking tarragon. The test point is the base of the throat.

Thyme

This widely used culinary herb has small lilac to white flowers that appear in the summer or fall. It is used as an antiseptic, carminative, and vermifuge.

This herb has an interesting or paradoxical effect in relationship to the spiritual properties versus some of the physical properties; it has a depressing or slowing down effect on the physical level. This also supplements spiritual properties which primarily consist of a deep stimulation towards action. This action can be taken in many different ways, but the person is brought more closely into contact with their reason for being, with the willingness to have action in the world. Thyme has been noted on occasion to relieve headaches, yet many people may even experience headaches when utilizing thyme. This is because of a willingness to release things that interpose themselves between your soul's purpose and the way you struggle with relationships, various difficulties, and blockages to the path of action. This yields a fascinating, extremely well-balanced effect with regards to the sedative properties of thyme. It is used to calm one down, and at the same time, one is gathering strength in action.

Its signature is related to this pattern on the level of the essential oil. The odor of thyme is better than the herb when taken as a tea to bring one to a calm space while gathering strength for action. Emotionally, there is an inward journey, but the journey is always directed by thyme to a place of action, a place from which things get done. This can be useful for people who need to spread information, who need to be involved in projects, or who need to bring the attention of the world to bear upon specific areas they are focusing on. Perhaps publicity or contact with the media is necessary. This is not the inward spiritual journey but is where the paradox regarding the sedative effects are so interesting. When thyme is initially taken, there is an inward sedation and calming effect, but this is more on the physical level. Energy is being drawn from the physical level deep inside the individual, usually to the unconscious mental level. Then it is brought through the etheric body into the mental body in a more conscious fashion, so that the individual has focus of attention.

It is also recommended to use thyme when a sense of direction is needed. This is not so much that it will provide the direction itself, but it will give more energy towards looking for it. And there is an increased ability to understand and relate to one's chosen destiny, to become more comfortable with it. This is useful in the final stages of releasing past life karma. Perhaps you have done past life regression or you have utilized channeling or other techniques to learn about past lives. You have balanced this by working on the principles in your life, and now it is time to point towards the future. Thyme is useful because, with this energy added to your own way of looking into the future, you can approach it with a sense of peace, with inner strength. In shaping projects and events with others, you may glimpse their futures more easily. This is not quite the same thing as prophecy, when directions and energies from many different sources are usually combined together to give a particular informative result. Rather, this is the energy of many individuals working together towards a common goal. That goal becomes clearer. A vision of the future may be enhanced, and such ideas of prophecy may be strengthened.

Smelling the aromatic oil develops the ability of clairaudience. The sounds that may be received will be within a given frequency range unique to each individual. They will be sounds that could be quite useful in bringing energy to the surface. Chanting is definitely assisted by the aromatic oil.

In Lemuria, the plant was developed over a gradual period. Much of the Lemurian civilization was exposed to the herb. It is a common flavoring ingredient today. In Lemuria, it was used in a similar fashion, though not for eating but for smelling. The aromatic oil was observed in nature to have a pleasant effect upon the constitution. And so the plant was looked at from many different points of view. It was seen then that it could indeed take on much of the understanding of will as it related to the Lemurian civilization. This working with will is a way in which action at the purest level is in communion with the energy of the Earth. This was one of the purer forms of energy in the Lemurian civilization. This is also why thyme has been recognized throughout mankind's history and utilized as an herb, spice, and aromatic oil.

In Lemuria, there was an intermingling with thyme, and in this intermingling many of the essential ideas of the Lemurian civilization came into this herb. However, it was also flexible enough that its will related to civilization as it was needed. On the current journey through Western civilization, it is necessary to have peace with oneself so one can take action. Thus, for the last few thousand years, and probably for the next few thousand years, this is the path that thyme will take. Its karmic purpose eventually will be to bring the understanding of the Earth through the facet of will to mankind. But this will be tempered by mankind's deeper understanding of love.

There is a strengthening of the third chakra, easing of difficulties in the second and fourth chakra, and a speeding up of the meridian flow in the liver, kidney, and bladder. The triple warmer meridian is balanced, the nadis in the wrists and ankles are stimulated, the syphilitic miasm is eased, and the third, fourth, and fifth rays are brought into greater focus for most individuals. The most positive aspects of planet Mars are enhanced by this herb. It would be best to use thyme when Mars is in trine with ruling or important planets in your chart.

The flow between the mental and etheric bodies increases in intensity. The physical body is affected at the cellular level, generally releasing past life information but more specifically cellular energy. This is usually transmitted from the astral to the mental body, and thyme enhances this process. Cells carry a history, or a record of one's life. This may extend back several generations. These are specific family generations, not just relating to past lives. This information is made more available to people. Patterns of eating, environmental conditions, and trauma that may have stressed the body, as well as events that have benefited the body, have associations with them. Some of these associations relate to time, place, or specific individuals. This information is made more available to a person through this herb.

This plant is useful for animals in many different ways. Because it has been on the planet for so long, there is a direct genetic confluence or concordance between most animals and the essential nature of this plant. Therefore, when it is available to them to be eaten, they may choose it in small quantities. In fact, when animals in the wild come across thyme, they often chew it as if they have been deprived of it in their lives. The test point is the neck.

Turnip

Turnip is a popular vegetable that produces small yellow flowers. It is used as a salve and poultice.

The tuber is the recommended part to be utilized. Turnip should be eaten raw, especially when shredded so it is more palatable. There is a strengthening of the astral body due partly to the way turnip, though of white color, grows underground and has a vibrational capacity to attract darker and more difficult energies from the Earth to purify them.

We have occasionally mentioned that the Earth is able to change forces of negativity and difficulty into energies of health and harmony for all beings on the planet. Many roots of various plants are able to do this. But of the plants that are accessible to humans, turnip has the ability to do this most easily for most people. When people are having difficulty with astral travel, are involved in the astral body in difficult dream experiences, or are having trouble in their waking life because of not understanding their dreams, it is wise to use this herb. Indeed, when the turnip tuber is eaten, there is not only a strengthening of the astral body, but dream recollection is intensified and enhanced. However, there will be a tendency for the dreams experienced, when turnip is eaten regularly, to be of an astral nature, that is, nonsymbolic dreams, not just relating to what happens to you during your day or your week, but dreams in which the astral body leaves the bedroom where you are sleeping and moves to levels in which it understands consciousness in many different fashions. Turnip enables one to integrate information. In itself, turnip, does not enhance astral travel. Instead, it strengthens the astral body, and thus with some willingness for astral travel, the understanding of what occurs will be easier for a person.

In addition, difficult or dark energies working with a person, particularly in the wintertime, are released by using turnip. Many times the release of such energetic forces can only take place on the astral level. This is because such energies are based on a vibration in harmony, or near a vibrational resonance, with the astral body of most people. Turnip is recommended for dispelling negative thought forms experienced while asleep.

This happens more in the winter. As the days grow shorter and nights longer, there is an innate encouragement of these darker beings. Many of them have their origins in the thought forms of other people. They are unconscious hatreds, energies of prejudice or difficulty. They are taken within the Earth for a time, but with an intelligence in and of themselves are generally released in the darker hours, perhaps midnight or 2:00 a.m. These energies proceed for a longer and easier time when the night is extended, so they are stronger in the wintertime. Turnip, with its ability to dispel these forces, relieves one of difficult sleep patterns, so it may be recommended, particularly in the wintertime, for people with insomnia. Do not eat it directly before sleeping. Instead, eat it in a salad at noontime or sometime during the day, so its effects may permeate gradually into the astral body. There is also a strengthening of the mental body, but the primary effect is on the astral body.

There is, of course, with the enhanced ability to understand astral travel, greater control over the process. This may allow some individuals a choice. They come to a place in the astral experience in which they may choose a much higher level of vibration. This generally involves a guide or helper, someone to point the way. Communication with such spirit guides in the waking state, with the conscious mind, is enhanced. If you have met such a guide in the astral state, it is wise to meditate and imagine that spirit guide with you again. Ask for the communication under the influence of turnip, and such spirit communication will likely be enhanced. Make this request the next day, and for three more days, because astral energies generally take about three days to permeate the physical level fully. As astral traveling is enhanced, there is a sense of greater peace in the astral state. For some individuals, this may mean that at first they recognize fear in the astral experience and are snapped back to conscious reality, but under the influence of turnip, it may be much easily to choose a path of greater calm and peace than have fear. As the energy is strengthened within them, the understanding of why they were afraid may come, and this is very important.

There will also be a strengthening at the physical level, and the feet may be stimulated. This is primarily because turnip juice is so cleansing. One can utilize this by imagining the energy proceeding from the base of the foot directly into the Earth. There is a deeper connection to the Earth. Do this technique while meditating with your spirit guides.

In Lemuria, this plant was seen as primarily decorative, and the root or tuber was quite small. The Lemurians noticed the glow of the root while astral traveling. It seemed to change their vibrational level while they explored the world around them on many different vibrational levels other than the physical. This tiny point of glowing light seemed to be able to enhance and work with their energy. It was as if one could smell, touch, and feel it on the astral plane. This was a curious phenomenon, but not of very much interest until the Lemurians recognized that working on the astral level might eventually become difficult for mankind. Then turnip was chosen, and the devic order brought to action with the idea of easing astral plane difficulties.

In Atlantean times, as more and more thought forms of a confusing nature were released to mankind, it appeared that turnip would need a new role. That was one in which the negative forces would have to be dealt with. We have spoken of the elementals, barely at the level of permanence or intelligence as you would understand it, but still able to create some havoc on the physical plane. Turnip was a natural solution for easing negative thought forms because of its ability to work on the astral level. The devic order associated with it gradually took on the task of relieving some of these energies. Its karmic purpose is to return to its former state, in which it dances in the astral light to aid in the enjoyment of life without a heavy burden or task being placed upon it. This is in harmony with astral travel, which is not just for gathering information, but is also for the enjoyment of this plane. Dancing is much easier without a physical body and with the symbols provided on the astral level.

There is some opening of the root chakra and stimulation of the crown chakra, but the primary emphasis is on the throat chakra. The throat chakra is opened and strengthened; energy is released from it. The kidney, lung, and pericardium meridians are strengthened. The nadis at the soles of the feet, throat, and top of the head are stimulated, and the third and eighth rays are clarified for most people. There is an easing of the cancer miasm. This may bring some people to a state of greater clarity about cancer and all that it works with on this planet. Some of the negative influences of the planet Neptune may be relieved by this herb. Usually, take it when your Sun is in square with Neptune. The test point is the soles of the feet.

Vervain

Small, pale-lilac flowers grow on this perennial plant. It is used to ease fevers, headaches, pleurisy, and ulcers.

Vervain helps to attain a deeper understanding of what occurs on the fourth dimension and how you interact on such a level, particularly with energy patterns that are formed on this other dimensional plane before they come into physical existence. One might say that this is the realm of the etheric body, but this is not entirely accurate. The etheric body is working specifically with source energies from the fourth dimension. However, the etheric body primarily exists as an interface between the other dimensions and the physical body and three dimensional world you are familiar with.

When vervain is used, many processes of interdimensional energy transmission, reception, and utilization take place. Part of this is a condensation; vast amounts of energy condenses in small quantities into the etheric body and then are transmitted to the physical body. Vervain assists this process by speeding it up. Individuals who understand manifestation or who work with creative visualization will benefit by using vervain.

The interesting shape of the stem of this plant is an indicator of many of its properties. On the dimensional level of understanding, this is a model to give you greater understanding of your world, how to coexist with other levels and work in many ways on the fourth dimension. It is hard to understand the nature of the fourth dimension when it is not easily tangible or seeable. Vervain reminds the individual of this.

Attunement to such higher energies affects psychic gifts and energy on the purer, undefined level of the intuitive process. Much of this higher energy can disturb some people. The possibilities and potentials that they see are available around them but are not clearly understood. In such individuals, there can be a great deal of nervousness and difficulty with sleeping. This is where some of the tranquilizer effects of vervain have a longer lasting and deeper effect. It is not merely from the various substances that it imparts, but rather it is from interdimensional energy attunement. An enhanced compression of energy happens when a person wishes to focus fourth dimensional energy, even when they are not consciously aware of the process.

This process aids in assimilating energy released by inert gas devices and homeopathic remedies in their lower potencies, from 12x downward. Many fourth dimension energies are easily unlocked by homeopathic substances and inert gas devices. There is greater relaxation about psychic abilities and less attention and focus on such gifts by the conscious mind. This does not mean that the abilities are lessened. Rather they are strengthened, because the conscious mind does not stand in the way. For instance, those troubled by the results of channeling will experience a definite enhancement of the channeling process by using vervain.

If vervain is taken with a flower essence or gem elixir, there will be a synergistic influence, because the essence or elixir would be more activated by vervain. However, not all individuals will be aware of this effect. This impact will partly depend on the person's sensitivity to the energies that are released at these higher dimensional levels.

In Lemuria, the plant was utilized in its early stages in ritual. It was then a lot smaller and grew much closer to the ground. Gradually, the energies of the Lemurians, focused through ritual and play, became a part of this plant's dance, as you might call it. Vervain became part of the ritual, so it naturally extended outward and the stems grew a bit longer. It was seen that, in mankind's future, the full understanding and vision of interdimensional energy would not be easy. The devic order associated with this plant was assigned to aid in this understanding, and the plant willingly took on this stimulation and focusing of energy from other dimensional levels. Indeed, at various times in Lemuria and more often in Atlantis, a loss of understanding multidimensional energy took place. Gradually, the understanding of multidimensional energy was greatly diminished in the Egyptian, Grecian, Western and many other cultures. This was when vervain came into its own. And that is why it is more useful today, as this understanding of energy is less understood on this planet. Thus, the karmic purpose of vervain is to provide this energy in a more focused form. Its ultimate purpose is to achieve multidimensional transfer of energy from the fifth dimension. Vervain will then be transformed and will attain some degree of consciousness in and of itself.

There is a stimulation of the fifth and seventh chakras. The liver meridian is cleansed, while the pericardium meridian is enhanced and energized. The nadis throughout the throat and forehead area are slightly stimulated, and the etheric body is brought into a temporary state of alignment in an oscillatory pattern. It swings between the mental and physical bodies in a regular rate at around the Earth frequency of 7.83 cycles per second. Individuals who feel particularly attuned to Earth energy may also benefit from vervain. The cancer miasm is slightly eased, and the fourth, fifth, and sixth rays are brought into a state of greater clarity. When animals are upset, acting out of ordinary patterns, or have difficulty sleeping, vervain is recommended. The test point is midway between the shoulder and neck.

Walnut

This tree produces male and female flowers in catkins. Walnut is used as a digestive aid and to relieve gout and gum problems.There is a definite strengthening of spiritual purpose. This takes place outside the will. The will is divine purpose as an individual manifests it. However walnut, particularly when the nut is eaten, brings greater alignment with your purpose because the purpose itself is strengthened. Unfortunately for many individuals, simply strengthening one's purpose is not sufficient to help in their understanding. Therefore, it is often best to combine walnut with its flower essence and other herbs such as chaparral, red clover, juniper berry, Chinese burdock, and dong quai, for women during menstruation. Then the will of an individual may be stimulated to focus upon one's purpose.

The way life purpose is strengthened by walnut results in a strengthening of the physical body for those who are aligned with spiritual levels. This is particularly useful for people who have a spiritual understanding of vegetarianism and yet are still addicted to meat. In breaking free from this, the first pattern is a mental understanding of what is to be. They then recognize some of their purpose, and energy that wishes not to harm, but only to love, is strengthened in them by using walnut in the diet. One, of course, must do this cautiously; walnut is quite rich and strong in certain oils. Some of these are beneficial. There is also its protein content that should be examined. In making the transition from meat, the physical body is strengthened along with the belief that it is best not to eat meat.

There is a clearer perception of the path and purpose of others. When developing psychic gifts, one is able to trust these more. This inner trust and strengthening enables the individual to hold energy within the physical body in various psychic states for much longer periods of time.

Walnut looks somewhat like the brain. It has a hard shell and rather tasty interior which is intertwined with the shell. People may notice this in attempting to extract the nut. Similar strengthening modes of the individual are intertwined with their life, their higher purposes, and the way in which their brain functions.

This has been a very interesting tree on the Earth and has been utilized as a food substance throughout history. The energies associated with the plant began in Lemuria strictly as a food that was used in certain rituals. The particular color associated with walnut was utilized for painting the body, and its odor helped people find their purpose in life. This was needed even in Lemuria. There were those in Lemuria who grew a bit depressed or anxious. The solution was a strengthening of their purpose, so that they would have the resolve and will to continue in the world. The devic order associated with walnut was given this task, and it saw that it would be extremely important for mankind. It was very difficult for this task to be fully revealed to the Atlantean people. This karmic purpose was often forgotten, or in some cases, repressed. It provided many genetic characteristics in certain latter day Atlantean experiments that created some difficulty on the planet. However, the final result of this was the wide variety of walnut that occurs worldwide. Walnut helped in some of the Atlantean genetic manipulation experiments, it was one way in which, at least on some small level, its devic order could permeate again into mankind.

There is a strengthening of the chakras in the knees as well as in the fifth, sixth, and seventh chakras. The eighth, ninth, and tenth chakras above the head are aligned temporarily. This causes a great flow of energy from higher levels into an individual, and there is a greater sense of purpose, peacefulness, and trust of oneself. There is added movement in the governing vessel meridian and extra energy in the nadis by the knee region. The etheric body is cleansed, the soul body is strengthened, and the mental body is stimulated. The psora miasm is significantly eased, and the seventh and eighth rays are made clearer and easier to understand. There is some benefit in the varieties of walnut being again brought together so that, ultimately, when entirely combined, an almost generic walnut would eventually be created again on the planet. This would strengthen its spiritual properties. The test point is the top of the head.

Willow

A tall tree found in Europe and the United States, willow is a popular Bach flower essence. As an herb, willow is considered an astringent, tonic, and anti-periodic.

There is some transfer of willow flower essence properties to the herbal use of willow. With grief, pain, and energy associated with sadness, there is additional assistance on a higher spiritual level in using this herb. Under most circumstances, the ability to release pain, to cry, and to allow inner sadness to come to the surface more easily can be intensified in people, and they can move through it quicker with this herb. Yes, it is pain-relieving, analgesic in some of its effects, but this is not only due to chemical action. It results more from bringing the pain to a person's conscious awareness, so that they may understand the reason for the trouble. Pain is always a sign of something amiss or something wrong.

In moving through levels of pain, one often understands more and gains a better grasp of the way of all things. When leaving behind an old pattern and coming to a new one, there may be pain, and it is sometimes hard to break through. The best thing for a person under such circumstance is not to question the emotion or the source of the pain. Rather, simply allow the feeling to pass by expressing it, by crying or allowing it to surface, and then when it is appropriate, have a moment of peace. In that moment of peace, you will be much more in touch with a sense of love, a sense of beingness. That is the time to express that love, even if it is only by imagining a beam of beautiful light pouring from you to another person or perhaps to the world at large. The entire process of visualization, releasing pain, and the ability to perceive new patterns are enhanced by using this herb. Indeed, there are a number of poems associated with weeping willow. It also has its own particular way of moving in the wind. Many of these resound unconsciously with people as they understand how this tree forms, and how the ability to release sadness is intrinsic within themselves.

Spiritually, there is a deep sense of sadness as one understands why this entire planet has been subjected to great difficulties, suffering, and levels of incongruities. As you understand the difficulties that many people have experienced on this planet, there is increased understanding that the suffering you also experience is shared for the purpose of greater joy. As sadness is released, you may discover a deeper understanding of God. This comes not on a mental level, not even on an emotional level, but at the level of pure joy on the cellular level, as if every cell is awakened at the etheric level, as if every part of your body becomes more alive. An appreciation of God's joy is enhanced by using this herb.

There is, of course, a consequent transfer here in which understanding another person's enlightened place is easier. And so it is useful to use this herb when seeking to assimilate the teachings of a master. And there is some connection here with understanding the ancient ways—the patterns in the past before mankind's civilization. For people to really understand ancient history, it is sometimes necessary to put aside many of the patterns and understanding that you have today. This is not, as it would seem, to put knowledge aside just so that new ideas do not confuse old ones. Rather, it is that, especially at the emotional level, one would wish to use old information immediately to make a better world and to gain greater understanding for yourself. If you do this, you may appreciate the rut mankind has got into. It is useful to be shielded from this so that you do not experience sadness too deeply. This is where willow helps, because one is able to assimilate these past levels of information and rather quickly move through levels of sadness to appreciate mankind's patterns and utilize the information for change. This gives extra capacity to philosophers and people with ideas of the future who wish also to delve into past history, and willow is recommended for such a purpose.

In Lemuria, the tree was utilized for shade and meditation. Its great beauty was well known with the people. It was also seen that some suffering and difficulty lay ahead for mankind. And many times the question was asked, "How may this be eased for mankind?" And so in meditations beneath this beautiful tree, an antidote was discovered; a place of great joy. It was in those moments of enlightenment that the tree extended a willingness and a love to the Lemurians, as if to say, "How may I also be a part of this joy?" The Lemurians saw the way sadness might block mankind from understanding God's joy, so they gave to the tree information and the capacity to change itself to remind mankind of how to release sadness and to experience God's joy. Its karmic purpose, obviously, is to continue to maintain this. Yet, at some point in mankind's future, it is also hoped that the plant will fully release all pain and suffering of mankind. Then its karma will be balanced, and the plant will likely change again. It is likely to grow even taller and to bring the ideas of God even more clearly into action by producing flowers of all different colors.

There is more balance in the second, third, and heart chakras. A strengthening of the pericardium and triple warmer meridians, as well as the nadis throughout the hands, feet, and chest takes place. The etheric body is cleansed, the mental body is energized, and the emotional body expands. The syphilitic miasm eases, and the fourth, fifth, eleventh, and twelfth rays are made clearer for most people. Animals are often attracted to this tree. If one is choosing a site for animals to roam free, it is wise that they be by this tree. The test point is the center of the chest.

Wintergreen

This native American shrub produces white flowers in the summer. It is a tonic, stimulant, diuretic, and aromatic.

There is an enhanced ability for sound to be directly converted into spiritual energy and force. The inner vibratory rate by which the life force enters an individual on a daily or momentary basis is not sufficient for most individuals to fully assimilate and work with wintergreen. As a result, there can occasionally be some difficulties combining this herb with homeopathic or other vibrational remedies. Homeopathic potencies higher than 30x will be particularly effected. This is not always the case, but for safety's sake it is probably best to avoid combining wintergreen with such remedies. One reason is that the great penetrating quality of wintergreen tends to shift an individuals vibration rather dramatically. This can have the effect that a homeopathic remedy will be fully presented in the body, but not able to properly transfer its energy to the person. Wintergreen can actually temporarily increase the life force energy, but to a degree that it is hard for the person to assimilate properly, so it will affect many things at subtle levels before it affects the persons' consciousness and physical body. Such energy spills over to the mental and etheric bodies, where the primary action of homeopathic remedies tends to take place. Wintergreen could be used as part of vibrational therapy, but it should not be done within the same time frame. Wait at least three days between taking wintergreen and a homeopathic remedy, flower essence, or gem elixir.

Its odor and penetration deep with the individual may enhance the ability to use sound in all its forms. As an individual chants, hums in meditation, or creates a simple Om sound there may be a deeper sense that the sound is vibrating in harmony with the individual. The penetration of the odor is its signature. It runs deep in an individual, especially within the skin. The skin is in many ways receptive to sound, and it is hoped mankind will better understand this auditory level.

As more individuals are accepted in society who have been given the particular cross to bear of being fully deaf from birth, they may find greater spiritual awareness of vibration in new ways. These are largely sensory. This involves not only the movement of subcutaneous tissue, but the skin's surface. These individuals will certainly find this property enhanced by the occasional use of wintergreen, particularly in aromatherapy. However, it is hoped that what they learn can also be transferred to hearing. Such individuals may learn to hear their own vibration more deeply. On a spiritual level this is of great assistance. There is a continuous and joining vibration throughout the universe. It is the life force of humanity and God's loving energy. It is sound at all times. Individuals able to more easily tune into this sound and merge with it, may find many inner visions stimulated, a greater sense of God within, and greater peace.

There is some enhancement of sound's ability to be used in healing to assist individuals in deeper states of self-love. There are enhanced clairaudience and deeper states of meditation in which all psychic abilities are then increased. This makes it easier to gather any form of data. The vibration of what it is you are gathering data from is the source by which the information appears to you. There will be enhancement of this technique using wintergreen.

This plant was used in Lemurian ritual to create an area of the Earth in which a particular ceremony or focusing of energy took place. Generally, this was a grouping of twenty or thirty individuals in a clearing or grove in the forest that was about a hundred feet in diameter. Wintergreen oil was placed around this area. Its odor was breathed deeply by the individuals, and then they invited the devic spirit to be with them to assist in sonic work. Such meditations were not always done for a specific purpose, as in providing more peaceful and healing energy to the Atlanteans or focusing devic energy on a given plant or animal species. Rather, it was often done just to make contact with and have a joyousness interchanged between Mother Earth and the Lemurians. The devic order associated with wintergreen recognized this penetrating capacity and attempted to gradually enhance it. Under the guidance and tutelage of the Lemurians, it was made permanent, and its karmic purpose remains to provide these potentials to humanity.

The sixth, seventh, and eighth chakras are brought into a temporary state of alignment. As a result, added energy, beginning on the sonic level, may move through an individual and beyond. This focusing of energy may then proceed into some of the other chakras for healing. There is some strengthening of the gall bladder meridian, the nadis in the ears are stimulated, and the etheric and causal bodies are strengthened. The fifth and tenth rays are also augmented. There are some positive effects in the symbolization of Uranus with individuals. Animals will often be drawn to this plant for its medicinal uses. It would be wise to give it to your pets two or three times a year, so they may choose to chew it. The test point is the earlobes.

Witch Hazel

This small tree or shrub is found in the eastern United States. It is an astringent, sedative, and tonic.

There is an enhancement of the ability for individuals to let go. The scaliness of the bark is a good indicator of the individual's ability to release what is external. This releasing pattern especially takes place on the higher chakra levels, but this is not always understood, since the letting go process is generally seen as primarily emotional. When engaging in spiritual practices, one often confronts techniques that do not work, that do not assist an individual on their path. These may be held onto out of habit. Witch hazel allows relaxation on a spiritual level for an individual's deeper path to emerge. This does not so much focus energy on the deeper path, but simply allows it to emerge more easily.

Witch hazel releases past life karma that is currently affecting an individual. Some of these properties also work with the witch hazel flower essence. However, witch hazel in the herbal form can be of special benefit for an individual to understand just why those karmic difficulties are no longer needed and to see how there can be change. In meditating upon difficulty in a relationship, there is some understanding of the karmic attributes when witch hazel is taken.

There is also some enhancement of the penetrating insight that is often necessary for fully understanding past life karma and for a willingness to accept new ideas. Individuals learning new techniques that are in contradiction to old processes may become less attached or nonattached for longer periods of time using this herb. This nonattachment can then allow reflection on paradoxes regarding difficulties about the two systems of teaching. This is useful because, in the inner discovery of information and understanding, a paradox is ultimately first resolved on an internal level. The paradox is not understood mentally as to which teaching is right, but rather it is known inside that both teachings are right and a sense of oneness results. This is the correct assimilation of a paradox. This is largely a mental process, but psychically it allows a deeper acceptance of several points of view, and ultimately an integration of these points of view into a process, meditation, or particular technique that is very useful. Thus, witch hazel is applicable in many areas of psychic inquiry such as new techniques of psychic development, healing, and telepathy where there is a contradiction in the techniques being learned.

Indeed, there are many avenues of psychic development that most individuals have not entertained even as possibilities of developing. For instance, the senses may develop so that an individual can, in a more conscious state, journey within the Earth with clear sight and vision, observing and seeing, almost being able to touch things within the Earth. There is also the ability to communicate on levels far deeper than people currently understand—as you receive information, so you give it. In this way, a communication vortex is set up that draws in the energy of the entire soul stream that you are communicating with. Instead of receiving information that can be quantified or separated into a single voice, it is received as many voices at once. There are many ideas around this that are not understood now, because mankind would not know what to do with these psychic gifts. They cannot yet be used in a practical way. It is possible that in the future many more of these gifts will be discovered. In fact, the guiding rule here is that, if it is something you can conceive of or can imagine, it is most likely possible.

In Lemuria, the plant was used for its penetrating odor. There is a continuing value in aromatherapy, although most individuals will today find the aroma quite distasteful. Certain individuals may, however, have a link with Lemurian times, when the odor was used to cleanse an area where a particular meditation or ritual was done for long periods of time. When it was seen that a change was necessary, this plant might have been used. There was, moreover, an attunement with the devic order to achieve this cleansing. Its cleansing properties were not utilized very much after Lemuria even into the current day, and this is partly due to the higher frequency of cleansing that is required. In most cases, cleansing required by Atlanteans and later civilizations was of a more direct fashion, relating to the emotional and etheric bodies, not so much the causal and soul bodies. But this latent cleansing capacity remains with the plant. Deep cleansing must also work on the higher levels. There must be cleansing on causal and soul body levels. This process will be available for individuals more and more in the future.

There is a slight cleansing effect in the root and seventh chakras. When witch hazel is applied to the scalp, there may be an additional benefit besides simply helping hair growth and the skin. This herb may penetrate deeply into the seventh chakra. However, the primary effect of witch hazel is on the higher chakras, especially the eighth, ninth, and tenth. There is some enhancement of the liver meridian flow, the causal and soul bodies are particularly cleansed, while the mental body is stimulated. The psora and gonorrhea miasms are eased, and the ninth, tenth, eleventh, and twelfth rays are all brought more into visibility and clarity for individuals. Positive aspects of Pluto, particularly in the natal chart, are good indicators of when to use witch hazel. The test point is the medulla oblongata.

Wood Betony

Wood betony is often found in wood regions throughout Europe. This flowering herb is still popular for treating bladder and kidney problems.

The ability to absorb and work with Earth energy and to share love between two people, perhaps on a purely physical level, is assisted by this herb. As for the signature, its reddish color and ability to combine with the Earth's energy are felt by those who project love to the plant. The connection with the Earth is inspired and enhanced by a loving vibration, because love is inherent in our connection with the Earth.

The negative thought forms associated with AIDS, as opposed to similar diseases engendered by even the same viral form, such as cancer, are eased. This is partly because the negative thought forms of AIDS come more clearly to view regarding sexuality. The lessons associated with AIDS are more important than the virus. This involves loving oneself, and the way sexuality is an intense, spiritual, and even precious part of that process. Lastly, the way sexuality relates to all of mankind is brought into greater clarity by wood betony.

Psychically, what develops is a greater merging ability, and tantra is activated. People can work better on various projects, such as co-authoring a book, because of a greater attunement with each other. Individuals who have some difficulty developing deeper intimacy with people they wish to be close to, especially with a spouse or another loved one, would benefit from wood betony. A merging takes place on a psychic level. Fear sometimes develops as a result of this because the two people involved begin to think each other's thoughts. This can be a little disturbing, but the pattern is eased by this herb.

The plant's origin predates Lemuria but was not fully brought into action until the mid-Atlantean phase, when full sexual differentiation became a problem. Then some of the attitudes around sexuality were a bit difficult to understand, and this plant helped ease such tensions. Wood betony works for both men and women.

The root and second chakras are brought into increased harmony and are better able to move energy up through the body. The circulation and spleen meridians are enhanced. There is natural spillover to the kidney meridian, but it is not directly affected. All the other meridians move more easily through the lower parts of the body, especially in the legs, thighs, buttocks, hips and abdominal regions. The emotional body is strengthened, and the gonorrhea miasm is eased. When Mars is in difficult aspects to other planets in the natal chart, this herb will often help. The test point is the place in acupuncture called 'conception vessel one.'

Yam

Wild yam is a perennial vine that produces small green-yellow flowers. In Chinese medicine, yam is used as a tonic and to ease diarrhea.

There is increased yin-yang balance in the physical body. When one is working on various spiritual levels, there can be temporary states of imbalance in the physical body that are significantly eased by this plant. Yam stimulates the body in a self-governing manner. There is also a strengthening of the individual's ability to merge divine will with personal will. At a certain level of this process the ego is tested.

The signature of this plant relates to its depth in the ground and its seeming appearance of an ability to move through the ground like a torpedo. The Earth around it is intimately cooperating with such movement. Its roots draw energy from quite deep in the Earth, yet some of this energy may be seen by those with etheric vision, even as it moves through the stem of the plant.

There is more balance for individuals struggling with willpower. They may have misused will, perhaps harming others by willfulness. Such individuals may be seeking to change the effect and power of their will on others. There is also an easing of difficulties relating to negative thought forms. This is not a direct action on the negative thought forms, but rather a strengthening of the will. Remote healing is also enhanced. This is naturally strengthened as the will becomes more aligned with divine will.

There has long been a particular association with this plant. It has the ability to concentrate energy. This was well known in Lemuria and was quite respected. At a certain point, this energy concentration was seen to be necessary for mankind, and then the question was posed by the devic order, "In what way would this energy be needed?" It was seen that, in the budding Atlantean civilization, the understanding of will might be lost. There is a certain sorrow that may be associated with this plant as one learns of its devic order, because this willfulness, this alignment of divine will with mankind's personal will, did not occur sufficiently in Atlantis. It was partly because of this that the tendencies and availability of energy in the current western civilization has taken its course regarding willfulness. Thus, the plant is once again coming into its own.

The third chakra is significantly stimulated. There is a transference of energy as this stimulation goes deep in an individual to the seventh chakra. The governing vessel meridian moves faster, and the etheric, emotional, and causal bodies are strengthened. The radiation miasm is slightly eased, and the twelve rays are activated. The eighth and ninth rays are brought more clearly into focus. When there are difficulties regarding planet Saturn, use this herb. The test point is the solar plexus.

Yerba Mate

This short evergreen tree comes from Paraguay and southern Brazil. It is the source of mate tea, a slightly psychotropic beverage popular in South America.

It creates a deeper sense of relaxation, almost a hypnotic state. This may be due in part to its psychotropic properties, but for the pure spiritual essence to be particularly strengthened, it is recommended that it be taken diluted in a very weak tea. One may then be more in tune with the spiritual effects, rather than the more chemical effects on the brain. The herb does not ease mental illnesses caused by psychochemical imbalances in the brain, as is the case with the plant's flower essence.The idea is not only the expansion of the etheric body, but the pushing out of the psychoactive effects of these drugs into the outer subtle bodies.

Many of this herb's effects are not due to chemicals in the plant, but result from stimulation of the etheric body. As the etheric body expands under the influence of this herb, there is a deeper sense of relaxation. For most individuals, there will be a feeling of oneness with many elements. This is not a way of discovery; it is a way of release. In becoming one with God, or with what one may be meditating on, there is a deeper sense of inner satisfaction. There is an increased ability to look deep in oneself in meditative states, to understand more about why one is on the planet, what one is working with, and who one is. These inner revelations are not particularly profound, they simply enable one to know that there is truth in the things that one discovers.

Dependency on this herb can develop, so there is a self-regulating effect that yerba mate has if it is used regularly in diluted form. Then this inner sense of oneness is more easily incorporated in a person. This is an important characteristic more associated with the whole plant than the flower or flower essence, because this deeper sense of relaxation is necessary for the entire being of a person. This is personified in the way the plant grows, but more importantly, its etheric signature indicates a continual flow of energy, as if energy pours from the Earth up through it and is then released to its entire surroundings. For this reason, it is sometimes of benefit to use in companion planting, especially with plants that are hybridized.

There is an obvious connection here to enhanced states of hypnosis. Again, there is a self-regulating effect. If one uses it for a month or so, even in weak dilutions, and does not have success with deeper hypnotic states, stop using the herb. After that time, there may indeed be deeper hypnotic states. The etheric body, as it affects the mental and emotional bodies which are intrinsic to the hypnotic process, has not allowed its full expansion or release of energy. After about a month of use, this expansion can take place on its own, and then the self-regulating effect of the etheric body will naturally communicate and coordinate the action of the etheric and mental bodies. Deeper hypnotic states can be utilized for channeling, past life regression, deeper understanding of how other people operate, and interesting and unusual psychic phenomena, such as levitation, movement of physical objects called psychokinesis, or interesting things associated with hypnosis that one might not otherwise accept as possible. Some examples of this include reading at a distance, remote viewing, or psychometry. Here it is the deeper hypnotic state that is the key. And as this is enhanced, remember it is a tool. If one misuses it, there will be the self-governing effect of yerba mate, and this misuse will lead to lighter states of hypnosis. These states take place because the etheric body is properly placed and properly regulated by yerba mate.

In ancient times, this herb was seen to have this gentler energy, this etheric flow as a natural result of the way it grew. This was strengthened in the plant so that these characteristics might be transferred to people.

There is a strengthening of the heart center and a significant release of energy held in the second and third chakras. This energy may easily be released to the Earth, and it often yields a deeper state of hypnosis and release of the etheric body. There is some strengthening of the pericardium, lung, and gall bladder meridians, and the fourth, sixth, and seventh rays are made clearer. Moreover, the petrochemical and heavy metal miasms are alleviated. As the heavy metal miasm settles deeper into the genetic code of people, the effects of certain herbs, flower essences, gem elixirs, and other vibrational medicines on that miasm and others changes. Vibrational medicines that have little effect on particular miasms may have even less impact, but remedies specifically attuned to certain miasms may go deeper in their cleansing effect. It is a condition of resonance that is set up; thus, if the frequency is out of resonance, it will have less effect. If it is in resonance, it will have a deeper effect. This principle applies to all miasms. The test point is the abdomen about two inches below the navel.

1 Gabriel Cousens, M.D. *Spiritual Nutrition and the Rainbow Diet* (San Rafael, CA: Cassandra Press, 1986).
Gopi Krishna, *Kundalini the Evolutionary Energy In Man* (Boston: Shambhala Publications, Inc., 1970).

CHAPTER XI

CONCLUDING REMARKS

It would seem apparent that individuals, in appreciating the way herbs are useful, will also add their energies to herbs. This is obviously in alignment with humanity's original purpose. The way this is done today is quite primitive. You may say, "Thank you for the healing," or, "I appreciate your beauty" to the plant, but deep inside there is little appreciation of the specifics of the plant—its signature, its beauty on the Earth, and what is unique about it. In the future it is hoped that, as mankind focuses more and more on the healing and strengthening power of love, this will be combined with the full appreciation of the qualities of individual plants. Then the energy added to them when they are grown, eaten, or utilized will add to the life stream and strengthen those characteristics most in harmony with the vibrations of love. The spiritual characteristics of plants will be taken more fully into people, and a beautiful and positive evergrowing cycle will be created. We hope many will explore how the spiritual and medicinal properties of herbs are combined. In fact, there will often be a much deeper effect when one appreciates the spiritual properties while taking an herb purely for its medicinal properties.

Plants are on this planet to aid and learn from mankind. They seek to understand and help, yet they learn this not only by action, but by seeing how mankind appreciates the plant kingdom. In honoring this principle, there is also a deep sense of the natural process in all things. A truly holistic view is taken. The way ecology is now being studied and understood, not just with individual plants, expresses a deeper appreciation for all natural forces. This is gradually creating a sense of deep love and praise towards the plant kingdom, which manifests a very powerful energy.

Very few people incarnated on or off the Earth are currently able to fully appreciate and work with this energy. However, those on the Earth who can work with this energy have seen a wonderful and powerful thought form. With this energy of praise, love, and understanding for the natural kingdom, it is possible for mankind to again be in greater comraderie, strength, and acknowledgement of plants. As this occurs, this energy may strengthen to a level beyond that which is capable of being mustered by any other race in this galaxy. A very powerful link will be created between the natural kingdoms and mankind. This link or bridge will allow beautiful energies to flow between mankind and plants. No longer will it be as it was in Lemuria, when plants were manipulated or worked with for specific purposes. Instead this deep appreciation in mind, body, and spirit in a direct assimilation of God's energy will be available through mankind to the plants.

In a historical sense, it will be like returning the favor that the Lemurians began by a similar path of love and appreciation. But now all of mankind, after many ages of learning and understanding with heart energy perfected and concentrated, will be available to the plants. The devic orders, in learning of this, could rapidly adapt to any conditions found on any inhabited world. Plants introduced into such a world would mutate and change to provide healthful and beneficial plants for the inhabitants. Their gifts would be shared. Some of the devic orders associated with these plants would also be released from these pathways and learn other ways of studying love and the deeper understanding of praise with mankind. This could even yield many new directions in plants and animals that would be created on the planet.

In the intermingling of life streams, the essential lessons of one are given to the other. By the vibration of each life stream reflecting to the other, the highest capacities on a vibrational level are extracted and communicated. This yields the purposes for each life stream more powerfully to the other. It is important that, when herbs are taken as food, individuals learn something about the habits and varieties of plants; this creates a much finer and more beautiful attunement with the nature kingdom and the devic spirit associated with the herb. The plant is able to transfer more of its spiritual properties into the individual.

There are many herbs that were very important in the past that are rarely used today. Examples here include soapbar, herbs for treating the skin such as devil's bit, and herbs utilized in other cultures that are not easily discerned by name. Some of these herbs used in Africa and South America do not even have Latin names for they have not yet been discovered outside of their native culture. Many of these herbs are not only difficult to obtain, but they are not accepted or understood by other people. Some are even difficult to describe. This situation may change as new herbs are discovered, named, and sources for them located, particularly from Central and South America.

Roses are also herbs with great spiritual value, but, with a few exceptions, the separate varieties cannot usually be obtained in stores. In time this will change. The leaves of roses are of some benefit, but one of the focalizers of energy for the properties of Vitamin C is, of course, the hips of the rose. Those bred specifically for higher quantities of Vitamin C will have the concentrated energies more present in the hips. Just using wild rosehips may be quite enough. There is a problem in taking roses for their spiritual properties. Many individuals are not yet attuned to a level of vibration at which they would be able to open sufficiently to the spiritual properties of roses. The first step should be with herbs and flower essences. That is why that material was first provided as an impetus and inspiration for many individuals.

An especially valuable herb that will be discussed in the second book in this series is Christ thorn. This is the bush that Jesus wore when he was crucified. Taking this herb opens the heart and brings one closer to Christ consciousness. Only a few herb shops in the United States now sell this herb, but it is available.

There are many trees, especially fruit trees, not commonly used as herbs that are especially valuable, although this is not understood today. Nearly all fruits have some beneficial or spiritual impact on the physical body. This includes plums, grapes, various bushes, strawberries, and fruits taken from various cultures outside of the United States. In tropical countries, this includes the mango and papaya. Nut trees are in many ways seen as fruits, in that they have a beneficial spiritual impact on the body similar to fruit. Examples here include the pecan, acorn, and macadamia.

The difficulty is that mankind's metabolism is sensitive to sugar, particularly the pancreas. Thus, some fruits and nuts are not yet easily assimilable by all people. However, as a general tendency, fruit and nut trees will become very important. This includes the lemon and orange and all varieties of citrus fruit. The various hybridized combinations also have some beneficial spiritual impact. There are the apple, banana, peach, and many others. This pattern will become more apparent as time goes on.

The spiritual transformation is now taking place in the West partly because so many more people are taking herbs. This is occurring even though most people are really not aware of these spiritual effects on the conscious mind level. People tend not to appreciate these spiritual properties when taking herbs because they take herbs purely for their physical body effects. They are usually not aware of the spiritual properties. The natural way spiritual enhancement must work is that an individual has choices. What happens is that a door, with certain capabilities or potentials behind it, is presented to the individual when they take an herb. It is up to the individual to open the door.

On a more complex level, thought form energy of a specific vibration is created that may or may not match an individual. Even when they open the door there may be a need for a little effort or attention on a particular spiritual area for some of these properties to be present. However, this is not always true. With most herbs some effort by the individual will be necessary for the herb's spiritual properties to work fully. These are capabilities that individuals may choose. However, for certain herbs such as chamomile, the relaxing properties are fully activated by the herb itself. Part of this is due simply to the herb's relaxing properties, but part of it is also due to the herb opening the mental and astral bodies together.

It is possible to activate the spiritual properties more than the physical healing properties of herbs. It depends on an individual's attitude while taking an herb. It is usually not a matter of taking them in a specific way, as for instance tincture versus a tea or the raw herb being eaten. However, with a few herbs a particular way to activate their properties is best. For instance, pine should often be rubbed over the third eye.

If mankind wishes to again walk through the door in these time periods when windows open on the Earth, as during the harmonic convergence in August of 1987, then these opportunities are given. Mankind must always be given a choice, and this is important. As more and more people choose the spiritual path, or look into levels of consciousness beyond that which they usually are acquainted with, an energy tends to gather. This energy is what helps create the current spiritual transformation.

The harmonic convergence will gradually have a broad impact on the way people are affected by vibrational remedies. The vibration of individuals on the planet is gradually being raised. Part of this is galactic, and some of it is specific to the Earth as it relates to galactic influences. The Earth is moving through a transition period, in relation to the central Sun of the milky way galaxy. This movement was charted by the Mayans and is what is denoted in the harmonic convergence time period. In this transition, energies are increasing. These energies will ultimately raise the vibration of most people on the planet. This can push them into whatever areas they are working in, and this is where vibrational remedies will have a polarizing effect. With individuals who magnetize towards lower vibrational areas of life such as greater power over others, greed, and hatred, vibrational remedies are likely to have less effect than before the harmonic convergence. However, individuals attempting to raise their vibration in harmonious areas to help others and understand themselves and their planet will be aided by these energies, and their vibration will be raised more than would otherwise have been possible. Vibrational remedies applied to such individuals will likely have a deeper, more long lasting effect, and will be more easily felt than if taken before the harmonic convergence. Those associated with life will move more towards life, those associated with darkness will move more towards darkness. This is a general tendency; there will, of course, be exceptions to this rule.

When an individual seeks to raise their vibration, there will be a more pronounced effect. Herbs tend to work on multiple levels at once with an individual. Thus, they will have a more profound effect because of the harmonic convergence. You will likely see the effects of herbs and all vibrational remedies increasing gradually with time. This also applies to various forms of electromagnetic medicine and other areas that do not use chemicals within the body, but rather activate overall patterns and vibrations.

The harmonic convergence will have less impact on activating the spiritual properties stored in most foods that are commonly eaten. There is a powerful influence from those inspired by greed and working with chemicals. This affects many food substances. Therefore, there will be contravening polluting influences on food. For most individuals these will likely balance out, so no overall positive effect from foods will be noted from the harmonic convergence. Things will continue at about the same pace. Individuals able to grow their own food or work with high quantities of organically grown or purely grown foods will notice a more pronounced change in consciousness from the spiritual properties of foods.

It is important for people to understand that many will not yet have the spiritual experiences with these herbs that are described in this book. Today, these properties affect people but at a more subtle level. However, as consciousness continues to shift and the respiritualization of society moves forward, more and more people will become sensitive enough to directly experience the spiritual properties stored within herbs. Ultimately, we will again experience a state approaching the consciousness of Lemuria, so that most people using herbs and vibrational remedies will innately understand and experience the total effects of these preparations in mind, body, and spirit.

Experiment with herbs and keep a journal to see how the herb's spiritual properties change your life, self-understanding, relationships, and day-to-day events. As these things are noted and written down, life may become more crystalized and clear. Also, look into the means by which you receive information and understanding. This is a subtle encouragement of your own channeling which is likely to continue expanding over the next few years. Herbs influence the progression to a new higher consciousness in many different ways.

VERVAIN

CROSS-REFERENCE TABLES

Psychospiritual	Adder's Tongue	Amaranthus	Balm (Lemon)	Basil	Beechdrops	Birch	Bird's Tongue	Birthroot	Bistort	Blackberry	Blazing Star	Buckthorn	Buttercup	Carrot	Cayenne	Chamomile	Chickweed	Cinquefoil	Clover (Red)	Cohosh	Comfrey	Currant	Daisy	Dill	Dogwood	Dong Quai	Echinacea	Elecampane	Everlasting	Eyebright	Fennel	Figwort
Affirmations																																
Angelic Attunement																										●						
Apply Teachings							●																					●				
Appreciate Beauty					●	●		●																				●				
Attune to Others							●																									
Christ Attunement																										●						
Communication																	●															
Compartmentalize																						●										
Earth-Nature					●	●	●					●									●							●		●		●
Ecstasy																																
Energized															●			●														
Fairies, Attunement													●																			
Fasting																																
Focalize Spritual Goals		●																							●							
Future Lives																																
God, Awareness of	●															●									●				●			
Group Interaction			●					●								●																
Group Meditation			●																													
Harmony																																
Higher Mind																																
Higher Teachings																																
Karma							●																									
Kundalini						●																										
Life Force																																

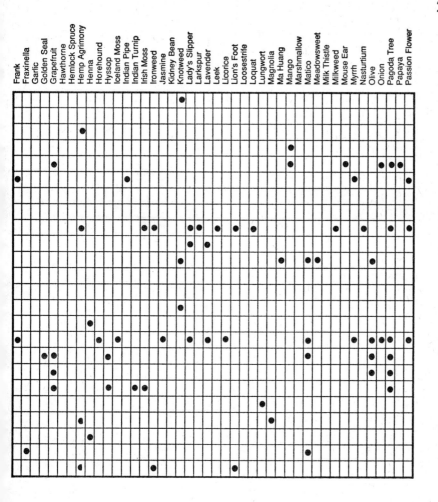

Psychospiritual	Paw Paw	Pear	Peppermint	Pimpernel	Pine	Pipsissewa	Pomegranate	Pumpkin	Radish	Raspberry	Rhubarb	Sandalwood	Sassafras	Schizandra	Self Heal	Shepherd's Purse	Squaw Vine	Strawberry	Sundew	Tamarind	Tarragon	Thyme	Turnip	Vervain	Walnut	Willow	Wintergreen	Witch Hazel	Wood Betony	Yam	Yerba Mate
Affirmations																															
Angelic Attunement												●																			
Apply Teachings	●											●											●			●					
Appreciate Beauty												●																			
Attune to Others															●																
Christ Attunement								●																							
Communication																															
Compartmentalize						●																									
Earth-Nature			●	●				●				●					●										●		●		
Ecstasy		●						●													●										
Energized			●	●	●	●									●									●	●						
Fairies, Attunement					●					●																					
Fasting	●	●															●														
Focalize Spritual Goals												●										●									
Future Lives												●																			
God, Awareness of								●																			●	●			●
Group Interaction																						●						●			
Group Meditation																	●											●			
Harmony																															
Higher Mind																															
Higher Teachings			●					●					●									●									
Karma																			●			●								●	
Kundalini								●							●																
Life Force																	●										●		●		

Psychospiritual

Psychospiritual	Adder's Tongue	Amaranthus	Balm (Lemon)	Basil	Beechdrops	Birch	Bird's Tongue	Birthroot	Bistort	Blackberry	Blazing Star	Buckthorn	Buttercup	Carrot	Cayenne	Chamomile	Chickweed	Cinquefoil	Clover (Red)	Cohosh	Comfrey	Currant	Daisy	Dill	Dogwood	Dong Quai	Echinacea	Elecampane	Everlasting	Eyebright	Fennel	Figwort
Love, Greater																																●
Meditation			●			●		●		●						●	●	●	●								●					
Negative Thoughts																									●				●			
New Concepts	●									●								●				●				●	●	●				
Obstacles Overcome										●								●														
Prana				●																												
Pregnancy								●																								
Relationships								●							●			●														●
Release																													●			
Soul Attunement									●													●										
Sound					●	●																										
Spiritual Acceleration										●				●																		
Spiritual Confidence																											●					
Spiritual Cycles																		●														
Spiritual Enthusiasm			●																													
Spiritual Patience									●																				●			
Spiritual Purpose						●	●				●		●	●								●	●									
Spiritualize Emotions																				●												
Spiritually Understand	●													●				●				●	●								●	
Tantra																																
Trust New Techniques										●																●		●				
Visions-Dreams																		●						●								
Yin-Yang Balance																																

Psychospiritual

	Frank	Fraxinella	Garlic	Golden Seal	Grapefruit	Hawthorne	Hemlock Spruce	Hemp Agrimony	Henna	Horehound	Hyssop	Iceland Moss	Indian Pipe	Indian Turnip	Irish Moss	Ironweed	Jasmine	Kidney Bean	Knotweed	Lady's Slipper	Larkspur	Lavender	Leek	Licorice	Lion's Foot	Loosestrife	Loquat	Lungwort	Magnolia	Ma Huang	Mango
Love, Greater					●							●		●			●									●		●			●
Meditation	●	●						●										●			●									●	
Negative Thoughts			●		●													●			●										
New Concepts																															●
Obstacles Overcome							●											●					●						●		●
Prana																											●		●		
Pregnancy			●																					●							
Relationships											●													●							
Release	●												●																		
Soul Attunement							●								●																
Sound															●																
Spiritual Acceleration																															
Spiritual Confidence							●																			●					
Spiritual Cycles															●																
Spiritual Enthusiasm															●																
Spiritual Patience							●																		●						
Spiritual Purpose	●		●	●								●	●	●						●			●								
Spiritualize Emotions																															
Spiritually Understand			●					●							●				●								●				●
Tantra																●															
Trust New Techniques					●					●															●						
Visions-Dreams	●		●												●																
Yin-Yang Balance																															

	Marshmallow	Matico	Meadowsweet	Milk Thistle	Milkweed	Mouse Ear	Myrrh	Nasturtium	Olive	Onion	Pagoda Tree	Papaya	Passion Flower	Paw Paw	Pear	Peppermint	Pimpernel	Pine	Pipsissewa	Pomegranate	Pumpkin	Radish	Raspberry	Rhubarb	Sandalwood	Sassafras	Schizandra	Self Heal	Shepherd's Purse	Squaw Vine	Strawberry	Sundew	Tamarind	Tarragon	Thyme	Turnip	Vervain	Walnut	Willow	Wintergreen	Witch Hazel	Wood Betony	Yam	Yerba Mate
				•								•		•		•			•	•					•		•				•	•		•		•	•		•	•			
	•	•			•					•						•	•		•			•								•								•		•	•	•	
		•		•											•																											•	
																											•			•		•											
		•																	•				•								•		•			•			•				
																										•	•																
		•										•											•																				
									•													•																					
	•												•																•					•	•	•							
			•									•																	•					•									
												•																	•					•									
																														•													
													•										•												•								
													•																			•											
													•																	•													
	•		•	•								•		•		•				•			•							•						•	•	•	•	•				
																														•													
		•						•					•		•									•					•	•	•	•	•		•	•	•	•	•	•		•	
																•														•													
		•			•							•											•										•										
•				•											•																												

Psychological

Psychological	Adder's Tongue	Amaranthus	Balm (Lemon)	Basil	Birch	Bird's Tongue	Birthroot	Blackberry	Blazing Star	Buckthorn	Buttercup	Carrot	Cayenne	Chamomile	Chickweed	Cinquefoil	Clover (Red)	Cohosh	Currant	Daisy	Dill	Dogwood	Dong Quai	Echinacea	Elecampane	Everlasting	Fennel	Garlic	Golden Seal	Grapefruit	Hawthorne	Hemlock Spruce	Hemp Agrimony	Henna	Horehound
Acceptance																										●									
Anger			●																															●	
Childish Enjoyment											●								●																
Confidence																										●							●		
Courage																		●											●						
Death, Preparation																												●							
Decision Making			●				●																								●				
Depression																																			
Ego Development																									●										
Emotional Balance														●	●	●		●								●							●	●	
Emotional Release																						●								●					
Empathy														●																				●	
Empowerment																																			
Expressive Ability	●				●																●					●									
Fear of Birthing																		●																	
Fear of Death																																			
Fear of Movement																																			
Fear of Old Age																																			
Fear of Psychism										●								●																	
Fear of Spirituality																		●																	
Fears																		●				●				●	●								●
Flexibility																					●												●		
Forgiveness					●										●																		●		
Freedom					●																														
Grief																																			
Guilt																																			
Hatred																						●									●				
Heart Opens													●													●	●								
Humility																																			
Inner Peace															●																				
Integration									●																									●	
Intimacy																																			

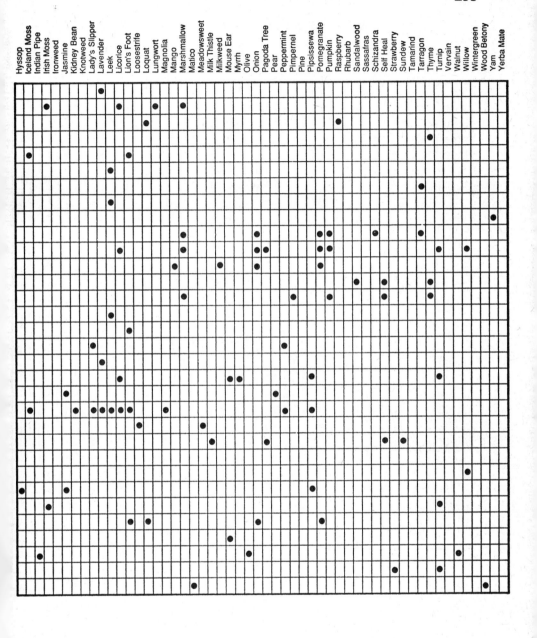

Psychological

Psychological	Adder's Tongue	Amaranthus	Balm (Lemon)	Basil	Birch	Bird's Tongue	Birthroot	Blackberry	Blazing Star	Buckthorn	Buttercup	Carrot	Cayenne	Chamomile	Chickweed	Cinquefoil	Clover (Red)	Cohosh	Currant	Daisy	Dill	Dogwood	Dong Quai	Echinacea	Elecampane	Everlasting	Fennel	Garlic	Golden Seal	Grapefruit	Hawthorne	Hemlock Spruce	Hemp Agrimony	Henna	Horehound
Joy																				●															
Judgmental																																			
Leadership																															●				
Loneliness																																			
Manic Depressive																	●																		
Negative Thoughts																																			
Patience								●															●			●								●	
Persistance		●						●																		●								●	
Praise																																			
Racial Prejudice														●																					
Relaxant			●											○	●		●																	●	●
Sadness																																			
See Others View												●																							
Self Image																							●							●				●	●
Self Love																																			
Sexual Image																		●																	
Sleep														●																					
Speak Clearer																																			
Stability																														●					
Stress																																●			
Suicidal																																	●		
Sympathy																			●															●	
Will Power	●							●		●																								●	

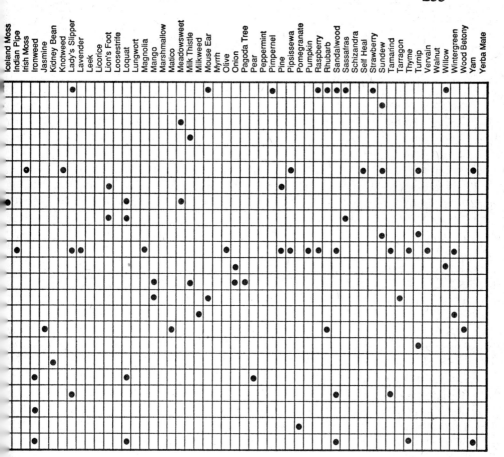

Psychic

Psychic	Adder's Tongue	Amaranthus	Balm (Lemon)	Basil	Beechdrops	Birch	Bird's Tongue	Birthroot	Bistort	Blackberry	Blazing Star	Buckthorn	Buttercup	Carrot	Cayenne	Chamomile	Cinquefoil	Cohosh	Comfrey	Currant	Daisy	Dong Quai	Echinacea	Everlasting	Eyebright	Figwort	Frank	Fraxinella	Garlic	Golden Seal	Hawthorne	Hemlock Spruce	Henna	Hyssop
All Psychic Gifts										●					●				●				●											
Astral Projection						●				●									●															●
Auric Vision														●			●								●		●							
Channeling																●																		
Children Psychic																				●														
Clairaudience																																		
Clairvoyance											●	●		●													●							
Dead, Communicate																														●				
Geomancy																																		
Intuition			●										●	●				●					●		●	●								
Levitation																																		
Life Force, See																					●													
Lost Distant Objects																																		
Manifestation									●							●																	●	
Past Life Knowledge		●														●															●			●
Prophecy						●																●	●	●	●	●								
Protection																								●					●				●	
Psychokinesis																											●							
Psychometry																																		
Remote Healing																			●															
Right Timing	●																																	
Telepathy		●		●	●							●			●																			
Third Eye Opens														●			●		●						●		●						●	
Trance Dancing																																		
Truth Perceived	●								●																●		●							

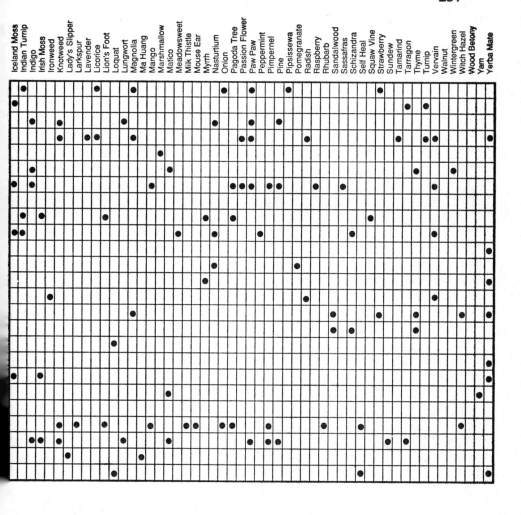

Professional	Amaranthus	Balm (Lemon)	Beechdrops	Birch	Bird's Tongue	Birthroot	Bistort	Blackberry	Blazing Star	Buckthorn	Buttercup	Carrot	Cayenne	Chamomile	Cinquefoil	Clover (Red)	Cohosh	Comfrey	Currant	Daisy	Dill	Dogwood	Echinacea	Elecampane	Eyebright	Fennel	Frank	Fraxinella	Garlic	Golden Seal	Grapefruit	Hawthorne	Hemlock Spruce	Hemp Agrimony	Henna	Horehound	Hyssop
Acupuncturist																																					
Alchemist																																					
Aromatherapy	●																									●	●		●								
Artist		●	●																																		
Astrologer													●				●			●					●										●		
Athlete																●																					●
Dancer																																					
Farmer								●		●	●						●	●											●						●		
Healing Abilities																		●		●			●	●									●		●		
Hypnotist																					●				●												●
Jeweler		●																																			
Managerial Job																																					
Martial Arts																																					
Massage Therapist																																					
Midwife				●																										●							
Mountain Climber																																					
Musician		●		●																																	
Past Life Therapy	●														●															●						●	
Physical Labor																																					●
Polarity Therapy																																					
Politician				●																																	
Psychic Counseling									●																					●							
Psychotherapy																		●																		●	
Reiki																																					
Scientist																														●							●
Sculpture			●																																		
Spiritual Healing												●																							●		
Student																		●																			
Veterinarian	●	●						●	●	●	●						●	●	●				●	●					●			●	●	●			●
Visualization																																					
Yoga Teacher																																					
Zoo Keeper	●								●						●			●					●														

	Iceland Moss	Indian Pipe	Indian Turnip	Irish Moss	Ironweed	Jasmine	Kidney Bean	Knotweed	Lady's Slipper	Larkspur	Lavender	Leek	Lion's Foot	Loosestrife	Loquat	Lungwort	Magnolia	Ma Huang	Mango	Matico	Milk Thistle	Milkweed	Myrrh	Nasturtium	Olive	Onion	Pagoda Tree	Paw Paw	Pear	Peppermint	Pimpernel	Pine	Pipsissewa	Pomegranate	Pumpkin	Raspberry	Sandalwood	Sassafras	Schizandra	Self Heal	Shepherd's Purse	Squaw Vine	Strawberry	Sundew	Tarragon	Thyme	Turnip	Vervain	Willow	Wintergreen	Witch Hazel	Yam	Yerba Mate
																								•															•														
				•						•						•	•				•								•																	•			•	•	
				•																																																
															•	•	•	•								•						•																				
						•										•	•						•						•	•																•						
				•								•	•			•		•																	•	•				•			•			•						
					•						•	•			•		•			•	•	•	•												•	•				•				•						•
											•						•																										•								•
																•								•																					•						
•																																																				
	•														•							•		•		•			•																							
•											•																							•																		
																																														•				•		•
																•											•													•				•					•		
																			•									•											•							•		•			
		•														•			•												•														•		•					
	•														•				•				•		•						•													•					○		
	•																		•																	•												•			
																						•																	•				•								
•	•											•	•			•				•		•	•	•	•	•	•		•			•	•	•												•	•	•		
														•																									•													
•			•	•	•	•	•			•	•						•	•			•		•		•		•				•			•			•		•	•	•		•		•		•	•	•		
				•												•	•												•							•									•	•					
																		•	•																																	
	•		•																																				•		•				•	•		•	•			

Chakras	Adder's Tongue	Amaranthus	Balm (Lemon)	Basil	Beechdrops	Birch	Bird's Tongue	Birthroot	Bistort	Blackberry	Blazing Star	Buckthorn	Buttercup	Carrot	Cayenne	Chamomile	Chickweed	Cinquefoil	Clover (Red)	Cohosh	Comfrey	Currant	Daisy	Dill	Dogwood	Dong Quai	Echinacea	Elecampane	Everlasting	Eyebright	Fennel	Figwort	Frank
All																				●		●			●								
Root		●	●	●											●		●														●		
Second				●											●					●											●	●	
Third		●	●	●			●		●		●					●	●		●	●	●	●									●		
Heart			●			●		●		●	●					●	●	●							●				●				
Throat	●					●		●								●	●	●	●				●	●					●				●
Third Eye								●					●	●		●		●	●			●	●			●		●		●			●
Crown		●									●									●						●	●					●	●
Eighth													●																				
Ninth													●					●															●
Tenth													●																				●
Eleventh													●																				
Twelfth													●																				
Abdomen																															●		
Arms																																	
Calves																																	
Ears																														●			
Face																														●			
Feet				●																											●		
Hands				●																													
Hip																																	
Kidney																															●		
Knees																																	
Liver																															●		
Neck																														●			
Pancreas																															●		
Thighs																																	

Fraxinella, Garlic, Golden Seal, Grapefruit, Hawthorne, Hemlock Spruce, Hemp Agrimony, Henna, Horehound, Hyssop, Iceland Moss, Indian Pipe, Indian Turnip, Indigo, Irish Moss, Ironweed, Jasmine, Kidney Bean, Knotweed, Lady's Slipper, Larkspur, Lavender, Leek, Licorice, Lion's Foot, Loosestrife, Loquat, Lungwort, Magnolia, Ma Huang, Mango, Marshmallow, Matico, Meadowsweet, Milk Thistle, Milkweed, Mouse Ear, Myrrh, Nasturtium, Olive, Onion, Pagoda Tree

Chakras	Papaya	Passion Flower	Paw Paw	Pear	Peppermint	Pimpernel	Pine	Pipsissewa	Pomegranate	Pumpkin	Radish	Raspberry	Rhubarb	Sandalwood	Sassafras	Schizandra	Self Heal	Shepherd's Purse	Squaw Vine	Strawberry	Sundew	Tamarind	Tarragon	Thyme	Turnip	Vervain	Walnut	Willow	Wintergreen	Witch Hazel	Wood Betony	Yam	Yerba Mate
All					•	•											•																
Root	•									•	•	•						•	•		•			•					•	•			
Second							•	•	•								•			•		•			•			•				•	•
Third				•	•		•	•	•						•	•	•		•	•	•			•				•				•	•
Heart	•			•				•					•	•			•							•				•					•
Throat			•					•	•				•	•		•	•					•		•	•	•							
Third Eye	•	•				•		•		•		•									•		•			•		•					
Crown		•								•		•				•	•							•	•	•			•	•		•	
Eighth		•																								•			•	•			
Ninth			•																							•			•				
Tenth																										•			•				
Eleventh																																	
Twelfth											•																						
Abdomen																																	
Arms													•																				
Calves																																	
Ears																																	
Face													•																				
Feet																		•															
Hands																																	
Hip																																	
Kidney																																	
Knees																		•									•						
Liver																																	
Neck																																	
Pancreas																																	
Thighs																																	

Subtle Bodies

Subtle Bodies	Adder's Tongue	Amaranthus	Balm (Lemon)	Basil	Beechdrops	Birch	Bird's Tongue	Birthroot	Bistort	Blackberry	Blazing Star	Buckthorn	Carrot	Cayenne	Chamomile	Chickweed	Cinquefoil	Clover (Red)	Cohosh	Comfrey	Currant	Daisy	Dill	Dogwood	Dong Quai	Echinacea	Elecampane	Everlasting	Eyebright	Fennel	Figwort	Frank	Fraxinella
All																				•													
Astral		•				•		•							•									•		•	•			•			
Aura																																	•
Causal	•			•			•																	•		•	•						
Emotional	•	•		•	•	•				•	•		•	•		•	•	•		•	•	•	•					•	•		•	•	•
Ethereal Fluidium																																	
Etheric		•		•	•	•								•		•						•		•		•			•				•
Mental	•	•					•	•	•				•	•		•				•	•	•						•	•		•	•	•
Soul																																	
Thermal																						•											
Integrated Spiritual																																	

Subtle Bodies

Subtle Bodies	Garlic	Golden Seal	Grapefruit	Hawthorne	Hemlock Spruce	Hemp Agrimony	Henna	Horehound	Hyssop	Iceland Moss	Indian Pipe	Indian Turnip	Indigo	Irish Moss	Ironweed	Jasmine	Kidney Bean	Knotweed	Lady's Slipper	Larkspur	Lavender	Leek	Licorice	Lion's Foot	Loosestrife	Loquat	Lungwort	Magnolia	Ma Huang	Mango	Marshmallow	Matico	Meadowsweet
All																																	
Astral	●						●		●								●								●								
Aura																			●														
Causal			●							●	●	●												●								●	
Emotional		●	●					●	●	●	●			●	●		●			●	●	●	●	●		●	●			●	●		
Ethereal Fluidium																																	
Etheric		●	●	●	●	●	●		●	●				●	●	●	●		●	●		●		●					●	●		●	
Mental					●	●			●	●	●	●	●	●		●	●										●	●	●			●	●
Soul									●															●								●	
Thermal																																	
Integrated Spiritual																																●	

Rays

Rays	Amaranthus	Basil	Beechdrops	Bird's Tongue	Birthroot	Blazing Star	Buckthorn	Carrot	Chamomile	Cinquefoil	Clover (Red)	Cohosh	Comfrey	Currant	Daisy	Echinacea	Elecampane	Everlasting	Eyebright	Fennel	Frank	Golden Seal	Grapefruit	Hawthorne	Hemlock Spruce	Hemp Agrimony	Henna	Horehound	Iceland Moss	Indian Pipe	Indian Turnip	Indigo	Irish Moss	Ironweed	Jasmine	Knotweed	Lady's Slipper	Larkspur	Lavender	Lion's Foot	Loquat	Lungwort	Magnolia
All																																								●			
1st		●																						●																			
2nd		●						●																●				●															
3rd		●				●		●	●									●						●													●	●					●
4th	●					●	●									●	●	●			●								●								●	●	●		●		●
5th	●	●					●	●										●		●	●								●	●													
6th									●									●			●																			●			
7th				●												●						●	●																●	●			
8th				●	●		●								●							●					●	●													●	●	●
9th										●												●						●												●	●	●	●
10th			●							●			●									●						●					●			●				●			
11th			●							●			●	●								●													●						●		
12th												●										●							●	●	●	●									●		

Milk Thistle, Milkweed, Mouse Ear, Myrrh, Nasturtium, Olive, Onion, Pagoda Tree, Papaya, Passion Flower, Paw Paw, Pear, Peppermint, Pimpernel, Pine, Pipsissewa, Pomegranate, Pumpkin, Radish, Raspberry, Rhubarb, Sandalwood, Sassafras, Schizandra, Self Heal, Shepherd's Purse, Squaw Vine, Strawberry, Sundew, Tamarind, Tarragon, Thyme, Turnip, Vervain, Walnut, Willow, Wintergreen, Witch Hazel, Wood Betony, Yam, Yerba Mate

Mango, Marshmallow, Matico, Meadowsweet, Milk Thistle, Mouse Ear, Myrrh, Nasturtium, Olive, Onion, Pagoda Tree, Papaya, Passion Flower, Paw Paw, Pear, Peppermint, Pimpernel, Pine, Pipsissewa, Pomegranate, Pumpkin, Radish, Raspberry, Rhubarb, Sandalwood, Sassafras, Schizandra, Self Heal, Shepherd's Purse, Squaw Vine, Strawberry, Sundew, Tamarind, Tarragon, Thyme, Turnip, Vervain, Walnut, Willow, Wintergreen, Witch Hazel, Wood Betony, Yam, Yerba Mate

Meridians

	Adder's Tongue	Amaranthus	Balm (Lemon)	Basil	Beechdrops	Birch	Bird's Tongue	Birthroot	Blackberry	Blazing Star	Buckthorn	Carrot	Cayenne	Chamomile	Cinquefoil	Clover (Red)	Cohosh	Currant	Daisy	Dogwood	Elecampane	Everlasting	Eyebright	Fennel	Frank	Garlic	Golden Seal	Grapefruit	Hawthorne	Hemlock Spruce	Hemp Agrimony	Horehound	Hyssop	Iceland Moss
All		●															●																	
Bladder					●			●					●	●		●		●						●	●		●				●	●	●	
Conception Vessel																																		●
Gall Bladder									●		●	●									●					●				●		●		●
Governing Vessel			●	●					●		●																							
Heart					●																		●											
Kidney			●											●	●	●									●		●							
Large Intestine																																		
Liver									●					●		●	●					●		●		●	●	●						
Lung							●																	●										
Pericardium														●															●		●			
Small Intestine																																		
Spleen						●			●									●					●										●	
Stomach	●					●			●							●										●	●		●					
Triple Warmer																																		

Miasms

	Adder's Tongue	Amaranthus	Basil	Beechdrops	Birch	Bird's Tongue	Birthroot	Blazing Star	Buckthorn	Carrot	Cayenne	Chamomile	Chickweed	Cinquefoil	Clover (Red)	Cohosh	Comfrey	Currant	Daisy	Dill	Dogwood	Dong Quai	Echinacea	Everlasting	Eyebright	Fennel	Figwort	Fraxinella	Garlic	Golden Seal	Grapefruit	Hemlock Spruce	Hemp Agrimony	Henna	Iceland Moss	Indian Pipe	Indian Turnip	Irish Moss
All																					●									●								
Cancer	●				●			●					●	●	●							●		●		●												
Gonorrhea		●		●				●								●						●	●				●											
Heavy Metal			●							●												●																
Petrochemical	●						●				●															●	●											
Psora									●	●												●					●			●	●	●	●					
Radiation						●																														●		●
Stellar																		●																	●			
Syphilis		●																						●						●		●		●	●			
Tubercular			●				●												●																			

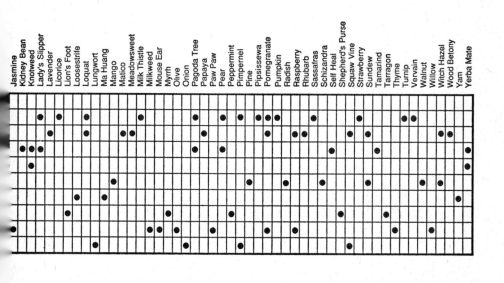

Nadis

Nadis	Adder's Tongue	Basil	Beechdrops	Bird's Tongue	Birthroot	Carrot	Cayenne	Chamomile	Cinquefoil	Clover (Red)	Cohosh	Currant	Daisy	Dill	Everlasting	Eyebright	Fennel	Frank	Garlic	Hawthorne	Hemlock Spruce	Horehound	Hyssop	Iceland Moss	Indian Pipe	Indian Turnip	Jasmine	Lady's Slipper	Larkspur	Lavender	Lion's Foot
All		●								●									●											●	
Abdomen								●																							
Arms												●																		●	
Back									●																	●					
Buttocks								●																							
Chest					●							●														●					●
Ears																●															
Eyes																●													●		
Feet			●				●						●				●							●	●						
Fingers											●																		●		
Genital																											●				
Hands			●										●							●			●						●		
Head				●												●	●		●							●					
Intestines																															
Jaw	●																														
Knees																															
Legs							●																●								
Neck																●															
Palms																															
Shoulder													●																		
Spine, Base			●																												
Throat	●		●											●																	
Toes																													●		
Wrist				●																											

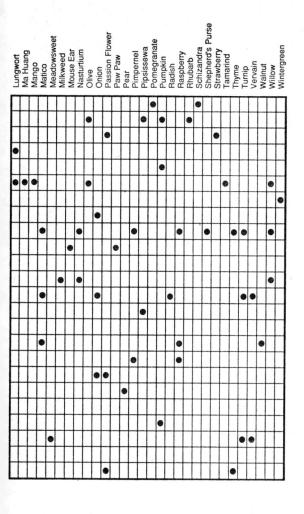

LIST OF 108 HERBS

Adder's Tongue
Amaranthus
Balm (Lemon)
Basil
Beechdrops
Birch
Bird's Tongue
Birthroot
Bistort
Blackberry
Blazing Star
Buckthorn
Buttercup
Carrot (Queen Anne's Lace)
Cayenne
Chamomile
Chickweed
Cinquefoil
Clover (Red)
Cohosh (Black or Blue)
Comfrey
Currant
Daisy
Dill
Dogwood

Dong Quai (Angelica)
Echinacea
Elecampane
Everlasting
Eyebright
Fennel
Figwort
Frank
Fraxinella (Gas Plant)
Garlic
Golden Seal
Grapefruit
Hawthorne
Hemlock Spruce
Hemp Agrimony
Henna
Horehound
Hyssop
Iceland Moss
Indian Pipe
Indian Turnip
Indigo
Irish Moss
Ironweed
Jasmine

Kidney Bean
Knotweed
Lady's Slipper
Larkspur
Lavender
Leek
Licorice
Lion's Foot
Loosestrife
Loquat
Lungwort
Magnolia
Ma Huang (Ephedra)
Mango
Marshmallow
Matico
Meadowsweet
Milk Thistle
Milkweed
Mouse Ear
Myrrh
Nasturtium
Olive
Onion
Pagoda Tree
Papaya
Passion Flower
Paw Paw
Pear

Peppermint
Pimpernel
Pine
Pipsissewa
Pomegranate
Pumpkin
Radish
Raspberry
Rhubarb
Sandalwood
Sassafras
Schizandra
Self Heal
Shepherd's Purse
Squaw Vine
Strawberry
Sundew
Tamarind
Tarragon
Thyme
Turnip
Vervain
Walnut
Willow
Wintergreen
Witch Hazel
Wood Betony
Yam
Yerba Mate

GLOSSARY of ESOTERIC TERMS

Astral body: One of the subtle bodies surrounding the physical body.

Astral projection: Also known as an out-of-body experience. The astral body temporarily separates from the physical body. This usually occurs when asleep, but can also occur when awake.

Aura: An invisible, luminous radiation or halo that surrounds the physical body. It varies widely in size, density, and color depending on the evolution of each person, and it exists around all life forms. Some psychic or sensitive individuals see it.

Causal body: An ethereal body that exists around the physical body.

Chakra: A spiritual energy center just outside, but connected to, the physical body.

Channel (Medium): An individual who serves as a vehicle or instrument for one's higher self and soul or for guides on higher planes to speak through. The person may be awake or in trance when this process takes place.

Chiron: This is one of the asteroids in the asteroid belt. It is associated with activating Christ consciousness.

Clairvoyance: A general term signifying many psychic gifts such as the ability to see things miles away.

Emotional body: A subtle body that exists around the physical body.

Etheric body: A subtle body that exists just outside and around the physical body.

Ethers: Seven or more dimensional states that vibrate faster than the speed of light.

Integrated spiritual body: This, and the term spiritual body, signify the combination of the spiritual properties of the subtle and physical bodies.

Life Stream: This is the soul group of a particular vibration associated with one specific path. It generally manifests in a given form as one particular type of life or being such as in a particular species or a particular sentient being. The life stream can continue across eons of time developing and changing yet remaining united in its common purpose.

Karma: A Sanskrit word meaning the sum total of a person's actions in their many lives. These past life traits are carried over into each new life with continuing opportunities for growth.

Kundalini: A powerful spiritual energy normally lying dormant in the physical body at the base of the spine. Once carefully awakened, spiritual growth ensues.

Mental body: A subtle body existing around the physical body.

Miasms: Various subtle imbalances residing in the cells and subtle bodies that are activated to cause numerous diseases when karmic patterns prevail.

Morphogenetic field: Patterns or vibrations that can be created by thoughts that exist over eons of time. It is a repeated process of a particular frequency of energy.

Nature spirits or **devas:** Souls living on a higher frequency than the physical plane that are intimately associated with the various forms of nature.

Rays: Incoming energies at subtle vibrational levels that create potential within the physical and subtle bodies. These are observed to generally enter the body from above, and there are characteristic colors associated with each ray.

Rife Ray: Inert gas stimulation by high frequencies that generate a subtle energy which has powerful effects upon living matter. This creates resonance and can be used to destroy microorganisms that are pathogenic to people, plants, and animals.

Soul body: A very ethereal subtle body that exists around the physical body.

Sushumna: This is an etheric part of the spinal column through which the kundalini energy rises from the base chakra to the crown chakra.

BIBLIOGRAPHY

Botanical Reference Material
Bailey, L.H., *The Standard Cyclopedia of Horticulture*, New York: MacMilliam Publishing Co., 1935.
Daydon, Jackson, *A Glossary of Botanic Terms*, New York: Hofner Publishing Co., 1965.
Hortus, New York: MacMilliam Publishing Co., 1976.

Vibrational Healing
Gerber, Richard, *Vibrational Medicine,* Santa Fe: Bear and Co., 1988).
Gurudas, *Flower Essences and Vibrational Healing,* Albuquerque, NM: Brotherhood of Life Books, 1983.
Gurudas, *Gem Elixirs and Vibrational Healing*, *Vol I* San Rafael, CA: Cassandra Press, 1985.
Gurudas, *Gem Elixirs and Vibrational Healing*, *Vol II* San Rafael, CA: Cassandra Press, 1986.
Hildegard of Bingen, *Hildegard of Bingen's Medicine*, Santa Fe: Bear and Co., 1988.

Herbs
Culpeper, Nicholas, *Culpeper's Complete Herbal,* Secaucus, NJ: Chartwell Nooks, Inc., 1978.
Garland, Sarah, *The Herb Garden*, New York: Penguin Books, 1984.
Grieve, M.A., *A Modern Herbal*, New York: Dover Publications, 1971.
Hoffmann, David, *The Holistic Herbal,* Forres, Scotland: The Findhorn Press, 1985.
Keys, John, *Chinese Herbs,* Rutland, VT: Charles Tuttle Co., 1981.
Kloss, Jethro, *Back to Eden*, Santa Barbara: Woodbridge Press, 1979.
Lewis, Walter and Elvin-Lewis, Memory P.F., *Medical Botany Plants Affecting Man's Health,* New York: John Wiley & Sons, 1977.
Lucas, Richard, *Secrets of the Chinese Herbalists,* West Nyack, NY: Parker Publishing Co., Inc., 1987.
Lust, John, *The Herb Book*, New York: Bantam Books, Inc., 1974.
Nickells, J. M., *Botanical Ready Reference*, Lakemont, GA: CSA Press, 1976.
Rose, Jeanne, *Herbs and Things,* New York: Perigee Books, 1983.
_____, *Modern Herbal,* New York: Perigee Books, 1987.
Santillo, Humbart, *Natural Healing With Herbs*, Prescott Valley, AZ: Hohm Press, 1987.

Schultes, Richard Evans, *Medicines From the Earth,* New York: McGraw Hill Co., 1983.
Stuart, Malcom ed., *The Encyclopedia of Herbs and Herbalism*, New York: Crescent Books, 1981.
Teeguarden, Ron, *Chinese Tonic Herbs,* New York: Japan Publications, Inc., 1984.
Tierra, Michael, *The Way of Herbs,* New York: Pocket Books, 1983.
Treben, Maria, *Health Through God's Pharmacy*, Steyr, Austria: Wilhelm Ennsthaler, 1983.
_____, *Health From God's Garden*, New York: Penguin Books, 1984.
Weiner, Michael A., *Earth Medicine,* New York: Collier Books, 1980.

For information on this continuing research, please contact:

Gurudas
P.O. Box 868
San Rafael, Ca. 94915

For information on purchasing the flower essences and gem elixirs described in this book, please contact:

Pegasus Products, Inc.
P.O. Box 228
Boulder, Co. 80306
800-527-6104

For information on doing private readings with Jon Fox and Hilarion, please contact:

Jon C. Fox
P.O. Box 1025
San Rafael, CA. 94915
415-921-7760

INDEX